MW01067598

TOP GUN MEMOS

THE MAKING
AND LEGACY
OF
AN
ICONIC
MOVIE

BY MEREDITH JORDAN

Copyright © 2022, Meredith Jordan
Published in the United States by Citation Press.
First Edition 2022
All rights reserved.
No part of this book may be used or reproduced
in any manner without written permission
except in the case of brief quotations when properly cited.

ISBN: 978-1-7337874-3-7 (Print)
ISBN: 978-1-7337874-4-4 (eBook)

CONTENTS

PREFACE

I was working at the Margaret Herrick Library one day in 2017 when I requested files from several different movies. The main repository of the Academy of Motion Picture Arts and Sciences is filled with amazing material and this was more for fun than anything. I needed a break from the work I was there to do, so I went fishing.

One of the folders contained Tom Cruise's contract for *Top Gun*. It was fascinating — it's in these pages — but my focus wasn't celebrities. I write about the lesser-known heroes of movie production, the artists, artisans and business people who contribute mightily to the art form from behind the scenes.

More compelling to me was Bill Badalato, executive producer of *Top Gun*. That movie was on my fishing list because I'd heard stories about it from his son, Billy Badalato, who'd been a production assistant (P.A.) on it. The younger Badalato, also a producer, was central to my first book, "Below the Line: Anatomy of a Successful Movie," about the making of *Last Vegas* (2013).

When I left the library that day I had copies of several interesting documents, all to be filed away for some magical day when I had no other obligations.

I met Bill Badalato in late 2018 for lunch, a casual meeting set in motion by Billy. We discussed a number of topics that day, just one of which was that Bill's agent had told him he should write a book about *Top Gun*. The next meeting, a few months later, focused solely on what a book might look like. I didn't hear from him for a few months after that, and when I did, it was to say he didn't think there was enough interest.

I didn't argue because I'd taken a job at a magazine, but I'd done enough homework to think there was both interest and a really great story to be told. One definition of what makes a film iconic is whether people debate its place in film history — including whether it was a good or bad movie to begin with — decades down the road. That *Top Gun* is still part of the dialogue 35-plus years later makes it one of the most enduring movies of the last century. And no one had ever written more than a chapter about the making of the movie, despite its rare longevity.

Several elements made *Top Gun* different. The obvious one was that there aren't many movies where the U.S. military supplies billions of dollars of its assets for sets, props and locations, and some of its best pilots.

Perhaps less obvious is how dangerous it was to make the movie. It was dedicated to Art Scholl, a well-known aviator and stunt pilot who died shooting plate footage, which were shots of real sky to go behind the actors in the mockups when they were on soundstages. Two other incidents might also have resulted in deaths. One involved the ocean rescue scene and the young Tom Cruise, who was pulled underwater by a prop parachute and cut free by Navy rescue divers. The other was on the side of a mountain outside Fallon, Nev., where movie crew was getting spectacular footage of jets soaring toward them. One jet turned late, narrowly averting a crash, the sheer force of it ᴴocking crew and camera to the ground.

Top Gun had two other defining features. The first is that ᴴ𝐚de with an incredibly small budget given what they accomplish. The $15 million budget in 1985 would `8.8 million today, when adjusted for inflation. ᴑ the $150 million circulated as the estimated *Top Gun: Maverick* (2022), a guestimate that ᴑ low.

extent to which the movie was fixed ᴘut any of the contemporary tools ᴛe that a movie comes together in the cutting room, but the editors of *Top Gun* helped reinvent the narrative in order to have a story.

I got a call from Bill on the last day of March 2020, a week after the pandemic hit and I was laid off from the magazine. *Top Gun* fans had been in touch in numbers, changing his mind about the level of interest in a book. Only he didn't want to write it. If I did, he would help where he could.

I'd like to acknowledge the impeccable timing of the call and COVID-19 for clearing my calendar of work and other remnants of a previous life. I'd like to thank Bill for his invaluable memos and notes, and his time over those interviews and emails, many of them friendly exchanges. I appreciate that he understood I would go wherever the facts led.

A reporter is said to be "gathering string" in preparing a story, and Bill's box of documents was filled with string. It led to many other sources of information, including access to private collections of production and studio documents. In the end, I had interviewed 90 people, most of whom had worked on the movie. Naval officers and personnel comprised another block of interviews. Writers and reporters who have covered the movie or someone connected to it, experts in specific areas of filmmaking and aviation, and cinema scholars, were another contingent. The last group included librarians, various museums and economic development people, and of course, fans.

All of that sits atop more than 1,250 pages of production, studio, personal, and government documents Many of them were memos, hence the title of this boo' Included in all that paper was an almost complete set daily production reports, or "PRs." Those daily rep summarize all other set documents used in a giver and, in the event the film ends up in court, are cons the controlling document. I write about the two pages in Chapter 8.

That paper provided a lot of details, from equipment to rejected locations, but also a lot of i the personalities of the filmmakers. Sadly, it also included the coroner's report on the death of Director Tony Scott. He leaped off the Vincent Thomas Bridge in Los Angeles on Sunday, Aug. 19, 2012, a day after returning from a scout to Nevada on the long-awaited sequel to *Top Gun*. Scott's last days are covered in Chapter 14 and his contributions to film in Chapter 15.

It's a strange thing to spend this much time studying the work of someone you can't observe or interview, even with the mountains of material of him talking about his most successful movie. Tony Scott was, in the words of Tom Cruise, "a great man and a great artist."

About halfway through the book I stopped thinking of the director as "Scott" and started thinking of him as "Tony." That change was triggered by an interview with a cameraman who choked up talking about him. By then I had interviewed dozens of people who had worked with Scott, many of them friends, and they all called him Tony. Collectively, they helped fill in the story of this brilliant, funny and complex man who was sometimes cerebral and visionary, other times telling jokes or scaling rocks and occasionally mountains, which he did as a hobby.

No one knew Tony Scott better than his wife. I made effort to interview Donna Scott early in the process, but was unsuccessful until the end. She's the last person I talked to for the book, and it made all the difference.

My initial assumption was that the passage of time might mean problematically disparate memories. There were occasional outliers, but always enough people to bring together a cohesive view of events, which could then, almost always, be found in paperwork. The movie's success helped keep memories alive.

The different vantage points of the movie crew and the aviators also helped. Try asking someone who has worked in the movie business for 30 years if they remember the base camp at any particular location. Ask the same question of a pilot who was only around one movie in his life, and he will remember it. One might even recall the smartass comments of a young movie star, as well.

This is the story of *Top Gun.*

Meredith Jordan, March 2022

Notes for Reading

This book is written, as closely as possible, as a chronology. All events are happening in 1985 unless otherwise stated.

Many people participated in the making of *Top Gun,* hence there are a lot of characters in the book. They can be hard to keep track of, so there is an alphabetical list for quick reference in chart form at the back of the book. The description uses the credit granted the individual as it appeared in the movie, if available.

There are a lot of references to other movies. Where movie stats are provided we have used the International Movie Database (IMDb), unless otherwise indicated.

You may notice that variations of the name, *Top Gun/* Top Guns/ Topgun. When the book refers to *Top Gun,* it's talking about the movie, or anything connected to the movie. "Top Guns" was the early name of the movie, while "Topguns" also appears in studio documents. Where the book refers to "Topgun," it's referring to the squadron, or the school, as that's the term used by most Navy personnel.

Note that movies are italicized in text, as in *Top Gun,* while screenplays and projects that haven't been made yet, are not.

Inflation numbers are calculated based on Consumer Price Index (CPI) data.

PART I
SIX MONTHS TO PREP

Late 1984-June 1985

PHOTO: C.J. Heatley

This shot of F-14s appeared in California magazine article that inspired the producers to invent and then make Top Gun. The photographer, Navy pilot LCDR C.J. Heatley, was to spend a lot of time assisting the movie production and Tony Scott.

CHAPTER 1
GREEN LIGHT TO PREP
1984

The story of how *Top Gun* came to life could be its own high-concept movie script. A filmmaker is reading a magazine story in a dentist's office, leaps to his feet to find his producing partner and proclaims, "This should be a movie!" And in three years it's on the big screen.

Just don't think it was easy or that its journey from conception to iconic film was logical. The seemingly simple idea for the movie — something about pilots at an elite fighter weapons school in sleek flying machines — required harnessing the U.S. Navy, which wasn't accustomed to being harnessed. It involved utilizing billions of dollars' worth of Navy assets. It meant finding a male ensemble cast, and filling two female roles, in a sea of young talent in Los Angeles in the mid-1980s. Add to those hurdles that Paramount set the budget at $13.8 million and stuck with it, although in the end it cost a little more than $15 million.

Consider the comparative technological limitations of the era. *Top Gun* was made in 1985 when routine tools associated with business operations today either didn't exist or were in developmental infancy. Cell phones, personal computers, email — the Internet — weren't in use. People wrote memos on typewriters and occasionally by hand. Even the fax machine wasn't in common use. When moviemakers needed to send a script somewhere, they sent it by courier or by overnight mail, which had become a huge business. Federal Express had $1 billion in revenue for the first time in fiscal 1983.

Top Gun struck a chord with the movie-going public despite being widely panned by critics. The movie had come out in a year of critically acclaimed films like *Platoon (1986), Children of a Lesser God (1986)*, and *A Room With a View* (1985), and critics saw *Top Gun* as too commercial, too MTV, too much a love letter to the military. Three weeks after it was released, word-of-mouth reviews took over. Paramount added 474 more theaters to meet demand, the opposite of what normally happens.[1] The movie ended up No. 1 at the box office in 1986.

More to the point, its popularity has continued for decades with legions of fans, and its worldwide gross, now at $357 million, continues to grow. And it was growing long before the sequel, *Top Gun: Maverick* (2022), began stirring up interest anew.[2]

Top Gun's impact on culture is undeniable. It is credited with helping turn the tide of anti-military sentiment in the post-Vietnam era. Dialogue from the movie dropped into the public lexicon and remains there today. The movie was credited with the boom in sales of white T-shirts and bomber jackets, which has never really fallen back. Merchandise linked to the movie — from T-shirts and hats to patches and pins — is still sold every day. Say what you will about *Platoon, Children of a Lesser God,* or *A Room With A View,* but there's no present-day market in T-shirts bearing the marks of those films.

Top Gun may be most often thought of as the movie that launched Tom Cruise's movie career into mega stardom. Easily one of the top movie stars of all time, Cruise is likely at the pinnacle of that elite group if the only measure is box-office proceeds. It's something few people besides Cruise and his agent might have predicted in 1985.

The Creative Producers

There are different kinds of producers. Creative producers take a project through from start to finish, usually with a script in hand. The job involves securing financing, or in this case, studio approval. They hire the talent needed, from the actors and director to key department heads, and post-production crew. They bring in the editors who sew it together, the musicians who write score and contribute songs, and they work to shape the final product into something with mass appeal. Then they bring the movie to market, another long, multilayered process.

The creative producers behind *Top Gun* didn't have a script. The vague concept for what would become the movie was published in the May 1983 issue of "California" magazine:[3] "Top Guns: At Mach 1 and 40,000 feet over California, it's always high noon." Written by Ehud Yonay with photographs by Navy pilot, LCDR. C.J. Heatley, it told the story of a fighter jet program at Naval Air Station Miramar in San Diego, which was founded to improve the performance of the Navy's most elite pilots, and had succeeded.

Holding up a single glossy image of a naval aviator in sunglasses in an F-14 to describe the concept for a major motion picture as criterion for gaining approval for a project wasn't the norm, even in the mid-80s.[4] But this was Don Simpson and Jerry Bruckheimer, the hottest producing team in the country thanks to *Flashdance* (1983) and *Beverly Hills Cop* (1984). In 1985 those successes led to a lucrative four-year exclusivity deal at Paramount Pictures.[5]

Bruckheimer told many reporters over the years of his visceral reaction to the magazine article. Perhaps most concisely, he described it as having "great visuals, call signs, all this wonderful stuff, a photo in the cockpit, reflections." Heatley said when he first met the producers they told him they'd seen the story — and his photographs — while at the dentist's office.[6] They'd been there at the same time for appointments and often did such things together.

Today, Bruckheimer is one of the highest grossing producers of all time, perhaps at the pinnacle if measured solely by revenue from movie and television titles. Back then he was the less-experienced half of Don Simpson/Jerry

Bruckheimer Films. Simpson had been president of production at Paramount, and Bruckheimer a freelance producer.[7]

Simpson, who died in 1996, had seen his stature rise quickly. His first job at the studio was executive assistant to the president of Paramount's movie division, and the last, before he founded his own company, was president of production. He had made it there in six years.

Being a studio executive wasn't what Simpson wanted to do, and of the many producers who had come through his office in his years at Paramount, he viewed Bruckheimer as the best. That's what Simpson told an audience at the American Film Institute in April 1988.[8] "He knew how to make movies, and I knew how to get movies made."

Among other things, Simpson and Bruckheimer were good at marketing and self-promotion, regularly accepting and inviting interviews. The pitch to Paramount leadership used compelling language that would cause any studio head to salivate: *Star Wars* on Earth! It was enough to get Jeffrey Katzenberg, then head of production at Paramount, excited. That enabled them to hire scriptwriters Jim Cash and Jack Epps, Jr.[9] At that point the writing duo had sold screenplays, although none had been produced.

Almost as an afterthought, Bruckheimer and Simpson realized they'd need to get the Navy on board.

The Pentagon

A lobbyist who represented studios in Washington, D.C., secured an audience at the Pentagon. Bruckheimer described the pitch meeting as taking place in a "capacious corner office on the third floor" in a "sea of ice cream suits, as far as the eye can see, extremely fit 50-year-old guys in white suits and gold braid, with a smattering of 30-year-old guys who look like bodyguards."[10]

Ultimately the idea of the movie won the approval of Navy Secretary John Lehman, Jr. but not all the Navy brass was keen on working with Hollywood. The Pentagon's last experience in partnering on a movie created a lot of internal strife. That movie was *The Final Countdown* (1980), the story of a modern nuclear-powered aircraft carrier that travels back in time to the Dec. 7, 1941, attack on Pearl Harbor. The film starred Kirk Douglas and Martin Sheen. A Navy investigation following production looked at whether members of the military had inappropriately accepted things of value from a producer, and subsequently charges were filed.[11] Recollections of what happened at the time varied among former Navy officers but all recalled a general reluctance to get involved with Hollywood after that. The sentiment was that getting anywhere near a movie could be a career-killer, and it was best to steer clear.

Navy leadership hadn't liked the next opportunity, which was *An Officer and a Gentleman* (1982). They didn't like the way the script portrayed the Navy, and declined to participate. Simpson, president of production at Paramount at the time, remembered how hard it was to make a movie about the Navy without them. That experience informed his strategy for the new movie.

The obvious question at the pitch meeting at the Pentagon about Topgun, as the Navy informally referred to the school, was what the movie was about. There wasn't a script yet and an 8x10 glossy of a pilot in an F14 didn't offer much detail. So, Simpson made up a story. Bruckheimer later said it turned out to be remarkably close to the one ultimately shot, but it was completely off the cuff. Whatever Simpson said, the Navy agreed to participate.

Simpson and Bruckheimer, properly solicitous, asked if the military could recommend a technical consultant. Someone suggested Rear Admiral (RADM) USNR (Ret.) Pete Pettigrew. He was a hero who had flown 325 combat missions in Vietnam before becoming an instructor at the Navy Fighter Weapons School, as Topgun was formally known.[12] The combination of being an insider, and retired, created distance that was desirable given what happened with *The Final Countdown*. Pettigrew soon went to work on the script with Cash and Epps in an effort to make it more palatable to those on the Navy side.[13] That would make it easier to get other needed permissions.

A script in progress

When the first Cash and Epps draft came in, Katzenberg and the others were disappointed. It had a lot of adrenaline but little story. They kicked it back for a second draft, which was returned six months later but left the moviemakers similarly nonplussed. That put the project into "turnaround," a positive-sounding term that means the studio is going to pass. Later, Bruckheimer would say the rejection had to do with a television show about the Air Force, "Call to Glory," which hadn't done well. Simpson and Bruckheimer just dug in deeper.

"We orchestrated a meeting with [president of Paramount, Michael] Eisner and Katzenberg. Don got on his knees and literally begged them," recalled Bruckheimer. "That got their attention."[14] But before long, Eisner and Katzenberg jumped ship to Disney. Now Simpson and Bruckheimer had to start over with the new Paramount chairman, Ned Tanen.

To their delight, Tanen approached them first, saying "the cupboard is bare" and he needed pitches. They told him they had a project featuring aviators, and he asked what it would cost. "We said $14, $15 million."

Tanen liked the idea, and the budget, but wanted to know which male actors they were considering. His approval, in late 1984, was what allowed the rest of it to move forward. "Tanen would only make the movie with Tom Cruise," said Bill Badalato,[15] whom Simpson and Bruckheimer hired as executive producer in January 1985. "That's how Cruise got in the movie."

Epps, however, says he wrote it with Cruise in mind,[16] and suggested the young actor to Simpson and Bruckheimer. "I thought he was the perfect Maverick: the guy you like even though he had some dislikable traits." Bruckheimer acknowledged that, saying they also thought he was a great choice. In the decade that followed the movie, Simpson and Bruckheimer consistently said Cruise was the only actor for the job.

But it isn't true that they hadn't considered other actors.

The actors (and an agent)

Simpson and Bruckheimer considered Sean Penn for the role of Maverick early in the process. Newspaper accounts, including some that quote Simpson, show that Penn and Mickey Rourke, along with Cruise, were of interest, and later that Cruise had been selected over Penn.

Syndicated columnist Marilyn Beck wrote a piece in July 1984 about actors being asked to do more to promote their movies.[17] That wasn't a contracted requirement, as it is today, and the story said Penn hadn't made himself available when one of his movies was released. The column also quoted an unnamed studio executive as saying, "If there's a choice between Tom Cruise and Sean Penn today, you can be sure we'll go with Tom because he is cooperative about promoting his films." The column appeared in some markets with a mugshot of Cruise and the words "Choice over Sean Penn?"

It was Penn who suggested to Cruise that he talk to his agent, Paula Wagner at Creative Artists Agency (CAA), to begin with. The actors met on *Taps* (1981), and Penn let Cruise stay in his guesthouse when he first moved to Los Angeles. Wagner represented Penn in landing *Fast Times at Ridgemont High* (1982).

In 1985 Wagner was rapidly making a name for herself at CAA, then at the 10-year mark of its storied history. A proponent of signing young actors early on, her roster included Val Kilmer and Demi Moore, who were also up for roles in *Top Gun*.

The role of Wagner in Cruise's career can't be overstated, given that they went on to create Cruise/Wagner Productions in 1993. In terms of box-office winnings, C/W operated at or near the top of the industry for 13 years, with grosses in excess of $2.9 billion.

"There are few things in life you just know, but [his impending stardom] was one of them," said Wagner,[18] who signed Cruise when he was 19. Wagner deserves full credit for Cruise landing the role in *Risky Business* (1983). "If Paula Wagner hadn't been as persistent and supportive of Tom, he quite simply wouldn't have been in *Risky Business*," said producer Steve Tisch.[19]

Separately, it's possible that Paramount later considered Kilmer as a backup for the role of Maverick. Kilmer's deal memo,[20] an internal studio document, showed the name of Maverick lined through, and made no mention of Iceman, the role Kilmer eventually played.

The casting department threw out as wide a net for actresses as for actors, despite the fact *Top Gun* had just two roles for women. The character who would eventually be called Charlie was the love interest of Maverick, while Carole was the wife of Maverick's radio intercept officer, Goose. Meg Ryan, in her breakout role, was cast as Carole.

One document titled "Charlie Possibilities"[21] appears to be the list of finalists. It includes Susan Hess, Linda Fiorentino, Jodie Foster, Kelly McGillis, Demi Moore, Julianne Phillips, Ally Sheedy and Daphne Zuniga. In total there were 32 actresses actively considered, and four who screen-tested with Cruise, including Demi Moore.

McGillis, who would ultimately play Charlie, declined. Among other things, she was under contract to Paramount and in line to star in *The Two Jakes*, the sequel to the *Chinatown* (1974) opposite Jack Nicholson.

Tom Cruise

Cruise, 22 when prep began, had three credits as a lead at that point. *Losin' It* (1983) had been forgotten quickly, while *All the Right Moves* (1983) received attention but didn't make a lot of money. It was *Risky Business*, which cost about $6.2

million and brought in about $64 million,[22] that placed him on a well-populated map of young male stars.

Cruise's earlier work, as part of the ensemble cast of *The Outsiders* (1983) and *Taps*, had been promising but slight. It was admittedly tough competition, given Penn and the other actors in those films, many of who went on to significant careers. *The Outsiders* featured Matt Dillon, Ralph Macchio, Patrick Swayze, Rob Lowe, and Emilio Estevez. *Taps* included Penn, Timothy Hutton, and Giancarlo Esposito.

In a 2020 interview, Lowe told a story about Cruise when they were young actors trying to get work. Initial auditions for *The Outsiders,* directed by Frances Ford Coppola, were held in Los Angeles. Dozens of actors tried out, and those who made the cut were brought to New York for a second audition. Most of the young men in the mix were thrilled. Cruise had a different attitude. When he discovered he would be sharing a room at the Plaza Hotel with Lowe, instead of having his own room, Cruise went "ballistic," according to Lowe, who called the episode "gnarly."

"The notion that an 18-year-old actor with a walk-on part in *Endless Love* and like a seventh lead in *Taps* could have that kind of wherewithal" made Lowe laugh. "But in the end, you can't argue with the results. He's had his eye on the ball since day one."[23]

Cruise's belief in himself was even stronger by the time *Top Gun* appeared on the horizon. He told Simpson and Bruckheimer that he wanted to be involved in the creative process. "So Jerry and I invited him into our process and he was with us on a daily basis," said Simpson.

Simpson and Bruckheimer, both 42 in mid-1985, knew the script needed help. The actor wanted the role of Maverick to be improved in a way that made the character more relatable.[24] "I liked it, but it needed a lot of work," was Cruise's recollection of the original script.[25] The producers welcomed the actor's assistance across the board.

Simpson called Cruise "a very smart guy" and said he had been "very effective in terms of his point of view." The actor "contributed a heck of a lot, to his character in particular, and to elements that we included." Cruise even weighed in on who would write the score. The actor also did what he could to help the movie, assisting producers in efforts to win over more people in the Navy during prep. All the while, Wagner made improvements to his contract. It was updated five times before the actor signed off — two days before principal photography began.

Cruise remained incredibly serious throughout production. It's striking because of his youth, but also because his peers were more laid back. By all accounts, the production of *Top Gun* was as much fun as it was hard work, and emblematic of the party culture of the mid-1980s. The other actors regularly partied with each other and with the crew, but Cruise didn't hang around for long. When he socialized it was generally with pilots and Navy brass, who found him solicitous and polite, or with Scott, Simpson and Bruckheimer. The result was that Cruise came off as aloof. There were minor hints of conflict that ended up in news reports, particularly between Cruise and Kilmer. That was explained as the men essentially being in character, and the characters didn't like each other.

When a member of the props department suggested to Cruise that he have a beer in a scene, the actor told him he didn't drink. The prop master explained to the actor that he didn't have to drink it, but if he held it on camera, the company would give him beer for the crew to drink. "Then I'll do it," said Cruise.[26]

"I think Cruise knew that this was his big chance," said John Semcken, who was the Navy's primary liaison with the production. "And that he may not ever get another chance."[27]

The Director

Many people involved in making the movie note a perceived assumption, built over the years because of Cruise's stature, that *Top Gun* was Cruise's movie. The actor was obviously key to its success. But it was Scott who made the movie — supported by a lot of below-the-line talent — and it is Scott's fingerprints that are all over it.

Hiring him to direct *Top Gun* seemed like a risk to some at the studio, but not Simpson and Bruckheimer. "We like to take directors when they're down, because that's the point in time that they are most amenable to guidance," Simpson said at an American Film Institute Q&A, a comment met with laughter.

Bruckheimer, who often stepped in to mitigate Simpson's blunter statements and actions, chimed in with a more measured explanation. "It's when somebody is down in their career, you know they're going to try 10 times harder to pull themselves up. And we like that, we want someone on the come, somebody who hasn't quite made it yet. Because it's not boring to them."

Scott was a commercial director whose only experience in feature films, *The Hunger* (1983), hadn't gone well. In its wake, with no other offers to direct a movie, he resumed making commercials. One, 1984's "Nothing on Earth Comes Close" for an automaker, intercut images of a Saab Scania and a fighter plane, with a final image of the aircraft taking off over a Saab driving on a tarmac. Simpson and Bruckheimer marveled at that specific visual and Scott later said the commercial is why he got the job.[28]

The creative producers got to know Scott on a rafting trip attended by a host of above-the-line movie industry people. The six-day trip down the Colorado River included the heads of Universal Studios and Disney, along with various directors and actors Danny DeVito, Tony Danza and Penny Marshall. It was a lot of fun with "a lot of tequila, a lot of chili and a lot of water — gone," Simpson told the AFI audience.

One night, sitting around a campfire, someone asked Simpson and Bruckheimer what was next for them. They had just returned from the meeting at the Pentagon and had approval for *Top Gun*, Bruckheimer said.

"Don was telling the story of the movie, and Tony said, 'Well whenever you get around to hiring a director, please make me at the top of the list. I'd love to do a picture like that,'" recalled Bruckheimer at AFI. "Later that night, we turn around, and there's Tony, about 30 or 40 feet in the air, climbing the face of the Grand Canyon — with his bare hands, and no guidelines! Tony is the kind of adventurer those pilots were, the pilots had the same kind of aggressiveness." He said the pilots weren't "quite as crazy as Tony, because they're dealing with the government and our money and those planes, so they have to be a little more careful, but their life is on the line, as Tony tries to put his life on the line."

Donna Scott, Tony's wife, said he told a different version of the event. Climbing the wall wasn't what really secured the deal — that was a dare from Simpson. The producer said that if Tony would swim Lava Falls, a Class 10 rapid, he could have the job. Tony put on two life jackets and a helmet and jumped in. "That's the story he always told," she said.[29] Later Scott swam Lava Falls again, that time when he was in the Grand Canyon on a Marlboro commercial, she added.

With commercials, which have much larger budgets per-frame than do major motion pictures, every second is managed to full effect. Scott knew how well sex sold, and the role music a la MTV was playing in the entertainment lives of young Americans, and he planned to tap both. Even the Saab commercial started with a handsome driver-model in sunglasses wearing nice clothes.

He relied upon one book, in particular, to guide the specifics: "Looking Good: A Guide For Men."[30] Written by Charles Hix, with photographs by Bruce Weber, it was described as "a grooming guide for men, with advice on caring for their hair, face, body, hands, and feet." Its real appeal was the pictures of young men. "It was his visual Bible for the way he wanted the men to look," said Badalato. "He carried it around during prep when he was sorting out the look he wanted the pilots to have."

Scott paid that intense attention to detail in making *Top Gun*. He weighed in on everything from how many planes were towed to a scene as props to whether the actors should be in jeans for the volleyball game. He helped place the patches on what became the famous leather jacket worn by Cruise. He often required two sets of furniture available for some scenes in case he liked one better than the other.

John DeCuir, Jr., production designer, recalled Scott being hands-on from the outset. "He was very concerned about the look of the movie. That meant the directorial spin he put on it, something that had his visual signature on it."[31]

"Tony was a perfectionist and he would constantly change things around," said Fred Baron, who worked in the production office and as an uncredited location manager on *Top Gun*, and went on to be a studio executive.[32]

Scott's love of the "magic hour," the time just after sunrise and before sunset, would be something many people remembered about Scott decades later. "He wanted to know where the sun would be on every location," said Baron.

Non-filmmakers recognize that time of day as twilight or gloaming, while camera people think of it more technically, for the brief time natural light is diffused evenly. "Tony wanted everything backlit," said Dan Kolsrud, the first assistant director, whose job was to run the set while also acting as the right-hand person to the director from when he started in prep through principal photography. "He wanted sunset behind everything. It was meant to be romantic rather than real."[33]

In very early stages Scott pictured something dark for the movie but soon came around to an almost opposite vision, one of "blue skies with silver jets, and rock and roll music." And good-looking guys.

The Navy

Top Gun relied so heavily on the use of the Navy's props and locations there was no movie without the service. The meeting in the big room at the Pentagon was just the first step. There was no guarantee the project would be embraced down the chain of command. The difference between naval officers — some in charge of squadrons of F-14s, A-4s and F-5s, others managing aircraft carriers and bases — assisting begrudgingly or enthusiastically was the difference between a hit and a miss. To get their support the filmmakers needed to build relationships.

It wasn't just the Navy, either.

Like any big star, the F-14 had more than one handler. The Navy agreed that the movie company could use and photograph the aircraft as long as no classified information got out. For cameras to be attached to the planes — something the creative producers felt was essential to telling the story — had to be approved by Grumman Corp., which developed and built the F-14.

The supersonic fighter jet was designed to find and destroy enemy aircraft at any time of day or night, and in all weather. It began service in 1972, and was at its peak in the mid-80s. The defense contractor would make 712 of the aircraft before retiring the line in 1991.

In the mid-80s, the F-14 was at its peak. It was sleek and stood 16 feet high, a remarkable military machine. Its full wingspan was 64 feet, which was slightly longer than its 62-foot length, but its wings also could be angled, or swept, to just 38 feet. Air moves more slowly over swept wings, which reduces turbulence. It also made the F-14 that much more versatile. The F-14 was also well known by the public by that point and for the storytellers, it was almost a character in its own right.

Bruckheimer had met with Dick Milligan, deputy director of public affairs at Grumman, in December 1984, which shows the importance the producers placed on Grumman's cooperation. Milligan already had one Hollywood patch on his jacket: He had been a technical advisor on *The Final Countdown*.

Milligan's follow-up letter to Bruckheimer, dated Dec. 21, 1984, thanked him for the meeting and reiterated his interest. He enjoyed discussing the "various problems involved in filming air to air sequences with modern combat aircraft." Bruckheimer copied the letter to Simpson, Dawn Steel, and Charles H. "Charlie" Maguire, respectively, president and vice president of production at Paramount.[34]

But bringing Grumman into the fold was something else entirely, and that fell to Badalato.

The Executive Producer

When Bill Badalato graduated from Cornell University in the mid-1960s, he wasn't thinking about being a filmmaker. His focus was on economics and labor relations. His father-in-law — Steven D'Inzillo, head of Local 306, Motion Picture Projectionists, Operators, Video Technicians and Allied Craftspeople — advised him that "if he wanted to do good for labor, be a good manager," recalled Badalato.

D'Inzillo introduced the young man to the president of Screen Gems, which ultimately led to a job in the television production division of Elliot, Unger and Eliot in New York. It still operates today as EUE/ Screen Gems Ltd., a film and studio production company with facilities in Wilmington, N.C., Atlanta and Miami.

"That was my first exposure to the basics," recalled Badalato. Living in the city enabled a different kind of education. "I could watch every film imaginable," he recalled. "I fell in love with filmmaking."[35] Two years later at EUE he was asked to accept an intern. It turned out to be Charley B. Moss Jr., whose family owned a well-known theatrical exhibition company with jewels like the Criterion Theater on

Broadway. The young men both dreamed of producing a theatrical feature film and soon became friends, eventually finding a horror script called "It Drinks Hippie Blood."

"Starting with nothing but our shared desire to make a film we were able to raise, through 'friends and family,' the funding necessary to make a (very) low budget movie," wrote Moss.[36] That included his father, who in addition to financing was involved in the casting process and in analysis of dailies. The younger Moss produced, Badalato co-produced, and John D. Hancock directed.

The $180,000 movie — more than $466,000 today when adjusted for inflation — was made without a distributor but found a suitor in Paramount. The studio's contribution was to change the name to *Let's Scare Jessica to Death* (1971). The movie became a cult classic, with Paramount issuing a DVD version in 2006.

Hancock brought Badalato on as "the line guy" on *Bang the Drum Slowly* (1973), Robert De Niro's second feature. The character De Niro played was a loner, and "Bobby was loner on set," recalled Badalato. He described the actor as "intense. He was so concerned that his baseball uniform would lose its worn look that he refused to give it to the wardrobe mistress for fear she would wash it." Badalato worked with De Niro again on *Men of Honor* (2000), that time as producer.

It was the offer of a production management job on *Jaws 2* (1978) that prompted Badalato and his wife, the former Jane D'Inzillo, to move to Los Angeles permanently. Badalato stayed at the studio after the release of *Jaws 2* to work on John Belushi's last film, *Continental Divide* (1981). Someone at Universal introduced Badalato to Bruckheimer, who hired Badalato as production manager on *Cat People* and *Young Doctors in Love*, both 1982, and then as executive producer on *Top Gun*.

"I was brought on early to basically figure out how to do the movie as there were no films before this with the extent of military involvement," he said. "I think it's accurate to say

Jerry knew and liked how I worked. I was budget-conscious and not intimidated by directors — I liked the challenge."[37]

Badalato was the first full-time hire for "Top Guns," as the project was still called. He knew as he drove from his home in the Hollywood Hills to the Paramount lot that first morning in mid-January 1985 it was likely to be a stressful production. He'd read the script and begun work on a preliminary budget and it was clear the $15 million they thought was approved by the studio wasn't enough to do what they wanted, even with a best-case scenario with the Navy.

What was clear, even without hard numbers, was that Paramount didn't want to spend a lot on the movie. That dynamic — the business side balancing the creative side — isn't unusual. Directors want to make the best movie possible, and executive producers are charged with controlling the purse. That created rich terrain for conflict.

The job of executive producer is sometimes referred to as line producer, a term that stems from lines on an accounting statement. Being the steward of the budget is a key responsibility, and decades later, many people would still remember him as "the money guy." The emphasis in this case should be on the word "executive" because of the extent to which Badalato designed and managed the complex physical production, something well documented in memos, interviews and internal Paramount paperwork.

Badalato had already given thought to the core structure of principal photography. The most efficient way to make the movie was in four parts: a ground story, a sea story, air-to-air, then a special-effects component, which was needed to tie the pieces together. Each of those would require different locations and have different requirements in production space, and, in some cases, crew. There were numerous other details that also fell to him. Picking up the initial communication with Grumman was just the start to a long process that had to play out before cameras were attached to an F-14. And, that was just one of the moving parts.

The extent to which it would fall to Badalato to rein in the stubborn Scott also is noteworthy. It doesn't appear that either Simpson or Badalato ever intervened to get more money for the production, although it is likely they stopped Maguire from cutting it as much as he wanted.

Pay packages and credits due

Today, the credits that appear at the end of movies, sometimes referred to as the scroll, are long. Listing everyone who contributed to making a movie benefits the production companies and studios. It shows the sheer effort in creating the art but also the substantial investment in personnel needed.

For decades, studios listed very few people in credits. Leadership could assert that screen time was costly, but it was also indicative of the cultural norm, which was that credit — and profit — adhered to the top. So did recognition for the work. "Above the line," which refers to the writer(s), director, actors and producers, began as an accounting term. The pay for high-level players went above a line at the top of the accounting statement. At the same time, strong unions rose up to help ensure movie workers received decent treatment and pay. Vestiges of the cultural norm remain today, particularly with profits, but also in terms of recognition.

Studio executives of the day fit somewhere between, with well-paying jobs and prestige, but not in the credits. As a result, mid-level studio executives, many of them in leadership roles, are largely obscured in the record. Most didn't have a financial stake in the movie, but they left their marks, just the same. Working on the Paramount lot in the first months of prep, as they did with *Top Gun*, meant close proximity to studio services, employees and executives.

People in top studio roles were written about, even if their names didn't appear in credits. Dawn Steel, one of the few high-ranking women executives in Hollywood, would eventually leave Paramount to run Columbia Pictures. Her most significant contribution to *Top Gun* likely was helping to get the screenplay right, because she connected the creative producers to the writer who fixed it, and shepherded him along, but she also provided top-level support during post-production and distribution.

When it came to *Top Gun*, Maguire, in particular, was a force to be reckoned with. As head of production, he applied pressure about the budget early on. It was also he that passed out the memo that dictated who was to get on screen credits. His job wasn't on the list.

Maguire was vice president of production at Paramount in the early 1980s, and moved into Simpson's former job as head of production in plenty of time for *Top Gun*.[38] His credits, which have been recorded, included working as an assistant director to Elia Kazan on *On the Waterfront* (1954), which was shot in New Jersey. His relationship with Kazan continued for several more pictures. Maguire moved to Hollywood and up the ladder, with roles as an associate producer on *Splendor in the Grass* (1961), *Fail Safe* (1964), and *Shampoo* (1975).

"Charlie was a very pragmatic studio guy who saw behavior and would make a call. He didn't spend a lot of energy on his choice of words," said Badalato, who would go on to produce movies like *Hot Shots* (1991), *Benny and Joon* (1993), *Alien: Resurrection* (1997), *Men of Honor* (2000), *About Schmidt* (2002) and *Around the World in 80 Days* (2004).

Like Badalato, Maguire hailed from New York, part of the larger group of Hollywood production executives who had come west to join the business. That influx, and one like it on the directing side from England that included the Scott brothers and others, was helping shift how Hollywood did things.

At the end of principal photography for *Top Gun*, Maguire went through and eliminated people approved by Badalato for onscreen credit, including Fred Baron. Baron had appeared on call sheets as location manager, and that was the expected credit. In reality he had done more for the movie, acting as a "a field [unit production manager]."

Badalato said he pressed for Maguire to give Baron the location manager credit, but there was no changing his mind.[39]

As executive producer on *Top Gun*, Badalato was above the line, and his credit appeared near the opening of the movie. That placement spoke to his importance to the overall making of *Top Gun*, yet he wasn't in the money. As a rule, creative producers and executive producers have different pay structures. Creative producers have a stake in box-office returns, whereas executive producers don't.

The creative producers were also the ones to take the movie on the road, talking about it and promoting it and themselves. That period lasted longer with *Top Gun*, given its success, which greatly enriched Simpson and Bruckheimer and anyone with a share in its backend profits.

The duo's AFI appearance in 1988 was striking for another reason. During the Q&A, Simpson called the making of *Top Gun* a "grievous undertaking," and it was, but he followed up with something else that was misleading at best. He credited Bruckheimer with designing the complex physical production, which met with audience approval. Bruckheimer stayed silent.

It typically falls to the executive producer to design and manage physical productions, and that was the case with *Top Gun*. Badalato decided on the four-part structure, built out the plan for principal photography like an architect with a blueprint, then saw it through construction. His intense efforts over many months are clearly reflected in internal Paramount memos, personal notes of various people involved, and both described and confirmed by numerous sources.

Badalato said he doesn't begrudge the fact he wasn't in the money on *Top Gun*. It's how the job is structured. "I felt like I was fairly compensated then, and I still think so today," he said. He was less circumspect about Simpson and Bruckheimer taking credit for designing the physical production, even cavalierly, at a Q&A. "That pissed me off," he said.[40]

Above-the-line pay

A Paramount Pictures Corp. form memo titled "FLASH Preliminary Deal Summary," dated Jan. 1, 1985, addressed most above-the-line costs. It included how much the company was paying for the rights to the underlying story to Ehud, to scriptwriters, to military consultant Pete Pettigrew, and the director. It also listed the producers, specifically Simpson and Bruckheimer, but said only, "Per their Overall Deal." There was no mention of Cruise.[41]

A flash memo signaled to people on the distribution list at the studio that it should be reviewed quickly. The same memo would be updated as a new issue when a change or addition was made. This one, Issue No. 6 for the Simpson/Bruckheimer Project, "Top Guns," was created by Greg Gelfan in business affairs and circulated to at least 19 people. There are two "received Feb. 21 1985" stamps on it. One stamp was Maguire's as head of production, and the other was Jim Fasbender, who signed the checks.

The memo is structured A-F, with five summaries preceding the above-the-line agreements. An asterisk near the bottom notes it reflects just one change from the previous flash memo. The change is the addition of another scriptwriter. Some of the language in the memo is straightforward but the parts that deal with the writers' deals are distinctly convoluted.

Yonay, who penned the article for California magazine, was in for a $2,000 option for the story, another $1,500 to extend the option for 12 months, and finally a purchase price of $20,000, "less all sums," if the project moved forward.

Tony Scott would receive $400,000 "pay or play," meaning he was guaranteed that much, regardless of whether the movie was ultimately made. The real prize for the director was that he would earn 7.5 points NP, or net profit. That would be $26.7 million if it were 7.5 percent of the worldwide gross for the movie, which in January 2022 was estimated to be $357 million. Net profit is different. It deducts all costs of making the movie, from production and salaries to marketing and distributing, and a host of other things, too, like the cost of managing the business of it over years, such as re-marketing expenses for releases of the VHS, DVD, 3D versions. Whatever the total, it's a very large number.

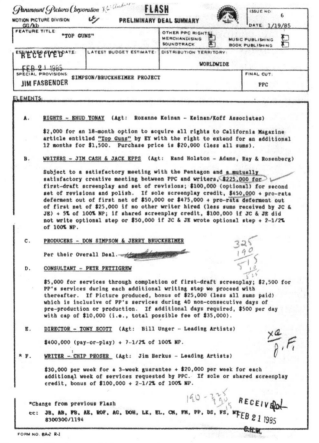

The paper "flash memo," this one guiding above-the-line costs of Top Gun, was once a regular fixture in in-boxes on desks throughout the studio.

All industries employ smart accountants to use creative methods, usually legal ones, to manipulate reported profit. The higher the expenses, the greater the ability to reduce (or even eliminate) taxes, royalties and the sums associated with points, agreed to as part of profit-sharing agreements. Deal memos were the fertilizer of creative accounting, using murky language to aid the studios in what they paid out. A huge variable was "distribution fees," where the distribution company associated with the studio would charge the production company, which had the effect of greatly reducing profits and what the studio had to pay out.

NP provided a huge orchard where Hollywood's creative accounting could blossom. Eventually high-profile legal challenges shined a light on the practice, and the marketplace had wised up and started demanding their points from gross.

It was the norm in the 1980s and the language of the flash memo, delivered in late February 1985 about "Top Guns" is a good example. Cash's and Epps' deal was "Subject to a satisfactory meeting with the Pentagon and a mutually satisfactory creative meeting between PPC and writers."

Plot, Hollywood Style

"The Top Gun Naval Fighter Weapons School is where the best of the best train to refine their elite flying skills. When hotshot fighter pilot Maverick (Tom Cruise) is sent to the school, his reckless attitude and cocky demeanor put him at odds with the other pilots, especially the cool and collected Iceman (Val Kilmer). But Maverick isn't only competing to be the top fighter pilot, he's also fighting for the attention of his beautiful flight instructor, Charlotte Blackwood (Kelly McGillis)."

Then they would be paid $225,000 for a first-draft screenplay and set of revisions plus an additional $100,000 for a second set of revisions and polish. It got a little more complicated from there. "If sole screenplay credit, $450,000

+ pro rata deferment out of first net of $50,000 or $475,000 + pro rata deferment out of first net of $25,000 if no other writer hired (less sums received by JC & JE) + 5% of 100% percent of NP; if shared screenplay credit, $100,000 if JC & JE did not write optional step + 2 ½% of 100% NP."

The part of the memo notated to be the change from the last flash memo was the plan to pay another writer, Chip Proser, $20,000 a week for three weeks, guaranteed, then $20,000 per week for each additional week of services. "If sole or shared screenplay credit, bonus of $100,000 + 2 ½% of 100% NP."[42]

Chapter 1 - Endnotes

[1] Tina McFarling, "Top Gun Shoots Back to Top Slot," *Screen International*, June 14, 1986.

[2] "*Top Gun* (1986)," The Numbers, https://www.the-numbers.com/movie/Top-Gun.

[3] Ehud Yonay, "Top Guns: At Mach 1 and 40,000 feet over California, it's always high noon," *California*, May 1985. *California* ceased publication in 1991. Article reposted, date unknown. http://www.topgunbio.com/top-guns-by-ehud-yonay/ [4] John Patterson, "Bruckheimer Goes to War," *Guardian*, October 27, 2000. Friday Review, 4. https://www.newspapers.com/image/259565057.

[5] Charles Fleming, "Days of Plunder," *LA Weekly*, April 22, 1998. https://www.laweekly.com/days-of-plunder/.

[6] C. J. Heatley, LCDR USN (Ret.), interview with the author, December 1, 2020.

[7] "*Top Gun*" Special Collector's Edition (2004), Los Angeles, Paramount Pictures Corp. (DVD commentary).

[8] "Harold Lloyd Master Seminar with Jerry Bruckheimer and Don Simpson," American Film Institute, 1988.

[9] Iain Blair, "Team Behind 'Top Gun' Brings Back Creative Producing," *Chicago Tribune*, May 11, 1986, 13-2. https://www.newspapers.com/image/388901401. [10] Paul Attanasio, "The Twin Titans of 'Top Gun'," *The Washington Post*, May 16, 1986, D1, D3. https://www.washingtonpost.com/archive/lifestyle/1986/05/16/the-twin-titans-of-top-gun/db86b5f9-f7ad-4f3e-bd97-81ccf6522c2a/

[11] For more information about the conflict surrounding *The Final Countdown*: "UNITED STATES of America v. Peter Vincent DOUGLAS, et al., Defendants. Civ. A. No. 85-436-N. https://law.justia.com/cases/federal/district-courts/FSupp/626/621/1398816/) Emory Brown, a former Navy commander, was convicted of accepting an illegal gratuity oft $5,563 from producer Peter Douglas, the son of actor Kirk Douglas.
"Virginia Naval Commander Loses Conflict-of-Interest Appeal on Film Making," Associated Press, February 25, 1985. https://apnews.com/article/ad5c71cf19d36d85423577b2a66b985b

Mary Jordan, "Navy Pilot Files Slander Suit," Washington Post. March 20, 1985. https://www.washingtonpost.com/archive/local/1985/03/20/navy-pilot-files-slander-suit/199555fd-81f8-4aae-b323-7f8562032684/

The scandal was also the subject of a 1984 "60 Minutes" episode on CBS.

[12] The Topgun training school is now formally called "United States Navy Strike Fighter Tactics Instructor program" and located in Fallon, Nev.; however, in 1985, it was the "United States Navy Fighter Weapons School" operating in San Diego, Calif. Source: Tony Perry, "An Era Ends in San Diego as Navy's Top Guns Take Off," *Los Angeles Times*, May 30, 1996: 1.

[13] Pete Pettigrew, RADM USN (Ret.), interview with the author, December 10, 2020.

[14] "*Top Gun*" Special Collector's Edition (2004).

[15] Bill Badalato, executive producer for *Top Gun*, interview with the author, January 26, 2020.

[16] Kurt Anthony Krug, "MSU Alumnus Jack Epps Reminisces About 'Top Gun,'" *Press & Guide Newspapers*, September 13, 2011.

https://www.pressandguide.com/2011/09/12/msu-alumnus-jack-epps-reminisces-about-top-gun/

[17] Marilyn Beck, "Hollywood is telling movies stars they need to be promoters too," *Courier Journal* (Louisville, Kentucky), syndicated by Tribune Media Services, Inc., July 31, 1984. https://www.newspapers.com/image/110746778/

[18] Dave Kronke, "He Accepted the Mission," *Los Angeles Times*, May 12, 1996, Calendar-94. https://www.newspapers.com/image/159271744/

[19] James Andrew Miller. *Power House: The Untold Story of Hollywood's Creative Artists Agency* (Harper Collins: 2016). 136.

[20] Dan Furie "Val Kilmer's deal," Paramount Inter-Communication, May 1, 1985, Furie to Greg Gelfan. TGC.

[21] "Charlies" Paramount Inter-Communication. May 14, 1985. MSP.

[22] The Numbers. *Risky Business* (1983), https://www.the-numbers.com/movie/Risky-Business.

[23] Armchair Expert (April 27, 2020). Rob Lowe, interviewed by Dax Shepard. Lowe recalled the occasion, using the word "gnarly" to describe Cruise's behavior. https://armchairexpertpod.com/pods/david-chang-jh2e9.

[24] Memorandum of Agreement, Paramount Pictures Corp. and Creative Artists Agency (CAA), January 31, 1985. TGC.

[25] Christopher Connelly, "Tom Cruise: Winging It," Rolling Stone, June 19, 1986, https://www.rollingstone.com/music/music-news/tom-cruise-winging-it-119000/

[26] Mark Wade, property master for *Top Gun*, interview with the author, April 29, 2020.

[27] John Semcken, LT USN (Ret.), interview with the author, November 5, 2020.

[28] "Nothing On Earth Comes Close," SAAB, 1984.

https://www.youtube.com/watch?v=PM3woO0AbCw.

[29]Donna Scott, interview with the author, January 5, 2022.

[30] Charles Hix, with photography by Bruce Weber, *Looking Good: A Guide For Men* (New York: Hawthorn Books, 1977).

[31] John DeCuir, Jr., production designer for *Top Gun*, interview with the author, May 12, 2020.

[32] Fred Baron, uncredited location manager for *Top Gun*, interview with the author, April 5, 2021.

[33] Dan Kolsrud, first assistant director for *Top Gun*, interview with the author, January 26, 2021.

[34] Richard Milligan, Deputy Director of Public Affairs at Grumman Corp., on Grumman stationery, to Jerry Bruckheimer, December 21, 1984. TGC.

[35] Badalato, January 26, 2020.

[36] Jonathan Kay & Charles Moss, Magic in the Dark: One Family's Century of Adventures in the Movie Business (Toronto: Sutherland House, 2021).

[37] Badalato, January 26, 2020.

[38] "Charles H. Maguire has been named senior vice president and executive production manager for the motion picture group of Paramount Pictures Corp., Los Angeles," *Los Angeles Times*, November 27, 1985, 43.

https://www.newspapers.com/image/401474516/

[39] Badalato, January 26, 2020.

[40] Badalato, interview with the author, November 1, 2021.

[41] "FLASH Preliminary Deal Summary," Paramount Inter-Communication. January 1, 1985. TGC.

[42] "Issue No. 6 for the Simpson/Bruckheimer Project, Top Guns," Paramount Inter-Communication. February 21, 1985. TGC.

CHAPTER 2
PREP BEGINS
JANUARY-FEBRUARY 1985

5555 Melrose Avenue

Prep for *Top Gun* started in the DeMille Building at Paramount, the domain of Simpson and Bruckheimer. Just being ceded use of the 8,451-square-foot building, just one building in from the twin arches of the Melrose Gate entrance, was visual evidence of the duo's power at the studio.[43]

Visitors of the day were brought to a reception area outside their office on the second floor. Nicely decorated with white linen couches, the wall featured platinum records for *Flashdance* and *Beverly Hills Cop* awarded by the Recording Industry Association of America.

A lot was made of the fact the two big-time producers shared an office. It made good copy for the reporters who came to write about them. More unusual was the fact they shared a desk, albeit a very large one with a partition. It was less surprising to people who knew the business. Producers of their kind spend a lot of time out of the office, and when they are there, the work is collaborative, like moviemaking itself. They each had their own copy machine.

A visitor with more than a minute to look at the office would have seen widely divergent spaces, which was "emblematic of our personalities," Simpson once said. "My area of the office is a sea of debris. I read periodicals like a maniac for ideas and stuff, so it's just, like, packed with newspapers. Jerry's is basically very well designed, and clean and precise."[44] In the mix on Simpson's side was a small, framed picture of six years worth of his business cards, reflecting his rise from executive assistant to president of production at Paramount.

The walls of the room featured two Andy Warhol lithographs of Mao Tse-tung along with a rack of televisions. The TVs were more for Simpson, while the quality sound system was Bruckheimer's domain. It was a big enough space that both music and television could be on. "I'll watch TV over here, Jerry will listen to music over here. So you got an overlay of images and sounds, and magazines here, and the pristine element here. We'll throw things up in the air and see where it sticks."

When an interviewer noted that there were side offices, so that if they wanted, they could make a private call, Simpson replied that he'd only used it twice, both times to meet with fundraisers from his college.

DeMille Building

Once known as the "Publicity Building," it was renamed by the studio in 1941 after Cecil B. DeMille, the famed producer/director. He was the force behind the classic blockbusters *The Greatest Show on Earth* (1952) and *The Ten Commandments* (1956).

Improvements had been made to the building over the years, including in 1951 when a second floor was added for DeMille himself. He occupied the flat-roofed, sturdy building with its cement plaster walls and wood windows until 1956. In those days, a visitor had to walk down the middle of a large, open room filled with desks to get to DeMille's office at the far end. Actress Betty Hutton, who starred in *Greatest Show*, described walking past his "21 secretaries" on the way to her interview.[45]

In 1985 the building still featured a long hallway with a large front office filled with cubicles for various assistants and secretaries, but now private offices lined each side. The hall ended at a reception area and the large executive office at the rear, as it had in DeMille's day.

Badalato's office, Room 104 in the DeMille Building, was anchored by a large desk and a credenza. The desk held a typewriter, which would get constant use, and a traditionally sized, blank-page flip calendar for notes, meeting schedules, start dates and deadlines.[46] As a New Yorker, Badalato stood out but he also looked like a producer, and he knew his way around. He was a mix of personable and tough, and he was smart. He crunched numbers but he also liked to talk to people.

The credenza was home to a strip board, a physical version of the shooting schedule. Each strip contained a scene number, how many pages were in the scene, the characters, and whether the action takes place in the day or night. He took it with him on every show until the creation of software.

Badalato's most immediate challenge was coming up with meaningful figures for what the Navy would charge. Many fans of *Top Gun* believe Paramount only paid for the fuel of the jets, but what the Navy agreed to was to bill at cost. But how much would it cost to operate aircraft carriers with thousands of sailors on board, or to fly F-14s and F5s, which would serve as enemy aircraft, or to fire missiles? How to determine costs associated with the ground crew who towed an F-14 from one hangar to another for set decorating? All of that had to be worked out.

Creating relationships with people in the Navy was the starting point. Navy Secretary Lehman had dropped responsibility for it at the feet of RADM Thomas J. Cassidy, Jr., commander of fighter and early warning aircraft for the Pacific Fleet and in charge of the 23,116-acre Miramar base. Now all focus was on Cassidy.[47]

The one thing everyone seemed to agree on was that significant changes to the script were required. With sheer force of will, Simpson and Bruckheimer, particularly Simpson, had succeeded in getting the project green-lighted at Paramount. Yet the problems that had put the script in turnaround to begin with remained, even in the second draft.

Pettigrew had worked on a weekly basis to assist Cash and Epps on the second draft, and there were improvements, but the second draft still wasn't workable.

Scott's breakdown of the script reflected that understanding. His Feb. 13 memo, "Rough Estimate — Shooting Days," went through the script by page number, start to finish, estimating how long it would take. It added up to 77 shooting days. Scott planned to use two cameras throughout filming, "other than SFX stunt sequences – 3 or 4 cameras," and "three or four special effects and stunt sequences, which would include the air-to-air scenes.[48]

While much of that would hold true, the memo is a good way to gauge the dramatic changes to the script over time. The early breakdown was dotted with references to crashes and explosions. The first mention, on page eight, was a crash on the aircraft carrier. The next, on page 77, was the crash of a helicopter, followed by the "twist and fall" of planes on page 88, including a half day with Maverick in a parachute. He reasoned that the Alpha strike on page 105 would take five days to shoot, one for "ground SFX explosions," one day for air-to-air, two for "stunt flying," and one day for gimbal photography, in this case a mechanized cockpit set built on soundstages to simulate the actors being in flight. Battle sequences, on page 118, would take nine days to shoot, two of them with stunt flying. He also included big-ticket items he would need for certain scenes, including 20-foot models of planes and the helicopter.[49]

It also shows that Scott always intended three days for the scene at the Officer's Club, and to spend time on the relationship between Maverick and the love interest, who at that point was named "Kirsten." He wanted two days just to shoot scenes of them meeting at Kirsten's gym, although he noted the scene was "to be changed."

That underlying reality — that the script would change in ways they didn't know yet — was on everyone's mind. The story was still laced with testosterone but weak in most other areas, with two key problem areas. The first was a lack of authenticity in the scenes involving Navy pilots and the Topgun school itself, although Pettigrew had helped. The other was that the lead characters were unlikeable or implausible, or both. One example was Kirsten. The character was a local exercise instructor, an unlikely serious match for a high-functioning elite pilot bent on proving himself. But the scriptwriters were "enamored" of the character and resisted the requests to change her for the second draft, according to Simpson.[50]

Even more problematic were issues with the character of Maverick. He wasn't a sympathetic figure and it was hard for anyone on the creative side to imagine audience buy-in. Cruise didn't like the script and with the 10-page Memorandum of Agreement dated Jan. 24, 1985, there was wiggle room if he wanted out.[51]

Miramar

Whatever Cassidy initially thought of the movie production operating under his command wasn't stated on the record. What is clear is that Navy officers assigned to Miramar, where *The Final Countdown* had been made, were even more leery of Hollywood than those who expressed concern at headquarters outside of Washington.

At issue was whether the commissioned officer of the squadron that provided support for *The Final Countdown* purposely accepted something of value. That's something strictly forbidden, and grounds for a court martial. Most thought that whatever happened was innocent. The precise consequences aren't clear or relevant except that it was viewed as severe. To some, it seemed as if the Navy had asked its people to do something irregular — like help a movie company — and then held them personally accountable when irregular things happened. Career officers, some of who were now being asked to participate in *Top Gun*, liked being in the Navy and didn't want or need the drama.

Badalato was at least peripherally aware of sensitivity about the previous movie, because he mentioned it in passing in a memo. The main focus was picking up the ball with

Pettigrew, who had plenty of connections at Miramar.[52] Even with both him and Pettigrew working on it, it still took until Feb. 12 to get an in-person meeting on base, although it was a big one. It was to include the chief of staff for the fighter wing, along with its commander, Thomas "Otter" Otterbein. Lt. John Semcken III, from public affairs, would be there. The planning memo noted Semcken had been sent a script in advance. LCDR Connie Haney, chief of information for the Navy in Los Angeles, would meet them at the gate.[53]

RADM Cassidy's name, upper-cased where other names in the itinerary weren't, was also on the memo, but only that he "possibly will attend." They needed buy-in from Cassidy if they wanted to gain traction within the Navy. If sailors in his command got the idea it wasn't something the admiral cared about, they might not, either.

Simpson, in particular, thought a big splash was needed to impress the Navy. The filmmakers would travel to San Diego in two different groups, each in Old English Livery stretch limos that featured bars and televisions. The drivers would wait and return them to the airport that night.

Badalato and Scott flew from Los Angeles early in the day Feb. 12 and met Pettigrew for lunch at Imperial House on Bankers Hill in San Diego. The classic steakhouse, opened in 1961, featured leaded-glass windows that overlooked Balboa Park. It was a nice setting for a business lunch and they sat in a circular booth with leather seats, linen tablecloth and polished silverware.

Pettigrew provided insight into his work with Cash and Epps. The consultant had worked closely with the screenwriters with some success, but he was candid about limitations. He'd been direct in telling the writers the Navy wasn't going to sign off on certain scenes, like the ones that depicted F-14s crashing on its aircraft carrier. Yet the scenes remained in the second draft. Scott, charming and funny, hadn't seemed concerned. He was confident they would get the Navy lined up, or find another way.

Simpson and Bruckheimer, who had left Los Angeles later, met them at Imperial House after lunch for the convoy to Miramar. Haney met them at the entrance and led the limos to command offices, which was when they found out the admiral would be there.

Personnel on the Navy side had been pulled together quickly. Semcken had barely come to grips with his new assignment. He had just been told, at a regular meeting of Fighter Wing staff, that he would be involved with the movie. That happened in Cassidy's office, all of them seated around a traditional Navy green felt conference table. The admiral asked anyone who had graduated from the Strike Fighter Tactics Instructor program, the official name of Topgun, to raise their hands.

Semcken said four hands were raised and lowered. Then Cassidy told them why: He needed a volunteer to work with the movie production. Not a hand went up, a reflection of what had happened with *The Final Countdown*. Cassidy announced it would be Semcken, to the relieved laughter of his peers.[54]

The grand entrance planned by Simpson happened. The stretch limos were too big for the parking lot at the command, so they had to leave them parked in front of the building, the drivers standing by. It was a Hollywood entrance, and a successful meeting that covered a lot of ground. While there hadn't been much communication from the Navy, they had done their homework.

A lot of things got resolved at the meeting, including what to do about the character Charlie. "In the original script Kelly's role was an instructor at a yoga studio and a waitress at a Bonanza steakhouse!" said Semcken. "Don Simpson did not like that — he wanted her to be a pilot! At that time women were not allowed to fly combat aircraft." It's hard to imagine Simpson didn't know that, but the matter closed when the admiral flatly told him no. Fraternization was forbidden in the service.

Semcken quietly suggested to Cassidy that they model Charlie after Christine Fox, a civilian analyst and consultant to the Department of Defense who worked on site. She was highly educated, carried a security clearance, and in a fictional world, would be a more reasonable match for someone like Maverick. Semcken said Cassidy stayed quiet, allowing the filmmakers to go on for a while, then suggested Fox.[55]

Basis for Charlie

In 1985, Christine Fox was a consulting analyst for CNA Corporation, on assignment to the Navy. She was a maritime air superiority specialist who, like the character based on her, instructed at Topgun. Fox initially had concerns that her association with the movie might hamper her work with the Navy but the opposite occurred, "The movie was so popular …it gives me an instant 'in' to talk to people in the aviation community."[56]

Fox's association with *Top Gun* gave her career another, more important kind of boost. "In the 80s the fighter guys were not thrilled to have a woman assigned to be their analyst. There was tremendous skepticism. When the movie came along it really propelled our excellent working relationships." [57] Since then, says Fox, "It's just kind of hovered in a powerful way that I had no expectation of."[58]

In turn, Fox vouched for the movie, particularly how it portrayed the Navy pilots, "What we ask these people to do is dangerous. That culture exists for a fundamental reason. As individuals they are smart, caring wonderful human beings, as you can imagine, but in a collective they are pretty aggressive, as the film portrayed them."[59]

Someone called for her to join them, and she stunned the room. "When she walked in Don Simpson looked up at her and said, "Do you have your Screen Actors Guild card?" I'll never forget that," laughed Semcken. Fox was "nearly six feet tall and blonde. And attractive." They had found the basis for Charlie, elevating the already bright mood in the room.

The other significant development at the meeting was the arrival of Otterbein and LCDR Bob "Rat" Willard, who was operations and executive officer of the Navy Fighter Weapons School, second to Otterbein. Otterbein's name had been on the memo but not Willard's. Rat and Otter, as they were known, had spent that day flying in Yuma.

Willard said he had heard rumors on base about the movie but was otherwise blindsided by the meeting. "We came back later in the afternoon, beat from a day of instruction, and were in our office to wrap it up," he recalled. Then someone arrived to tell them the admiral wanted to see them. They were told to come as they were. "We had our hats and flight suits on when we went over there, no idea what we would find."[60] The command center, in a building that was cater-cornered from Hangar 1, was close enough for them to walk. They saw the limousines as they approached. Even if they had fit in the parking lot, limos were a rare sight on base.

"Inside it was a bunch of people, Jerry Bruckheimer, Don Simpson, quite a crowd," recalled Willard, who would become key to the movie and ultimately rise to second in command of the Navy. Amid introductions, the pilots were told the film company "had an interest in making *Top Gun*, and the Navy was interested in supporting it." The screenplay sat squarely on the desk.

Willard understood what the admiral wanted. "The idea was that we would help close the gap between the way they were portraying school and Navy and what we would consider to be acceptable." When they got to that point, the admiral's office would forward it to Washington. At some point, Otter looked at him and said, "You've got it, XO," effectively assigning him responsibility for it, although the CO would have limited involvement in the background.

Badalato also managed to get a few answers about how they could account for things. His notes, on an itinerary from that day, read "take off to landing g, 2,000 gallons = $1,800 fuel." That confirmed the Navy's agreement to charge only when they had planes in the air. It represented a savings to the movie company, although exactly how much wasn't clear. There were numerous other associated costs that had to be determined, beyond the cost of fuel once it was airborne.

But the best evidence the meeting had been a success was the fact that the next meeting was scheduled. It would involve a new scriptwriter touring the base and meeting with Fox.

Fixing the script

Bruckheimer and Simpson landed on the idea of bringing in scriptwriter Chip Proser in January. He was a director and television cameraman who had sold one script to Zoetrope Studios.[61] It was acquired by Paramount, which was how the studio knew who he was.

Proser, who officially started on Feb. 11, had initially been reluctant to work for Paramount because the studio had allowed his script to languish, but the pay was right: $30,000 a week for three weeks, guaranteed, then $20,000 for each additional week. It was more than they wanted to spend but there wasn't a lot of time, and everything rested on getting the script right.

Badalato quickly organized the next meeting at Miramar, this one an overnight for Scott and Proser to meet with "Rat, Otter and Flex." On Wednesday, Feb. 20, they flew to San Diego and again enjoyed the transportation services of Old English Livery, and a driver who waited until after the first meeting to take them to their rooms at the Mission Valley Inn. In addition to the meetings, they would have a tour of Miramar. Proser would rewrite the script, and meet with Fox to reimagine the role. Paperwork shows the fee for Proser approved as of Feb. 21.[62]

To prep for the meeting with the filmmakers, Willard, Otterbein and Semcken read and marked up the same script, using different colored felt pens. Semcken, last on the list, used a purple pen. He said he liked the story "but there were a lot of mistakes." The comments of the ranking officers were more fact-based, with some things highlighted as unacceptable. "I was on the making-it-cool side," he said.

Willard agreed with that assessment and noted a primitive element. "The early screenplays looked like something we did in school for a project," he said, "not fancy, at all." They were on a thin, crepe paper, the other comments written in green and blue.

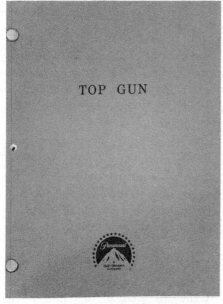

Several people from the Navy worked on the script for Top Gun, including RADM (Ret.) Pete Pettigrew and Admiral (Ret.) Robert F. Willard, owner of this copy.

PHOTO: Virginia Hawkins

The division of work had Willard in charge of anything happening in the air and command decisions, and overseeing the Navy's line edit of the movie. Semcken would also participate in improving the script while being the Navy point person for the movie on the ground, managing day-to-day interactions. A host of others would assist, dozens of pilots, and hundreds of Navy personnel, but what that actually meant remained to be seen.

Within a few days, Otter and Willard briefed their squadron of pilots and Radio Intercept Officers about the movie. Lt. Dave "Bio" Baranek, a RIO, said there were numerous meetings from there, casual bagged lunches in the ready room for pilots who weren't in the air where Willard read from the script. It had "several misunderstandings" and terms that were "misstated or misused." The most often quoted example is the use of "going ballistic," because there is no controlling a ballistic plane. Baranek reported that the "small errors caused great amusement in the ready room."[63] Willard acknowledged as much, saying it had prompted him to reach out to Washington. They told him the movie was going to be made, so "he'd better help fix it if he didn't want Topgun to be embarrassed."

Everyone on the Navy side understood the script would change, certainly more than Scott did. With Otterbein punting the project to Willard, it was understood that Willard would fix it, with Semcken in the background to deal directly with Scott. In the meantime, Willard would continue with his full-time duties as XO [Executive Officer] of Topgun.

All of those meetings teed up an official scout to Miramar, which Badalato was scheduling for early March. Generally, a scout was to find and confirm locations and to make creative decisions about the movie. This particular scout was already ambitious. First, the Navy would oversee the scout, and second, Tom Cruise was expected to be in the mix.

Badalato realized the scout could also advance efforts with Grumman. The process of installing camera mounts to the aircraft began with an evaluation of whether it could be done safely. Every step was time consuming, and they had to get moving. On Feb. 27 he sent a memo entitled "Dick Milligan – Grumman" to Scott, Simpson and Bruckheimer that Milligan would join them at Miramar. "Pending our meeting and everyone's approval of Milligan we will be able to employ him through Grummans [sic] as a technical advisor." Exactly how wasn't known yet, but it was a step forward.[64]

Badalato sent a more urgent memo the same day to the same people, and this time he added Maguire. The meetings at Miramar had confirmed that plans to begin shooting in May weren't realistic with the Navy. "Given the lead time required by various departments within the Navy to accommodate our filming requirements, we will not be able to begin shooting Top Gun before June 3."[65]

Things were changing in the physical board on Badalato's credenza, moved around in the course of organizing the production. "Please note as the rewrite has not been completed the number of days devoted to each sequence could vary," wrote Badalato.

Maguire, for his part, knew that the changes underway made it difficult to sign off on an accurate budget. The script was in flux, and financial information was still largely unknowable. That didn't stop him from pressing Badalato for the "B and B," the "budget and board," but the budget still lacked meaningful numbers.

Chapter 2 - Endnotes

[43] Iain Blair, "Team Behind 'Top Gun' Brings Back Creative Producing."

[44] "Harold Lloyd Master Seminar with Jerry Bruckheimer and Don Simpson," American Film Institute, 1988.

[45] Margaret Bean, "La Hutton Proves Claim as Fabulous Entertainer," *Spokesman-Review* (Spokane, Washington), March 15, 1953, 38. https://www.newspapers.com/image/569541552/

[46] Bill Badalato, Interview with the author, January 8, 2021

[47] Bill Badalato, "Top Guns – Tuesday, February 12, 1985," Paramount Inter-Communication, February 12, 1985. TGC.

[48] Tony Scott, "Rough Estimate — Shooting Days," Paramount Inter-Communication, February 13, 1985. TGC.

[49] Production department script breakdown. TGC.

[50] Attanasio, "Twin Titans."

[51] Paramount Pictures Corporation. Memorandum of Agreement, contractual terms and conditions for Tom Cruise, January 24, 1985. TGC.

[52] Pettigrew, December 10, 2020.

[53] Bill Badalato, "Top Guns – Travel and Miramar Schedule," Paramount Inter-Communication, February 20, 1985. TGC.

[54] Semcken, November 5, 2020.

[55] John E. Horton, 87; Movies' Longtime Link to Pentagon," *Los Angeles Times*, June 12, 2006, 150. https://www.latimes.com/archives/la-xpm-2006-jun-12-me-horton12-story.html

[56] Left of Boom podcast, "Meet the Real Charlie from 'Top Gun,'" Hope Hodge Seck interviews Christine Fox. https://www.military.com/podcasts/left-of-boom/2020/09/03/meet-real-charlie-top-gun-christine-fox.html

[57] Lisa Goldapple, "Atlas of the Future: The Pentagon's real Top Gun," July 18, 2019. https://atlasofthefuture.org/futurehero-christine-fox-the-pentagons-real-top-gun/

[58] Left of Boom podcast, "Meet the Real Charlie from 'Top Gun'."

[59] Goldapple, "Atlas of the Future."

[60] Robert 'Rat' Willard, LCDR USN (Ret.), interview with the author, December 2, 2020.

[61] Zoetrope Studios was renamed American Zoetrope in 1990.

[62] "FLASH Preliminary Deal Summary," Issue No. 6 of the "Simpson/Bruckheimer Project, Top Guns," Paramount Inter-Communication originating January 1, 1985 and dated February 21, 1985. TGC.

[63] Dave Baranek, *Topgun Days: Dogfighting, Cheating Death, and Hollywood Glory as One of America's Best Fighter Jocks*, (New York: Skyhorse, 2012), 215.

[64] Bill Badalato, "Dick Milligan – Grumman," Paramount Inter-Communication, February 27, 1985. Badalato to Don Simpson, Jerry Bruckheimer, Tony Scott. TGC.

[65] Bill Badalato, "TOP GUN – Shooting Schedule & Production Notes," Paramount Inter-Communication, February 27, 1985. TGC

CHAPTER 3

CASTING THE DEPARTMENT HEADS

MARCH-APRIL 1985

Business at the DeMille Building had quickly turned to finding department heads. The next hire, after Badalato, was Casting Director Margery Simkin, who officially started Feb. 25.[66] She had worked with Simpson and Bruckheimer on *Beverly Hills Cop*. The casting director's job doesn't generally involve picking the top stars, because that happens at the studio level. But Simpson and Bruckheimer had a lot of sway. And Tom Cruise's agent was pushing for $1 million.[67]

"Don wasn't happy about it." said Simkin. "He wanted to know who else was out there." The actor had received a lot of attention for his last role, in *Risky Business,* but his pay was perhaps a quarter of what he was asking now. Simkin said that seemed high to Simpson. He and Bruckheimer had already agreed to $750,000. The call revealed what she saw as the division of labor between the two super-producers: Simpson focused on above the line talent, while Bruckheimer was production side, although both did it all.

Simkin got out her notebooks and looked over the name of every young actor she knew. Then she called Simpson back. "I said, pay him." Cruise was undoubtedly the best candidate for Maverick. Some of the names on the list were right for other parts, she reasoned, and there were many of those. She also got to work finding the female lead.

Many of the actors being considered for roles in the movie had little previous exposure. Simkin contrasted opportunities for fledgling actors in 1985 with today's casting environment: "Film now is not as open to introducing unknowns as it was in 1985. When I put together the cast of *Top Gun* almost nobody had done anything. That cast would not be possible today."[68]

Simkin's contract allowed either a personal assistant or a casting assistant, and she opted for the latter. She hired Jeff Greenberg, who was assigned a cubicle in the front section of the building where a previous casting assistant had worked.

"The desk was piled so high — it was like a joke desk. Papers and pictures and notebooks were stacked up. I had to excavate it," recalled Greenberg. Buried in the debris was a checklist of 30 things that had to be done "to the taste of the casting director, who was abnormally demanding," he said. Badalato said that was a nice way to summarize Simkin, who had a reputation for being blunt.[69]

"So, I'm blunt," Simkin laughed. "It's that kind of job."

Normally the production designer, who oversees the art department and shapes the look of the movie to the will of the director, would be an early hire. At this point Scott believed a production designer could play a secondary role, even part time, because could just shoot the Navy being the Navy, although that didn't turn out to be the case.[70]

The producers were acutely aware that they should find department heads with experience in making movies about the military. It was the main line of inquiry in the interview with James "Jimmy" Tyson for men's costume designer. He recalled Scott, Simpson and Bruckheimer talking a lot about *The Right Stuff* (1983). It was fresh in everyone's minds for its depiction of the military. At the end of the interview he said they leveled with him: "We like you, Jim, but we're looking for a very special person, the guy who did *The Right Stuff*. If he's not available, we'll let you know."[71]

Tyson told them as he left that he understood. "Because of the success of the movie, everybody who worked on it for one day — one day — had put it on their resume," he explained. What Tyson didn't say was that he had been the

"the head guy" for costumes on *The Right Stuff.* He had received attention for it, particularly for having built the astronaut suits. It was pre-Internet, pre-IMDb, and it wasn't possible to click a few buttons to check credits.

A few days later the power trio called him back. "They were like, 'What are you, an asshole? You can't tell us that you ran costumes?'" Tyson laughed at the memory. It became a bond among all of them, something they joked about for years. "Tony, he was a guy's guy, so were Don and Jerry. And so am I."[72]

He hired Bobbie Read, who was credited as costume designer for women on *Top Gun,* For a long time, major movie productions had two costume designers, one for men and one for women, particularly for period films. After the end of the studio era, the tradition of having a men's costumer pull the costumes remained, at least in part. In contemporary films, however, the practice hung around longer. [73]

Bobbie Read described herself as more of an assistant to Tyson. There was also a more practical split in the division of labor than gender needed for the movie. "He did the uniforms, I did the streetwear," Read recalled.[74]

Tyson's experience with uniforms went back more than a decade. It was his experience at Western Costume Co. that helped him land the job on *The Right Stuff.* The company, a mainstay in Hollywood for more than a century, remains in operation to this day, and had been behind a film presentation on American military uniforms for the U.S. Bicentennial. "I had to do every uniform from 1776 to 1976, for Army, Navy, Marines and Coast Guard. So I had pretty good knowledge of where to get stuff, well before *Top Gun.*"

Tyson again turned to Western Costume for assistance with costumes for Maverick. Polaroid photo archives, noted by scene numbers, show Tom Cruise in flights suits as well as in the famous jacket.[75] A memo from Paramount that listed "Top Gun Licensees Sales" was circulated to staff at Western. The memo listed Novelization (Pocket Books); Model Kits

(Testor Corp); Headgear and embroidered patches (Joy Insignia); and T-Shirts (Nexus Industries.) Aviator clothing (Avirex Ltd.) was for retail sales through the "The Cockpit" mail order catalogue. The list also included a board game (Fasa Corp), which would not be available until summer.[76]

A four day scout

Badalato made the most of the information from the Miramar meeting. His biggest asset was Semcken, who as the naval officer designated to monitor and help the production, was now assisting from his office on base. He helped Badalato secure a sequential shooting schedule from the Navy in part by putting him in touch with others. While tentative, it provided the Navy's availability in shooting scenes on the aircraft carrier and the air-to-air sequences. It was vague, but it was progress.[77]

Semcken was working on his own system because he knew whatever numbers he provided required close accounting. He and Willard were committed to creating a paper trail that was both thorough and easily explained, another nod to what had happened with *The Final Countdown*. It was all wheel-invention at that point, because there were no existing estimates on the hourly cost of flying an F-14, an F-5 or an A-4. The Navy didn't account for its assets that way.[78]

The scout to San Diego was four days, March 10-14. It began with a dinner meeting in Los Angeles Sunday night. Scott, Milligan and Badalato met at La Parc Hotel, where Milligan was staying.[79]

The purpose of the meeting was to discuss air-to-air sequences, and for Scott to get to know Milligan, but it was noteworthy for the display of the director's drawings. Scott was a graduate of the Royal College of Art who originally wanted to be a painter. He was an exceptional sketch artist and as a budding movie director used that talent to do his own storyboards.[80] Storyboards are graphic depictions or illustrations presented in sequence, a little like a black-and-white graphic novel, to help get a vision across.

The next morning the three flew to San Diego, as did Simpson, Bruckheimer and Cruise, and their arrival at Miramar was again choreographed. Each group traveled separately. Scott, Milligan and Badalato would arrive at the gate first and be met by Lt. Sandy Stairs, who had the title of CHINFO/Los Angeles. CHINFO, or chief of information and the Office of Information, was headquartered in Washington. Haney would meet Simpson, Bruckheimer and Cruise half an hour later.

Cruise was there for several reasons, not the least of which was to impress the military. He still had longish hair from *Legend* (1985) his last movie, which hadn't immediately won over the Navy with their regulation shorthair. But he had been eager to learn from them, which had been noticed, and the overall impression was good.

The first meeting of the day was with the Navy brass, with focus on carriers. Lunch included a slide show and discussion on water survival. Cruise welcomed a mandatory three-day safety class on water survival.

That afternoon the group toured the USS Kitty Hawk, the first real look at what they would be dealing with in shooting on an aircraft carrier. From there Simpson and Bruckheimer left for the airport.

But the others, including Cruise, went to the Hyatt Islandia on Mission Bay for the night, and returned to Miramar the next day. That day's itinerary included a scout of the Topgun school, after which Cruise and Milligan took off. Badalato and Scott stayed another night, scouting locations around San Diego with a member of the film commission, a nonprofit organization sponsored by the city to assist and promote film and television production. They flew home Wednesday night.[81]

One significant change was made after they returned from the scout, although its origin is unclear. From then on, the movie would be called *Top Gun*. The first script had been

"Top Guns," plural, while people in the Navy informally referred to the squadron as "Topgun."

A biography on Warren Skaaren, who was to do a lot of work on the script, posits the change was to reflect the increased focus on the character, Maverick.[82] However, the change in the name, following the intense meeting with the Navy, drew a line between how the Navy referred to its school and the Hollywood version, and happened two months before Skaaren's hire.

At this point, a different writer was at work improving the script.

Proser rewrite v. film budget

Chip Proser's first rewrite of the script dropped at the DeMille Building about the time they returned from San Diego. It wasn't considered finished, but it did give them a way to gauge progress. Badalato quickly dug in, hoping it contained specifics that would improve his budget estimates, or even better, lead to insights on how they could save money. But instead of scenes that would rein in costs, the script was going in the other direction.

At about the same time, Maguire told Badalato the studio wanted the *Top Gun* budget cut to $13 million. The executive producer wrote a detailed memo about it, effectively punting it into the big office in the DeMille Building. "The movie we are currently preparing cannot be made for [$13 million]," he wrote to Simpson and Bruckheimer on March 20. It was possible they could do it for $15.5 million, "if we get lucky."[83]

Badalato wrote that the budget was already "high risk," and that the visual effects and flying sequences would have a life of their own once they got started. Decisions had to be made and once that happened "there is no turning back." Most of all, they needed a firm number to make the movie.

What made Proser's script expensive, Badalato continued, were the extensive flying sequences and added special effects. Those scenes had to be "pinned down and simplified." Badalato had also counted 40 speaking parts, and noted the already significant costs of the cast. But it didn't make sense story-wise, either, he wrote. "Major characters are not in focus as there are so many characters in the story." He recommended combining characters. That would not only save money, but also tighten a script that badly needed it.

Badalato had laced the memo with attempts at subtlety like "[P]reparation time is going by rapidly," before getting to the larger point. "TOP GUN is not the kind of project that the studio should play games with in terms of holding back on a decision to add more money to the budget. The project requires an amazing amount of planning."

Generally an EP doesn't focus on the creative side, but Badalato's efforts dovetailed with business. Getting a handle on the budget meant getting a handle on the story. Given it was mid-March, the more effort put forth toward solutions, the better for Simpson and Bruckheimer. They were benefited by the ideas, many of which they adopted, but also by virtue of it providing cover for them with Scott. There isn't any documentation that they minded, and Badalato would continue to write fulsome memos throughout production. "If they didn't like what I was doing, they never told me," he said.[84]

In the immediate term, the March 20 email bolstered Simpson and Bruckheimer's defense for the conversation with Maguire about the budget. It was up to them to run the play.

A few weeks later Maguire was still pressing to cut the budget. Fasbender, on the accounting side, had a look at the numbers and sent Maguire an internal memo May 1 that supported the larger number. A $13.1 million budget didn't include the $639,573 draw that was due to Simpson and Bruckheimer, and $88,318 in prep-production expenses from 1983, 1984, and the first two months of 1985, he wrote.[85]

Fasbender also flagged other needed areas that weren't included in the lower number. There was $1.4 million for "miniatures," which was how they were anticipating getting some of the special effects; and it didn't factor in non-LA based cast. That was sliding into dangerous terrain. "Unless the casting is completed quickly, the casting director will exceed the basic contract amount budgeted," he wrote, presumably because they were running up costs by bringing people in.

Badalato's copy of the memo included a note to himself: "We have money in extras casting to cover when Margie Simkin leaves."[86] Badalato had budgeted for background actors before learning that no one in the Navy could be paid under Navy rules. Any Navy "extra," as they were still called, would have to volunteer. The budget anticipated paying them, which meant there were funds that could be reallocated.

But as powerful as Maguire was, he didn't have the clout of Simpson and Bruckheimer, who worked with the studio to arrive at a total somewhere in the middle. The figure arrived upon doesn't seem to be contained in any contemporaneous documents, although it would become clear later. The main point was that the grip of the studio was upon them to keep costs down.

Proser's final "revised" version of the script landed April 4. While he had improved on earlier versions, specifically with regards to use of military language and in developing Maverick's love interest. She was renamed Charlotte Blackwood, or "Charlie." He'd come up with additional characters, perhaps too many. Meanwhile, he hadn't gone far enough in fixing other issues. Most notably, the character of Maverick remained unappealing.

In the Proser script, Maverick had become a darker, more conflicted character, his relationship with an openly critical Goose was more nuanced, and Carole, Goose's widow, never explicitly forgave Maverick for his part in Goose's death. One unidentified observer described the Proser script as more "morally inquisitive" and less feel-good than either the Cash and Epps original or the eventual final product.[87] Simpson and Bruckheimer, though, had a formula for success and angst was not one of the ingredients. Don

Simpson, blunt in all things, summarized the Proser script, "He saw Kafka, and this ain't Kafka."[88]

Badalato directed his efforts to problem solving by writing a five-page memo titled "thoughts about story and budget." Dated April 6, it highlighted 12 key issues and ways to fix the script. Most were cost-saving measures, but his comments also took on specific scenes, locations, and challenges to scheduling. He noted depictions of military life that weren't accurate and wrote about character development. Some of his ideas, like making Goose a more sympathetic character as well as Maverick, were ultimately adopted.

But his strongest message in the memo was about the budget: "The only portion of this production that's conducive to being really on the money is the ground material." He said air-to-air sequences should be modified to cut costs. He saved the punch of the memo for near the end: "For the time being I think the most important task is to get the Navy's approval and create a budget that will get the picture made."[89]

Separately, he moved forward in hiring Milligan from Grumman, who had met everyone's approval. Milligan wanted to remain a full-time employee of the defense contractor, and it wasn't clear how the movie company could hire him. Badalato reached out to Paramount's representative in Washington.

Lobbying the Pentagon

John E. Horton, who had gotten Simpson and Bruckheimer the initial meeting at the Pentagon, had continued to work on behalf of *Top Gun*. That included networking on a golf course in neighboring Bethesda, Md., to finesse the situation with Grumman. Getting cameras attached to the sensitive military aircraft, which was something only the maker of the F-14 could do, wasn't progressing quickly enough. Horton scheduled a day on the links with Tom Connolly, retired vice admiral of the Navy, and John Carr, the vice chairman of Grumman. Horton and Connolly were friends, and members of Burning Tree Country Club, a golf and sporting club. It's men-only membership, a rule that remains in effect today, was just starting to draw criticism in the mid-1980s. By the end of the decade it would prompt politicians to resign their memberships.[90]

It was lush ground for deal-making that brisk winter day in early 1985. While frowned upon for members of Burning Tree to sign deals at the country club — Horton himself disavowed it — it was par for the course to sort out details. Connolly had played a role in the U.S. Navy Test Pilot Program, which had been the basis of the "California" magazine story that inspired *Top Gun*, and he had made a significant contribution to the development of the F-14 Tomcat. Meanwhile, Carr had a big job at the defense contractor.

After the golf game, Horton followed up with an April 11 letter to Carr reminding him of the meeting, and the goals of the movie company to speed up its work with Grumman.[91] Horton sent Badalato a letter the same day about hiring Milligan from the defense contractor. It told him who specifically he should contact at Grumman to make it official, and said the charge would be $500 a day, plus expenses. "He did not say anything about additional charges for the camera mount, which I told him I wanted — so I assume these are included in the $500.00 per day."[92]

Horton was wrong about that.

Finding Warren Skaaren

Simpson and Bruckheimer already knew they had to do something about the script, but they weren't certain the solution was jettisoning Proser. He hadn't had that much time to work on it. Simpson told Proser the budget was pinched, and that they have to cut his salary to $5,000 a week, or about $13,213 today, when adjusted for inflation. Proser, interviewed in 2020, said that was unacceptable. "I told him to find a $5,000-a-week scriptwriter," he recalled.[93]

In late April the duo turned to Steel, a champion of theirs and the first woman president of production at Paramount. "Don's strength is the story and script; he has the ability to recognize a great idea," she said. "Jerry has the eye for detail, for the physical side of the film, for the set and what's going on there."[94] It was Steel who had pitched *Flashdance* to the studio. She fought through opposition to get the project — their first as an independent company — into development. In the few years since she had overseen a string of hits, including their other big success, *Beverly Hills Cop*.[95]

Steel consulted with them on how to fix the script and recommended they hire Warren Skaaren. The Austin, Texas-based writer had worked miracles on another project, and she liked him. His work on the screenplay for *Captive Hearts* (1987), proved him to be responsive, thorough and fast. Steel told the producers she would reach out to him personally.

Skaaren recalled Steel's call on Thursday, April 25, which he summarized as "Problem with a script called Top Gun."[96] He said he was flattered, but he had just committed to a Warner Bros. project. Steel asked him to have a look at the script anyway, and he agreed. Simpson had it overnighted to Austin. Skaaren read it Friday and "immediately" saw both character development and structural problems. Immediate was good, from the filmmakers' perspective, but it didn't change the fact Skaaren was under contract with Warner Bros.

Shortly thereafter, Skaaren heard from David Kirkpatrick, a Paramount production executive under Steel. It was subtle pressure, that he was needed and that shooting was "nearly upon them." Skaaren, who believed his commitment to Warner Bros. left him little choice, called his agent. Mike Simpson, at the William Morris Agency, explained to Skaaren that he wasn't necessarily locked in. A studio with a troubled script well into production meant that Skaaren's pay to fix it could be substantial. Better still, if

Skaaren accepted, it would be up to Paramount to sort out the agreement with Warner Bros.[97]

That sounded good to Skaaren, who came up with a proposal on what he would change. His strength was character development, and he had ideas on how to make Maverick more likable. The scriptwriter detailed a plan both in written form and in a call with Simpson and Bruckheimer.[98] What Skaaren didn't know, at least at that point, was that Tony Scott didn't want to hire him.

Scott had sent a scathing one-page memo, also on April 25, mocking the writer. Skaaren's writing in *Captive Hearts* was "theatrical and cute — goes for the most boring obvious aspects of people — saccharin cute." "Of East and West," the screenplay about Nepalese soldiers penned by Skaaren that had landed him an agent and the attention of Paramount to begin with, was "boring expositional — bad BBC." The effort had "miles of description without selection or point." Scott called Skaaren "an intellectual who has become a writer."[99]

The memo was sent to Badalato, who was supportive of Proser's efforts. At the same time, Badalato knew the studio, in the person of Maguire, as well as Simpson and Bruckheimer, didn't really care what Scott thought at that point. Principal photography was looming and they had a script that no one was happy with, including the lead actor they were hanging it all on. The producers were happy to let the studio be the fall guys in terms of dealing with Scott.

To Skaaren's amazement, Warner Bros. let him out of his other obligation, and it happened fast, thanks to Steel's connections. That enabled him to temporarily put other work on hold. It also required that he work exceptionally fast. An internal Paramount memo summarizing his deal, dated April 26, required the first rewrite by May 7, while he was only officially assigned to *Top Gun* on April 29.[100] That memo valued Skaaren's deal at between $150,000 and $350,000, depending on credits. For instance, if he was the only credited screenwriter, he would make more than if he shared that credit. This would become controversial later.[101] Skaaren sequestered himself at home in Austin and got to work.

Separately, the studio pushed principal photography out a week, to June 26.

Hiring Harold Faltermeyer

Simpson and Bruckheimer were also interviewing people to work in post-production, the last stage of photography, then about six months out. Post-production may be the most overlooked stage of making a movie. Editors work for months, or in the case of *Top Gun*, much longer, to sew the pieces of raw footage together, gradually layering in special effects and audio, and later the soundtrack, to create a final product.

The creative producers already knew they wanted Billy Weber as the primary editor for *Top Gun*, because they liked his work on *Beverly Hills Cop*. They also knew they wanted to have Harold Faltermeyer write the score. The musician met Bruckheimer when they were recording the soundtrack for *Beverly Hills Cop*.

Faltermeyer said he heard about the movie when it was still in its infancy. "He said it was about jets," said Faltermeyer, whose first reaction was no. He was new at writing score, and he wasn't an American. "What does a little German guy have to do with such a patriotic movie?"[102]

But eventually Bruckheimer called back to ask Faltermeyer to come in for a meeting. That's the first time he heard "rock and roll in the sky." They said, 'Look, those guys are 20-something-year-old pilots. No fear, they are just going for it." They described a pilot sitting in the cockpit of an F-14, canopy still open, listening to Billy Idol in a Walkman. Faltermeyer agreed to do it.

A few weeks later — he wasn't sure exactly, but not long — they called and asked if he had a theme. Faltermeyer said he did, "I was not lying, but…" he paused, "I was lying because it wasn't really finished."[103] The producer asked to hear it. Faltermeyer explained it was in his head, ideas, not records. "Don Simpson said, great, then you can play it to me." The musician tried to push it off, saying it was just a couple of bars, but they insisted. They took him to Oasis Recording Studio, then on Lankershim Boulevard in North Hollywood.

The musician went inside the sound booth and sat at a grand piano while the others went to the control room. "I was all by myself, trying to remember what I had for the *Top Gun* anthem," said Faltermeyer. "I started to play and repeat, modulate into different keys, just a couple of bars. I was trying to talk my way through." Then he saw the guys in the control room nodding, as if they liked what he was doing, "like I did something right." That spurred him forward to the dominating chord in melody, the fifth in the key structure, "some kind of climax," he said. "Now it was taking off," he said. "It hit them big time, and I was in business."

But the test wasn't over. Simpson and Bruckheimer wanted Cruise to hear it — that night. It was about 10 p.m. so Faltermeyer resisted. Bruckheimer said something like, "We know you are a fast worker. Make a demo to play for Tom," and it was clear he meant now. The musician agreed and called a guitar player who was there by 11 p.m. "At 2 a.m. in the morning Cruise, Bruckheimer and Simpson show up."

He had worked "Top Gun Anthem" to the extent he could. They had him do that early rendition five or six times. "Tom was blown away," he said. They made cassettes for Cruise, Simpson and Bruckheimer to take with them.[104]

Transportation, Stunt Coordinators

R.A. Rondell was ensconced in something at Stage 4 on the Paramount lot one day when he saw his friend, Randy Peters. They both lived in Woodland Hills and spent time at the Sagebrush Cantina, a popular watering hole. Both had worked in the industry for a decade, albeit on different paths.

Peters had just gotten the job as transportation captain on *Top Gun* and Rondell, who was from a family of stunt people, said he wanted to work on the movie. He was more than qualified with stunt credits that included *National Lampoon's Animal House* (1978) and *Blues Brothers* (1980). Peters suggested they go talk to Cruise, who was on the lot for a screen test.

Rondell had met the actor on *Taps* through his brother, Reid Rondell, who had doubled for Cruise. Reid also worked with the actor on *Risky Business* and *All the Right Moves*. Just months earlier, Reid, 22, had been killed in a helicopter crash while filming "Airwolf," a television series that ran 1984-1986. It obviously devastated the Rondell family. It was reportedly hard on Cruise, too. The news had reached him while shooting *Legend* in England.

Cruise recognized Rondell right away. The actor asked if he still rode motorcycles, and did he want to double for him on *Top Gun*. When he nodded yes, Cruise said to follow him. "We walk right up to Tony, and Tom says, 'He's going to double me,' and Tony said, 'Okay.' It was just like that," said Rondell.[105]

Peters' path to the movie business had routed through Chuck Norris' studio, where he was a karate instructor. One of the clients was actor Steve McQueen, who took a liking to the young man. McQueen required a gym on his movies and would invite Peters to come work out. One day at Metro Goldwyn Mayer, Peters told McQueen he couldn't work out because he had to go to Contract Services to apply for a job.[106]

The actor said he wanted to apply for a job, too, and Peters soon realized he was serious. At first no one recognized McQueen, who in the mid-70s was one of the biggest stars on the planet. He had grown his hair long and had a mustache. "We looked like we were in the porn industry or something," joked Peters, who also had long hair. But it hadn't taken too long for the powers at Contract Services to figure it out and be won over to the idea of hiring Peters. The problem was he needed 30 days of experience.

At the same time, a producer working with McQueen was getting tired of the actor hanging around with a PA He let Peters know that he wouldn't mind if he ran along. Peters suggested the producer write a letter that credited him with the 30 days, which would get him the job, and he agreed. Peters stayed friends with McQueen until his death in 1980.

As transportation coordinator, Peters would oversee all production movement, from getting trucks and trailers to base camp and getting cast and crew to set each day. It also included procuring picture cars, which are any vehicle used on camera.

Rondell, as stunt coordinator, would handle the on-screen driving, Maverick on his bike trying to evade Charlie in her Porsche, motorcycle shots on the beach and pier, drag racing the F-14. He hired drivers when needed, including someone to drive Charlie's car, but drove most of the scenes himself.[107]

Chapter 3 - Endnotes

[66] Margery Simkin. Contract for services between Paramount Pictures Corp. and Margery Simkin, February 12, 1985, MSP.

[67] Margery Simkin, casting director for *Top Gun*, interview with the author, September 16, 2021.

[68] *Italy On Screen Today*, New York Film &TV Series Festival. Casting directors panel discussion with Simona Nobile, Lilia Hartmann Trapani, and Margery Simkin. December 2020. https://www.youtube.com/watch?v=GscBx_SlVhw.

[69] Jeff Greenberg, casting assistant for *Top Gun*, interview with the author, March 8, 2021.

[70] Kolsrud, January 26, 2021.

[71] James Tyson, men's costume supervisor for *Top Gun*, interview with the author. June 6, 2020.

[72] Ibid.

[73] Leighton Bowers, director of research and archives, Western Costume, email to the author, March 1, 2021.

[74] Bobbie Read, women's costume supervisor for *Top Gun*, interview with the author, January 11, 2021.

[75] Undated collection of photos, Western Costume Co.

[76] "Top Gun Licensees Sales," Paramount Pictures Corp, Studio - Merchandising & Licensing, undated.

[77] Badalato, January 26, 2020.

[78] Semcken, November 5, 2020.

[79] Bill Badalato, "Top Guns – Travel and Miramar Schedule," Feb. 20, 1985. TGC.

[80] Bill Badalato, "Top Gun," Paramount Inter-Communication, March 20, 1985. TGC.

[81] Badalato, "Top Guns – Travel and Miramar Schedule," TGC.

82 Alison Macor, *Rewrite Man: The Life and Career of Screenwriter Warren Skaaren* (Austin: University of Texas Press, 2017), 15.

83 Badalato to Simpson and Bruckheimer, March 20, 1985. TGC.

84 Badalato, January 26, 2020.

85 Jim Fasbender, memo from to Charles H. Maguire, regarding *Top Gun* budget allocations. May 1, 1985. TGC.

86 Ibid.

87 "Top Gun screenplay: Chip Proser," By the Lens. Undated, unattributed script summary. http://bythelens.org/examples/example13.php

88 Don Simpson, telephone conversations with Warren Skaaren, April 24 and April 25, 1985. WSP.

89 Bill Badalato, "Re: April 4 Top Gun Script," Paramount Pictures Corp., April 6, 1985, memo to Jerry Bruckheimer, Don Simpson. TGC.

90 Emily London, "Burning Tree Golf Club: Sexism isn't up to par," *The Black and White*, June 10, 2019. https://theblackandwhite.net/64693/opinion/burning-tree-golf-club-sexism-isnt-up-to-par/

91 John E. Horton, letter to John Carr, April 11, 1985. TGC.

92 John E. Horton, letter to Bill Badalato, April 11, 1985. TGC.

93 Chip Proser, interview with the author. May 15, 2020.

94 Bernard Weinraub, "Simpson and Bruckheimer, Part 2," *New York Times*, March 14, 1994. C11.
https://timesmachine.nytimes.com/timesmachine/1994/03/14/458120.html

95 John Taylor, "Bright as Dawn Strong as Steel: The Most Powerful Woman in Hollywood," *New York Magazine*, May 29, 1989, 45-46.

96 Warren Skaaren, journal entry, May 8, 1985, WSP.

97 "Top Gun--phone notes" (April 30, 1985). Audio recording of telephone call from Paramount Pictures Corp. production executive to Skaaren and Skaaren's verbal notes regarding call (C 2832). WSP.

98 Audio recording of Warren Skaaren telephone conversation with Don Simpson, Jerry Bruckheimer, April 30, 1985. WSP.

99 Tony Scott, "Warren Skaaren," Paramount Inter-Communication, April 25, 1985. Scott to Bill Badalato, TGC.

100 Greg Gelfan, "Top Gun" Paramount Inter-Communication, Gelfan to Ralph Kamon regarding contractual terms and conditions for "G. WRITER – Warren Skaaren", April 26, 1985. TGC.

101 Sonny Bunch, "The Bulwark Goes to Hollywood: Alison Macor on screenwriting 'Top Gun' and 'Batman'," *The Bulwark*, November 19, 2020.
https://bulwarkhollywood.thebulwark.com/p/alison-macor-on-screenwriting-top.

102 Harold Faltermeyer, interview with the author, July 3, 2021.

103 "Combat Rock: The Music of Top Gun - Behind the Scenes - Top Gun 1986," Cine Extras. https://www.youtube.com/watch?v=SFPzc-3H16g

104 Faltermeyer, July 3, 2021.

105 R.A. Rondell, stunt coordinator for *Top Gun*, interview with the author, July 19, 2021.

106 Randy Peters, transportation coordinator for *Top Gun*, interview with the author, August 3, 2021.

107 Rondell, July 19, 2021.

CHAPTER 4
THE ACTORS
MAY TO MID-JUNE

Casting board

By early May, Scott had met with a lot of actors, most at his office in the DeMille Building.[108] The office was comfortable, with stylish black furniture, including a big desk and comfortable chairs. Each male actor who auditioned read the same scene. A Polaroid of him would be tacked to a board on the wall of Scott's office. Gradually the board filled with candidates. Greenberg remembers getting fabric to cover it, so actors coming in to be interviewed wouldn't see the competition.[109]

A large number of candidates became less desirable with time, and Scott was slow to sign off on actors. It's fairly common among directors to wait as long as they can. With time it became frustrating to the casting department given the sheer number of roles to fill. Scott was encouraged to make some decisions.

Cruise told an interviewer he suggested Anthony Edwards for the role of Goose to Simpson and Bruckheimer,[110] although Simkin, the casting director, said she wasn't sure about that. Edwards had one of the more impressive acting resumes of the young men on the board, with credits like *Heart Like a Wheel* (1983) and the starring role in *Revenge of the Nerds* (1984).

Simpson stayed closely involved in the process, Simkin said. She remembered doing battle with him over actors Edwards and Tom Skerritt. Simpson wanted more of a comedian for the role of Goose, and thought Skerritt wasn't tough enough for Viper, the commander. She went to bat for both, and dug in. She recalled Simpson shouting at her. "I just gave it back to him," she said.[111]

Edwards was the first actor with a signed contract, and his pay was near the top of what they paid any actor, save Cruise. They agreed to pay Edwards $150,000 but he also got a merchandising royalty of between 2-1/2 and 5 percent, which most of the other actors wouldn't get.[112] Scott and the producers, working with the casting department, decided on whom they would hire, but the studio handled all contract negotiations.

Meanwhile, casting Charlie was proving to be the biggest challenge of all. Simpson and Bruckheimer were dissatisfied with the candidates. They had contacted dozens of agents and had come up with numerous qualified candidates. In his first draft of the reworked script, which arrived ahead of the aggressive May 7 deadline, Skaaren had significantly improved the character, which presumably would widen the appeal of the part. He drilled down on each character, considering their individual motivations and emotions, and created arcs he could chart on graph paper.[113] Each arc was plotted using a different color. The technique provided insight into what the characters lacked. It was an extremely analytical process at a time that wasn't commonplace among screenwriters.[114]

Skaaren, who recorded many of his calls, had received one from an elated-sounding Bruckheimer soon after his first rewrite arrived. "Excellent job. Excellent," gushed Bruckheimer. "Even Tony, who we thought wasn't going to like this because he doesn't have the kind of heart we want this movie to have, loved it." The producer noted that Cruise, who was traveling, hadn't seen it yet, but he and Simpson were certain the actor would like it. The feel of the script was right, and instead of big structural or character hurdles, now they were looking more at "line changes," he said.[115]

Skaaren demurred at the praise, noting that the script was too long and that he had avoided things like the flying scenes, unsure of which were "sacred cows." Bruckheimer agreed, saying the O Club scene, in particular, was too long. But they were on the right track.

"One thing to understand about us, we're, unfortunately, brutally honest," the producer continued. "If we don't like it, we'll say it the way it is."

"We're all trying to make it right," Skaaren replied.

"You did a brilliant job," Bruckheimer continued. "You really went for the stuff that needed to be worked on. Great job with the girl," referring to the role of Charlie, "she's much, much better. I don't know how the fuck I'm going to cast her. Scares me. Don't know when we're going to find a girl with this laugh," apparently referring to a detail Skaaren had attached to Charlie. "The girls here, unfortunately, are pretty awful."

"The girls you have a shot at?" asked Skaaren.

"The girls that are available, that are out there — nothing real exciting at that age," the producer said, apparently dismissing all available actresses in their mid-20s at that time.

Skaaren said he knew of an actress who could be perfect, but couldn't think of her name. Bruckheimer said they would "take any help" they could get. If Skaaren ever recalled the name, there is no record of it. The main point of the call was to get Skaaren to Los Angeles so they could give him notes and he could get back to work.

Skaaren's contract specifically enabled him to work from Austin, but he was happy to come out.

32 actresses, four screen tests, no Charlie

Bruckheimer, given the benefit of the doubt, might not have been fully aware of how much top talent of the day had been accessed. A two-page document, entitled "Charlies" and dated May 14, covered the search. Broken into five sections, it included the names of 32 actresses. The sections were: actresses who would test with Cruise; actresses the director hadn't met but could still be considered; four who had rejected an audition; a section headed "NY"; and one headed "LA."[116]

The women Scott hadn't met included Rosanna Arquette, Catherine Mary Stewart, Lori Loughlin, Elizabeth McGovern and Andie MacDowall. A note by Arquette's name read: "Avail/agent int. in pursuing getting $500,000 for next pic--agent would explore less $."

The New York list included Tracy Pollan, Dana Wheeler-Nicholson, Haviland Morris, Kim Greist, Amy Steel, Melissa Leo, Sean Young, Karen Sillas, Liane Langland and Pamela Lynch. Next to Pollan's name were the words "Taped/Young NO."

The LA section listed nine actresses who each had a "NO" by their names: Cecile Callan, Patricia Duff, Jodie Foster, Linda Hamilton, Helen Hunt, Jennifer Jason Leigh, Virginia Madsen, Michelle Pfeiffer and Mare Winningham. The document noted that Pfeiffer was doing *Sweet Liberty* (1986). It also showed Foster, despite the no, was still in the game: "Met Tony/NO — wants to test Monday if ng on tests." Assuming ng meant negative, or no go, it left the door open to bring Foster in if the first round of women to test with crew didn't lead to a selection.

The actresses who had passed on the movie, according to the casting memo, were Linda Fiorentino, Ally Sheedy, Meg Tilly and McGillis. Simkin had made a special effort with Sheedy on March 13, sending a handwritten note on a Paramount card, before the actress declined. "Ally — Sending you this as per Tony Scott (who is away on a location scout)," wrote Simkin. "Please have another look at "Charlie" — this is a first draft by a new writer (still needs work but is in the direction we want to go). We are all very excited + would still love to get you in to read with Tom. All the best, Margie."[117]

The next step was a screen test for the four actresses who had made the cut: Susan Hess, Demi Moore, Julianne Phillips and Daphne Zuniga. All were given the same underlying contract, albeit with different negotiated rates. It included an uppercase sentence in the paragraph about sex scenes. "NO FRONTAL NUDITY BETWEEN WAIST AND THIGHS

WITHOUT ARTISTS CONSENT." Of course, Hollywood didn't shoot genitalia in mainstream movies anyway. Even *Basic Instinct* (1992) was years away. The essential meaning was that the actress agreed to show her breasts on camera.

A casting memo was sent on May 16 about the tests the following day. It was a tight schedule: Phillips at 7 a.m., Moore at 9:30 a.m., Zuniga at 12:30 p.m., and Hess at 2:30 p.m.[118]

All four women were at various stages of new careers. Phillips was known at that point for being married to rocker Bruce Springsteen. Hess had done a television movie and miniseries. Zuniga had the most television credits. Moore was the best known and was being offered the most money.

All had to sign a test option agreement, which was a commitment to take the part if they were offered it. The memo showed which scenes they would read with Cruise. There were three: classroom, dinner and airport. All of them were to read the classroom scene. Phillips was told to also prepare for the dinner scene, and Moore the airport scene. Zuniga and Hess had been advised to prepare for all three.

Hess, who had already auditioned for Simpson and Bruckheimer and would later work with Scott, remembers them putting her at ease. The audition was held off of the Paramount lot but close by at the Professional Artists Studio at 845 North Highland. There wasn't a makeshift set or any props, as was sometimes the case. She recalled this as being a sparse rehearsal space, with one make-up room and one costumer. Hess, who saw Zuniga leaving as she arrived, could tell she was near the end of the lineup.[119]

"It felt like an assembly line," she said. She remembers Cruise being polite and reserved. "There was respect for the actress, definitely," she said, "but there was a boundary he wasn't going to go past." Some actors will try to connect with the other in a situation like that, she explained, but he didn't do that. "He was compact, a short guy, cute, and very driven." She didn't know if the actor had a say in who got the role.

One thing she recalled vividly was that Cruise lost his temper when he learned he wouldn't be able to make his workout. She was surprised, because he had otherwise been very controlled and professional.

Casting and shaping Charlie

Negotiating for Cruise, Kilmer and Moore in the same window of time had to have been tricky for Wagner. The most recent updates to Cruise's agreement were made April 25. Kilmer and Moore's respective deal memos and contracts, which both mentioned the other, were negotiated in May.

Moore's background included three years on "General Hospital" when the soap opera had soared in popularity. She had starred in a movie called *No Small Affair* (1984), and just wrapped *St. Elmo's Fire* (1985). Moore had something else going for her when it came to *Top Gun*: She was championed for the role by Tanen.[120]

Moore reflected on her audition when she was promoting her book "Inside Out" in 2019. The interview had gone well but she had "shanked" the audition, she said, in part due to insecurity. "I think I just got nervous on the whole and didn't own it."[121] She declined an opportunity to talk about the contract in January 2021.

But it's hard to imagine that Moore, 23 at the time, didn't feel pressure. Her contract had been sent the day before she and the other actresses would test with Cruise.

"At the risk of being presumptuous, but in the interest of time, enclosed are three copies of a proposed Test Option Agreement," wrote Paramount attorney Daniel Furie. The letter instructed Wagner to have two copies signed and returned to him. "As you know, we cannot allow anyone to test who has not signed a Test Option Agreement."[122]

The contract, which also named Moore's company, Pajama Party Productions, had her earning $100,000, with $16,667 per week prorated per SAG agreement. It was more than any of the other actresses had been offered. Moore had to make changes quickly, presumably with help from Wagner, to have it done before the 9:30 a.m. screen test the next day.

The second change eliminated the paragraph that aligned her deal, by name, with Kilmer's. Moore would receive third billing. The version Moore signed struck out any reference to Kilmer and added the words "above the title in 2nd position to all cast members" except the title star. It was the same credit McGillis would ultimately receive.[123]

The $100,000 fee for Moore remained the same, but on-location expenses changed to the greater of $100 per day or $1,250 per week. It also tightened the window that Paramount had to decide whether it could cast her, which freed her up to accept other work sooner.

The third change was to the nudity clause, which was lined out in pen with the same stroke reflected in Moore's signature, meaning she wasn't agreeing to the nudity clause.

Kilmer's contract, which also invoked Moore by name, was also being negotiated. Kilmer had agreed to do two more pictures for Paramount, as part of his contract to do *Top Secret* (1984),[124] a spy spoof. He'd also made it clear he didn't want to be in *Top Gun*. Paramount attorney Greg Gelfan notified the CAA legal department on May 1 that the studio was exercising its option to hire Kilmer for "an additional picture at $100,000." The letter noted the *Top Secret* option agreement would expire the following day.[125]

Kilmer's 2020 autobiography, "I'm Your Huckleberry: A Memoir," doesn't mention having been under contract to Paramount and touches only lightly on negotiations for *Top Gun*. He writes that his agent, "who also represented Tom Cruise, basically tortured me into at least meeting with Scott." Wagner isn't mentioned by name.

Kilmer writes that he was so disinterested in playing Iceman that he purposefully dressed in weird clothes and read his lines indifferently at the audition. "And amazingly, I was told I had the part. I felt more deflated than inflated. I had to get out of there."[126]

As he was leaving, Scott followed him onto the elevator. Kilmer said the director acknowledged that the script was "insufficient" and tried to charm him by talking about how cool the planes were. Scott acknowledged that the role wasn't the lead, but said he would make Kilmer feel like it was. Kilmer said that sentiment, and Scott's general youthful exuberance, won him over.

Kilmer's contract, signed May 30, was for $150,000 for *Top Gun*, up from the $100,000 stipulated for his second picture in the contract connected to *Top Secret*. It also eliminated the requirement that he do a third picture. Notably, his screen credit provision included a sentence that if the leading lady receives credit above the title, Kilmer will be accorded credit in first or last position of below-the-title performers.

Transportation to set was non-exclusive but no less favorable than that provided to any other cast members, except the lead star. That meant he wouldn't have a private car, but neither would any of the other actors, save Cruise. Expenses and dressing facilities were the "same provision as in the Demi Moore agreement."

People in Paramount must have seen it as a victory. In Kilmer they had someone who could play Maverick, if they needed him. Gelfan sent an internal Paramount memo that the deal with the actor had been finalized on May 30. "We have engaged Val Kilmer to portray the role of "Maverick" in "Top Gun,"" with Maverick lined through but visible. The memo, which outlined all provisions of Kilmer's contract, didn't state the role of "Iceman" anywhere.[127]

Moore didn't get the part.

Screenwriter Warren Skaaren had been blunt with Simpson and Bruckheimer that even after the Kirsten-to-Charlie transition, the character remained "flat." He proposed making Charlie more "ballsy," aggressive, and ambitious.

Cruise seized the initiative to work one-on-one with Skaaren and together they achieved more depth for the two characters. In scheduled meetings and late night telephone conversations the two men — with the blessings of Scott, Simpson and Bruckheimer — began building out a much more robust Charlie, adding screen time and dialog. It was the actor who insisted the script show that Maverick's interest in Charlie went beyond the physical.[128]

Company moves to location

The search for production space and housing in San Diego had focused on areas in relative proximity to Naval Air Station Miramar. Eventually Badalato leased most of the Travelodge at 3737 Sports Arena Boulevard for the next months.

The hotel, with its freshly painted blue and white signs, was big enough and had easy access to the highway. It could accommodate all primary needs of the production company in one place. One building contained 28 rooms on two floors, and they had three of them for the duration. Also in Travelodge's favor: a big pool and bar. Most importantly, Travelodge had worked with the production on its irregular requirements at a good rate. It wasn't fancy, and many people would later remember it as a "dump" and the best evidence of a restricted budget.

Badalato, who moved in on May 6, was the first one there. It was referred to as a suite, but it was more accurately duplicate hotel rooms with a door between, one of which had the bed removed, which he used as an office. From there he laid out the space for departments, scrawling notes on the map of the hotel. There was some existing office space they could use, but most would be created out of hotel rooms, as his had been. A large space was designated a conference room/makeshift theater where dailies could be shown at night.

The production department bullpen was in the middle of everything, the accounting offices next door. The Costumes department was on the side with the parking lot, so the costume truck could be adjacent to the office door. The props office was next to the art department. While the rooms had phones, they went through a central circuit. Some departments needed direct lines to the outside, so those were installed.

The hotel rooms on the second and third floors were to house the dozens of crew. The production managed all of the room assignments, part of its deal with the Travelodge. There were enough overflow rooms for people above the line, should they need private space closer to the production offices for meetings or to stay on site. Most were staying elsewhere.

First Assistant Director Kolsrud started in mid-April. The other department heads to start April 29 were John DeCuir, the production designer, Jimmy Tyson, men's costume designer, and Randy Peters, transportation coordinator.

Other department heads and managers filled in from there. They moved to the Travelodge at different times, some staying in Los Angeles to work. All were asked to prepare budgets by the end of May.

Kolsrud remembered the role of the production designer being diminished, or even part-time. "The attitude was that we were shooting the Navy" so the focus was on the camera. Rather than building sets they would incorporate the Navy's real estate. But that would not be the reality.[129]

Production Design, Transportation

"The design issue of merit with *Top Gun* was that it was a 100 percent location show," said DeCuir, and the position was certainly full time. He wasn't dealing with soundstages, although some would be built later for cockpits of the F-14s for special effects by others. "It's not the same thing as if you're filling 12 stages full of sets," he explained. "But location film is equally demanding," he said. He still had to design and build sets, but on location. "You're not getting on a stage but you're still supporting the narrative."[130]

Scott soon decided that shooting all of the ground story on Miramar wasn't realistic or desirable. The Officer's Club, where the Maverick-meets-Kelly scene takes place, was the best example. The club on base had low ceilings, so it wasn't well suited to the scene he envisioned. Scott also wanted a circular or oval bar, and remodeling it was out of the question. They found an alternative but it would be pricey to build out, so the search continued.

In total, DeCuir's breakdown reflected 60 sets, more than half of which required some kind of buildout. Some, like the Officer's Club, were extensive. If anything, that number was growing as Scott sought to improve the sets.[131]

"This was not a big design show, it was more about the camera," agreed Baron. He called it a "modern film with a realistic look, with car stuff and houses," when they weren't on base. He was responsible for securing locations off base, via lease or insurance or permit, and anything related to the site.[132]

The transportation department opened up on one side of a room at the Travelodge designed to hold gatherings. It featured an accordion wall that could be dragged across to cut it in half. The job involves getting vehicles lined up and organizing rental vehicles for people who were approved for them, finding picture cars and hiring drivers, then coordinating the movement of cast and crew to and from location. With *Top Gun*, Peters had to coordinate with Miramar officials for clearance for everyone. It was a much simpler process than today, but still difficult terrain.

Simpson and Bruckheimer told Peters which cars they wanted to drive in San Diego. Rumors were out there that their deal with Paramount included a hefty allowance for vehicles, but it didn't extend to the *Top Gun* budget. (Their famous matching Ferraris would come the following year.) He found plenty of options, writing a memo to the producers to list them.[133]

There was a Mustang convertible available, but it wasn't a 5.0 GT, and it cost $1,000 a month. A 1985 Corvette was available for $2,000 a month. A Pontiac Fiero GT, "loaded with everything," was $1,000. A Firebird and Camaro Z-28, each $1,000 a month, were available, as well as a convertible Chrysler LaBaron for $700.[134]

"The transportation budget reflects rental cars at about $600 a month," wrote Peters. "These cars are in excess of that price and would have to be cleared through Bill Badalato for budget purposes." Badalato said they could have whatever car they wanted, but the production would only pay $600 of the cost and they would have to cover the rest. Peters remembers switching cars out for them several times.

It also fell to Peters to figure out how to teach Tom Cruise to ride a motorcycle. Peters organized a safety class and private lesson for May 23 at the Motorcycle Training Center, across from the Hollywood Bowl.[135] The trainer would pick up the actor, along with a check for the training center, at 3:45 p.m. at the production offices. Peters also asked Billy Badalato, the executive producer's son, to help with the lessons. He had hired the younger Badalato, then 18, as a PA Peters reasoned that a young person, particularly one who owned a Kawasaki 500 Ninja, would put Cruise at ease. He didn't tell Badalato whom the lessons were with until after he agreed.

Badalato described Cruise as "a quick learner, capable" and very serious. The actor got upset with himself for not getting it faster. "The hardest thing is to ride at slow speeds," he explained. "He never dropped the bike, although he came close." The actor was intent on getting it right and they spent hours at the center. By that evening he "would drive around the parking lot, ride around the yard and come back."[136]

The younger Badalato, who was credited on the movie as Simpson's assistant, recalled taking the producer's cars to the car wash. He dallied the first time he took one so Simpson would associate the process — which involved going two blocks away — with a longer time frame. David Kelson, the cable operator in the sound department, said he remembered seeing Billy doing donuts in the parking lot. Badalato, now a producer, did not deny it.

The props department was also having challenges around the budget. Mark Wade, the prop master, realized early that the Navy wasn't going to help him. Efforts above-the-line had led to relationships between the production and high-level officers, which was facilitating movement on base and the use of big-ticket items. But the smaller things were left to people lower in rank that hadn't been ordered or instructed to work with the production.[137]

"The Navy wasn't cooperative at all at first, not to me," Wade said. "They didn't like the script, so they were not going to supply anything to me." He still had to come up with anything an actor would touch on screen that appeared in a script. And it wasn't going to be cheap.

He was also collecting props for other scenes, like the ones planned for Charlie's house. Initially Scott had wanted Charlie and Maverick to have drinks in the scene, but Wade made the pitch for California wine. Product placement was in its early adolescence and the props department handled things like that with only moderate studio interaction. Wade didn't have a source on wine, but he found one in Charles Krug, a Napa Valley winery owned by the Mondavi family, then on its own way to superstardom. Wade recalled Bruckheimer seeing it on camera those first days and inquiring if he had obtained clearance.

Mixing filmmakers, military, and civilians

There were now filmmakers, civilians and Navy personnel actively advancing the project. Commander Haney delegated to Lt. Stairs in the Los Angeles office of CHINFO the same way Otterbein had delegated to Willard. That gave her some ability to approve — or at least move — things to the next level. Stairs was the Navy "task masker," according to Badalato. He considered her a military version of a "unit production manager" in terms of decision-making. She was there to make sure the production did everything to Navy standards, a mix of public relations and ensuring nothing classified was inadvertently compromised.

It was Stairs who delivered on the request for estimated costs of operating Navy aircraft. The memo, from the comptroller of the Navy to the chief of information referenced the *"Top Guns"* request, noting that the rates were expressly for the purpose of the movie production. It was dated May 9 but it wasn't stamped as received until May 17. It included prices for the F-5, which they would use to depict enemy jets, at $4,262 an hour. There were two helicopters on the list: The SH-3, A CH-46, which was a transport helicopter, came in at $1,772. The list of four aircraft did not include the F-14, the star of the skies for *Top Gun*, but it still greatly advanced his mission. Now Badalato had something on paper he could rely on to crunch real numbers.[138]

The Navy was working with them in other ways. For instance, the meter on the planes would run from takeoff to landing, rather than the moment they began to prep the plane to when it was returned.

Willard and Semcken were in charge of making the script work from the Navy and Topgun's perspective. Willard was interacting directly with Paramount, while Semcken had begun working with the production, including spending time with Tony Scott. After the meeting with the filmmakers in the office of RADM Cassidy that day, Paramount had begun delivering the script to Willard at his home, in care of his wife, Donna. "I would open it at night, kids crawling on my back, edit it, and give it to the driver the next day," he recalled. He had to do it from home, because he still had his full time job as XO of the Topgun school. "I think the heroine was a gymnast in the first one and by the time we were through, we had the instructor at TG.[139]

It was up to Semcken to deal directly with Scott about scenes in the script the Navy — essentially he and Willard, as the task had been delegated to them — found objectionable. Early in the process he flagged several things to Scott. One of them was the way Goose was killed, which at that point involved two planes crashing on an aircraft carrier.

Semcken's best argument was implausibility. The current version of the script reflected the Navy losing three jets in 90 minutes. "We were the best pilots in the Navy, flying the best airplanes in the world at that time," he said. "We didn't lose planes like that." The director told him "I'm not making a documentary!" The topic was dropped in the short term, but Semcken knew it wasn't going to happen, even if Scott didn't.[140]

The production hired Richard "Dick" Stevens as aerial coordinator. His job was designing and managing Navy air-to-air support, which included Grumman, but at that point Badalato needed his help sorting out a strategy with the Navy to help break the logjam around approvals. Stevens had served in the U.S. Air Force as a photographer and cameraman during the Vietnam War. Key in his hire were his contacts with other aerial photographers who were either in the military or retired from it, because the Navy required a special rating for a photographer to go up in its F-14s.

On May 19, Stevens and Badalato sent a broad memo about all production requirements for the air-to-air scenes.[141] The plan was to circulate the memo to everyone involved on the Navy side until they got answers. They soon figured out that while the production now had contacts in the Navy, it wasn't the same thing as getting approvals. People who it seemed could sign off on specifics didn't think they had the authority or, even if they did, were reluctant to do it. It had to come from higher up.

Ultimate approval had to be at the level of the Pentagon, because the movie touched many different aspects of the Navy. The scenes that would shoot on base and the air-to-air photography were two distinct components. At that point, they assumed they would be filming the flight scenes at the China Lake naval air base in the western Mojave Desert. The chain of command at China Lake was also distinct from that on the aircraft carriers at sea, and for air sea rescues, and at Miramar.

Badalato updated Simpson and Bruckheimer, who were headed back to the East Coast to meet with Navy brass on the importance of their mission. "It is essential that Paramount representatives meet with the Navy at the highest command level," he wrote, including the list of various approvals still needed.

Stevens and Badalato prepared a proposed schedule for when they wanted to shoot the different segments and presented it to Semcken and Willard on May 19.[142] They also gave it, along with another memo dated May 20, to Bruckheimer, who ended up with a May 21 meeting with Navy brass.[143] The 13-item memo entitled "Aerial Requirements" included a broad list of things "from general to technical specifics" that needed approval. They needed an aircraft that could stand in as a MiG, and the feasibility of painting it for the "appropriate look of a real world threat." They needed aircraft carrier crew to assist with "simulated tire blow out," and permission to do a low-level flyby. They needed clearance for the actors to fly in the back of an F-14, to shoot a missile, to advance the cause of the Grumman camera mounts and permission to film at the carrier at sea on specific dates, Sept. 3-Sept. 10.

The goal was to have the powers in Washington make whatever changes they saw fit and sign off on it, so they could get a final version to Lt. Stairs by the end of May. Then they could move forward because they had approval from the highest ranks. That presumed that Semcken and Willard, who had been given responsibility for it, wouldn't have anything to say.

Chapter 4 - Endnotes

[108] Badalato, January 8, 2021.
[109] Greenberg, December 21, 2020.

[110] *Danger Zone: The Making of Top Gun* (2004), produced by David Crowther & Charles de Lauzirika.
https://www.youtube.com/watch?v=Knz5LM_FzEE&t=1167s
[111] Simkin, September 21, 2021.
[112] Dan Furie, "Top Gun" Paramount Inter-Communication, May 16, 1985. Furie to Greg Gelfan, re Anthony Edwards. TGC.
[113] Warren Skaaren. Intensity chart, *Top Gun*, (Series I). WSP.
[114] Macor, *Rewrite Man*, 84.
[115] Macor, *Rewrite Man*, 98.
[116] "Charlies" MSP.
[117] Margery Simkin to Sheedy, March 13, 1985. MSP.
[118] Margery Simkin, "Top Gun – Casting Schedule," May 16, 1985. TGC.
[119] Susan Hess, interview with the author, January 4, 2021.
[120] Badalato, January 26, 2021.
[121] "Howard Stern Show," Howard Stern interviews Demi Moore. Aired Oct 9, 2019 on SiriusXM 100 and 101.
[122] Dan Furie, "Top Gun / Demi Moore Test Option Agreement," Paramount Pictures Corp. May 15, 1985. TGC.
[123] Ibid.
[124] Dan Furie, "Top Gun – Val Kilmer," Paramount Inter-Communication, May 1, 1985, Furie to Greg Gelfan. TGC.
[125] Gregory Gelfan, Paramount Pictures Corp., to Shelly Srolof, Creative Artists Agency, May 1, 1985. The cover letter references Kilmer's original contract with Paramount for *Top Secret*, which has an option to do another movie for PPC for $100,000. TGC.
[126] Val Kilmer. *I'm Your Huckleberry: A Memoir* (New York: Simon & Schuster 20,20), 115.
[127] Greg Gelfan, "TOP GUN – VAL KILMER" Paramount Inter-Communication, May 30, 1985. Gelfan to Dan Furie, CAA legal department. TGC.
[128] Audio recordings and Skaaren's notes from calls, April - May 1985. WSP.
[129] Tyson, June 6, 2020.
[130] DeCuir, May 12, 2020.
[131] *Top Gun* Art and Production department documents (multiple documents, including script breakdowns, several dates, 1985). TGC.
[132] Baron, April 5, 2021.
[133] Randy Peters memo to Mark Fridkin, Jennifer Christi, and Barbara Weintraub. June 3, 1985. TGC.
[134] Bob Griffith, Dollar Rent A Car, Inc. to Randy Peters, May 10, 1985. TGC.
[135] Randy Peters, "Tom Cruise — motorcycle lesson," Paramount Inter-Communication, May 21, 1985. TGC.
[136] Billy Badalato (William Badalato, Jr.), production assistant on *Top Gun.* July 15, 2020.
[137] Wade, April 29, 2020.
[138] Department of the Navy, "Reimbursement Rates for use of Navy Aircraft," From Comptroller of the Navy to the Chief of Information, May 9, 1985. TGC. [139] Willard, December 2, 2020.
[140] Semcken, November 5, 2020.
[141] Bill Badalato and Richard Stevens, "Navy Air-to-Air Production Requirements," Paramount Inter-Communication, May 19, 1985. TGC.
[142] Bill Badalato and Richard Stevens, Proposed Shooting Schedule, Paramount Inter-Communication, May 19, 1985. TGC.

[143] Bill Badalato and Richard Stevens, Aerial Requirements, Paramount Inter-Communication, May 19, 1985. TGC.

CHAPTER 5
LAST WEEKS OF PREP
JUNE 1 - MID-JUNE

The Director

Over the months of prep Tony Scott had interacted with almost everyone. He was demanding and disinclined to pick his battles, which meant he wanted everything. Yet he was almost universally liked. He was charming and funny and won people over, even those he exasperated.

Scott's warmth to people on the crew, and by now members of the military, created a sense of friendship that many described years later. Photographer C.J. Heatley, whose day job was operations officer of VF 124, the largest squadron in the Navy, was one of those people. Scott knew who "Heater" was from his magazine photos, but reached out after seeing his oversized Cibachrome images on the walls of the lobby of the Officer's Club.

Heatley still remembers Scott's entourage that first visit. It included an English woman with the contemporary look of pop star Annie Lennox, something very unusual on base at that time. The woman flipped through a roll of $100 bills to pay him for his images. "I said, Jesus, Tony! I am on active duty. You can't pay me for anything!" Heatley said he would give him the slides, Scott could pay to have them developed, and return them. He invited the director to his home to pick which slides he wanted. To Heatley's amazement, Scott came over that night.

"He was leaning over my giant light table, going crazy!"[144]

The director stayed long enough for Heatley's wife to bake cookies and serve them. It was an easy visit and they talked comfortably. Scott repeated something he had said to others about his early vision for the movie, which was dark, as in the bowels of an aircraft carrier, and similar in feel to *The Hunger.* "I said that was true inside the ship, but that's not fighter aviation."

Scott set aside a stack of slides, which he took with him. He came back for a second visit and got even more, according to Heatley.

Badalato recalls liking Scott, even though by that point in prep he was increasingly at odds with him. There's an inherent conflict between the executive producer and director on any movie with a tight budget. With *Top Gun* it was in part because Badalato was expressly directed by the studio to keep Scott in check. "I always felt like we were good foes, but we were foes," he said.[145]

The other person whose job was to challenge Scott was Semcken. Many months earlier, Pettigrew had told the original scriptwriters that the Navy wasn't going to approve many airplanes crashing onto aircraft carriers. Virtually everyone involved with the movie who knew the Navy had told them the same thing. The writers liked Pettigrew. They asked if they could use his call sign, Viper, in the script. They also changed Maverick's first name from Evan to Pete. Meanwhile, Cash and Epps resisted changing several of the scenes flagged by Pettigrew.[146]

Scott certainly didn't want to change the scenes that were most explosive. The upper ranks of the Navy said there had to be changes, but they weren't specific, which had to have emboldened the director. In reality, what happened was that responsibility moved down the chain of command. Shaping the script into something that reflected well on the Navy had been delegated to Willard and Semcken and specifically Semcken in terms of the day-to-day, when it came to telling Scott.

"At that point there were three F-14s crashing in the script," said Semcken, who insisted it wasn't accurate.

"Topgun pilots were the best of the best. They weren't crashing planes like that."

Scott was seemingly unconvinced he couldn't have his way. "Tony was always pushing," said Semcken. "Always."

Scott also had proof that holding to his vision often yielded good results. There were two examples, the first being the early scene where Cougar loses his nerve in the air, and Maverick helps bring him in. It's a pivotal plot point, because Maverick ends up replacing Cougar, played by John Stockwell, at the Topgun school. Scott wanted to depict a bad landing of an F-14 where it snaps the hook and skids across the aircraft carrier, a concept that was gaining traction.[147]

But another one, which involved a midair collision over an aircraft carrier, was considered a non-starter with the Navy. And Scott wasn't giving up on that yet, even if he had to shoot it elsewhere. It fell to Semcken to tell the director there would be no midair collision depicted. He predicted his response: "I'm not making a documentary!"

The lieutenant, who had a diplomatic approach that had endeared him to the movie crew, decided to be blunt. "I said, 'Tony, think about it! If it's midair, they both die. The planes are each going 600 miles an hour. If they hit, everything comes apart and everybody dies." Even if a pilot lived, hitting something was career-ending. "If Maverick didn't die, he wouldn't fly again!"

"Well," the director said, "you need to kill him and it can't be Maverick's fault!" Semcken said he would come up with something, although in that moment, he wasn't sure how.

Several people, including Willard, recalled only one situation in which a radio intercept officer had been killed where the pilot wasn't at fault. The pilot and RIO had ejected from a failing aircraft and the canopy, the part of the aircraft that covers the seat, struck and killed the RIO. The Navy learned from the incident, and changed its processes. Semcken researched it and found the records: The pilot had been exonerated. It was the perfect solution. Semcken provided the details to Skaaren, who was working away in Austin.

While Semcken would butt heads with Scott, he also offered up gems. One was alerting Scott to the TACTS Trailer. The acronym stood for Tactical Aircrew Combat Training System, which was contained in a trailer with a briefing room. Technology, cutting edge and classified at the time, enabled the tracking and recording of the planes in the sky. That meant pilots could review their flight performances from the day before. It was also brilliant for the story, and a scene where Maverick's flying is reviewed in class.

In the meantime, Scott kept pushing for the scene where Cougar crash-lands across the aircraft carrier, and another that featured a flat spin. Because the Navy's oversight of the script only applied to the use of its resources, Scott figured whatever he couldn't shoot with the Navy he'd shoot elsewhere.

Camera, Grip and Electric

The dynamic between directors and cinematographers is different from movie to movie. Some directors rely on their directors of photography (DPs) to make all camera calls. Some, like Scott, exert a lot of direction. He knew cameras, lighting and equipment from his work on the commercial side, but more than that, he loved cinematography and studied it. With *Top Gun*, he intended to leave a strong visual footprint.

Cinematographer Jeffrey Kimball now had a team in Ward Russell as gaffer, or chief electrician, and Tom Prophet as key grip. The camera, grip and electric departments work hand-in-hand. The electric department covers any equipment that carries a volt or leads to it. The grip department handles everything else needed to support camera and electric.

The first task for each department was to organize equipment. Prep involves getting bids for equipment, then testing it. The camera department would have two cameras, which was standard, and referred to as A and B for the first part of photography. More cameras would be added with the air-to-air segment. They were committed to using Panavision, which was one of only two real options in the mid-1980s for major motion pictures and the dominant one in the United States.

The company, founded in 1954, designs and manufactures film and digital cameras and lenses, and has been at the forefront of their development. Its initial focus was on projectors, since theater owners needed lenses to accommodate the widescreen format the studios were delivering. Panavision had steadily grown since then, both in leasing cameras to television and movies and in improving camera optics, including through the development of anamorphic lenses.

Scott loved anamorphic lenses, which capture a wide image on the film frame by stretching it, and he intended to use them on *Top Gun*. An undated document for a Panavision rental compared the costs of the same equipment side by side. The weekly rental for anamorphic equipment was just shy of $3,000 while standard equipment was less than $1,900.[148]

Badalato explained the issue in a memo to Simpson and Bruckheimer. It wasn't just about cost. Anamorphic lenses would be heavier and more cumbersome than regular lenses in a game where ounces mattered. It would increase the likelihood they would waste more film, and that there would be more problems in post-production, while limiting the format in which it could be released.

Some of the concerns didn't carry weight, but there was the larger issue of Grumman. Principal photography wasn't far off, and filmmakers still didn't have the defense contractor's approval for regular lenses on the aircraft, much less anamorphic ones. And the executive producer needed Grumman to sign off. He suggested Super 35 in the memo, which meant someone had told him about it, since it was still somewhat unknown.

Super 35, perfected in 1983, removed the sound track area on the edge of the film stock so a lens could cover the entire width of the 35mm film. The sound track was recorded separately, and an optical squeeze of the image would be added in post-production to create the theatrical release prints needed. It meant the lens could see more.

Ultimately it wasn't the battle with Badalato that changed Scott's mind but a meeting with camera crew at Miramar. Scott and Kimball were skilled cinematographers, but aerial photography was something different. This meeting included David B. Nowell, an aerial cameraman who worked for noted aviator Clay Lacy, although Lacy wasn't at the meeting.

When they called Nowell, they asked him to come to base with a small camera he had written about in American Cinematographer magazine, new technology at the time. "I brought the small helmet-cam to show him and Jeffrey."

The May 10 meeting, a date Nowell checked on an old calendar, was the first time he ever met Scott. He and Kimball and other camera crew were standing around an F-14. Scott climbed up into the cockpit with a Panavision camera with an anamorphic lens. "The problem with these lenses is that they were big, heavy and their close focus was around 4 1/2 to 5 feet," explained Nowell. That just wasn't enough room to film the pilots in the cockpit.[149]

Scott, now convinced on his own terms that he couldn't shoot anamorphic, was all ears when Nowell started talking about Super 35. The young cameraman had just worked with cinematographer Dante Spinotti in filming *Choke Canyon* (1986), and Spinotti had used it.

Shortly thereafter, Scott told Badalato he would use Super 35.[150]

At about the same time, his request for filters from RSA Films Limited in London was approved. Light filters are put over lenses to shape light. This order was for "Colour Grads, hard and soft," meaning the filters were graduated — grads — with different effects and densities. The list sounded exotic: blue grads and glass blue grads, pop grads and coral grads, polar screens, 85s and Straight NDs, which stood for neutral density. Sunset grads had the otherworldly effect of prolonging a sunset by adding shadow detail.

RSA agreed to lease the filters for $609 a week, or about $1,578 today with inflation. Insuring them added another 12.5 percent. The rental ran from June 25 to Sept. 30. There was also the cost of shipping them, along with Scott's personal filters, from London.[151]

The grip equipment was in the same cost ballpark: $760 a week, about $1,969 today. Grip equipment ranges from dollies and tracks to ladders and tripods, which move the camera, and from flags and gobos to silks and sticks, which help shape light. That was nothing compared to what the camera and electrical equipment would cost.[152]

As gaffer, Russell's job included arranging the power and ensuring safe operations. The department had to review every location to determine power sources and where cables would run. He knew early in prep that *Top Gun* would need more power than most movies.

"To achieve the distinctive look the director and director of photography are seeking for *Top Gun*, numerous arc lamps must be used," he wrote in a memo that made the case for renting a specific high-capacity generator. It was typical to use two generators on a movie, he noted, but one was for backup. With *Top Gun*, both generators would be used "almost constantly at higher amperages than normal," he wrote. They needed to be able to use both AC and DC.[153]

Russell also submitted a preliminary equipment list that was seven pages long. The movie would need both an incandescent and arc package for lighting. Movies of the day were gradually phasing out carbon arc lamps, but Kimball and Scott were committed to using them. They were extremely bright, but could be tempered in a way that incandescent lights couldn't. *Top Gun* was one of the last movies to use them. The cost of the incandescent package was about $3,250 per week, while the arc package added $1,300.[154] That would translate to $11,790 today.

The Panavision lens rental was $2,000 a week, or $5,182 with the inflation adjustment. All told, the rental came in at about $8,000 a week, $20,729 today. That didn't include department salaries or the camera truck lease or the salaries of Teamster drivers who would move the truck.

Carbon arc lights

Carbon arc lights were the first widely used electric light, once used as street lights in large cities, along with many other uses. "It was Jeff's signature light," said Russell. "All the studios used them back then but he was one of the last people to go to HMI," a type of light that uses an arc lamp instead of an incandescent bulb. Carbon arc "was a different quality of light," he continued. "It was an actual, burning flame. You'd put in two sticks of carbon, feed it in and touch it together, and it bounced around and flickered." With a lens in front of the lamp, the result was a softer bright light. They would set them up outside and "blast them in from outside the window." Carbon arc lights were rarely used by the mid-1980s, and not just due to the environmental issues associated with emitting UV-A, UV-B and UV-C rays. They were prone to starting fires, they created radio frequency interference, they were heavy, and they made a loud buzzing noise. They also had to be closely monitored, which meant dedicated crew for each lamp to control output. "But the light was amazing," said Russell.

With the various department packages squared away, additional crew was hired. Crew start times were sent to the studio to "sign up." One memo shows sound, camera and electric crew coming at the same time. That included John T. Connor as camera operator, and Bob Duggan as best boy, second in charge of the lighting department. Lamp operators — needed to manage the carbon arc lights — also were in the mix.

Bill Kaplan was hired as the sound mixer. He had 10 years of experience, including on movies like *High Velocity* (1976), *The Blues Brothers* (1980), and *Romancing the Stone* (1984). It was his job to capture all dialogue and ambient sound on location or the soundstages. In this case, ambient noise was going to be an issue. Working sound on an aircraft carrier would be an entirely new challenge.

The production department set up a space to watch dailies at the Travelodge on the other side of the large room occupied by the transportation department. It featured an accordion wall, which could be pulled across to create two spaces.

Editor Billy Weber was also on board. He would be starting two weeks into photography and work from the Paramount lot. He would review film as it came in, keeping in close touch with Scott and the producers. He would also start cutting — putting film together to create scenes — right away. Then, on Sundays he would drive to San Diego and show them what he had pieced together.

Costume Department and Maverick's Jacket

The costume department didn't turn in its budget by the end of May, as had all other departments. Tyson, with help from Read, was flummoxed by the task of creating a realistic budget. Scott worked with them on specific details, including high-end items, which added expense. Costume crew stayed in Los Angeles longer than the others to have easy access to wardrobe vendors there.

They shopped around the city while also patronizing the legendary Western Costume Co., one of the oldest businesses in Hollywood. The Navy was not going to provide all of the costumes the movie needed and the famous costume house had an almost unparalleled collection of military uniforms.[155] Tyson, having worked there, knew it well.

Scott weighed in heavily on details. He wanted to accentuate the actors' good looks, and continued to show people *Looking Good: A Guide For Men* to get across his vision, which addressed civilian clothes. More than anything, he wanted a distinctive look.

The things the director wanted could be pricey, and Badalato was there to remind him of costs. Scott, growing weary of it, told his assistant they would dodge the executive producer at every opportunity. Catalaine Knell met Scott while employed by agent-producer Scott Ufland and found Scott's personality more amenable. By this point in the process she knew she liked the director, and was more than happy to run interference. It was her job, but she also wanted to do it.[156]

Scott's strategy of bypassing Badalato was designed to avoid conflict while the director got his own way, or at least as close to it as he could. Scott candidly told a BCC interviewer decades later he didn't take no for an answer. He described himself as "very childlike in terms of being a spoilt brat. If I'm told I can't have something, I'll just take it."[157] What that looked like at that point in the production of *Top Gun* was that Scott told department heads what he wanted, and that he would worry about Badalato later. And he remained very hands on with departments.

"Tony liked everything aged, and knocked down, old-looking and vintage," recalled Tyson. Scott wanted blue jeans and denim, for example, which meant Tyson and Read hunted through second-hand stores. "There were a lot of vintage stores on Melrose in the '80s; that's where the leather jacket came from," Tyson said. Read found the jacket Charlie would wear, which, while noted by fans, never reached the iconic status of Maverick's bomber jacket.

Most people believe it was a G-1 but one dedicated fan, Matt Lawlor, doubles as a researcher and has done homework about it. "I believe Maverick's jacket is a G-1 variant known as a 55j14 made in the late 1940s," he wrote in an email. The difference between the two may seem subtle to the casual observer: The 55j14 is a bit looser than that of the standard G-1, wider at the waist and slightly longer. "One of the big identifying features is the front pockets," wrote Lawlor, adding that the 55j14 was made by a company called L.W. Foster. There is a small slot in the left front pocket designed for a pen. Over time, the G-1 pocket flaps became more V shaped than curved, and finally straight. Maverick's jacket is more rounded. Collectively, the details convince Lawlor that Cruise the jacket Cruise wore was a 55j14.[158]

It was the boots that came up in a costume budget phone call between Tyson and Badalato. Scott felt strongly that Maverick should wear fancy cowboy boots, although they weren't something typically worn by Navy officers. Costume departments buy multiples of things to make sure a damaged item can be replaced, one more element adding to the bottom line.

Other budget items came into the production department in May, as Scott met with all department heads. Badalato sent a new memo to all department managers on May 30, asking that they reevaluate their budgets accordingly.

"As you all know, we are operating on a very tight budget. It is therefore doubly important that Tony have an opportunity to decide for himself what will or will not be deleted from a scene," he wrote. "Let's not surprise him!" Departments were asked to schedule meetings with Badalato to discuss any foreseeable overages. "Please delay any major purchasing until your budgets have been evaluated."[159]

Scott's vision, and personality, was such that he was going to make the movie as he saw fit, even if it meant circumventing constraints. "He was a young director at that point," said Baron. "His commercial work was brilliant and he was still finding his way in features."[160]

In 2021, Badalato played down the degree to which he had to manage the director. He noted that Scott was under a lot of pressure. Scott was director non grata after the lackluster performance of *The Hunger* and needed to redeem himself. "I think he was less worried about the budget battles which he waged than not producing great dailies and thus keep his job," said Badalato. "Tony was not out for me. Tony was out to survive the job."[161]

MAVERICK'S FLIGHT SUITS

#1: First Act - Crash   #2: Post Crash   #3: Final Act

CREDIT: Matt Lawlor

The average person might not have noticed the subtle difference in patches on the flight suit costumes worn by Cruise over the course of the movie, depicted here by act.

At the same time, reports that Scott was threatened with being fired — something the director joked about many times in interviews — have been overblown, in Badalato's view. "Not true during production. It's part of the 'living in the danger zone' vibe that Tony loved and projected." Studios are loath to fire directors during shooting, he continued. "It's a huge deal involving contracts, studio reputations and the [Directors Guild of America]," explained Badalato, who went on to produce, or executive producer, many movies, including *Around the World in 80 Days* (2004), *About Schmidt* (2002), and *Alien: Resurrection* (1997).

Production Design

Within the week Badalato had his updates. It's normal for departments to beef up budgets, knowing they will be trimmed, but there were real pressures. Even DeCuir, who thought his department would be among the least pinched since they were shooting so much on base, was over by $40,000, according to his revised budget.

Under the latest script, the art department determined 55 sets would be needed. The production designer's line-item summary marked 24 of those sets "NA," meaning zero costs. Those sets were places like the deck of the aircraft carrier, the flight line at Miramar, or special-effects sets to be built at the end of the movie, which were budgeted differently. That still left 31 sets, which he calculated at $240,000 to build out as Scott wished. His budget was $190,000.[162]

The executive producer had balked when he saw the art department budget. DeCuir met with him to explain each cost. Scott had been firm that he would shoot the Officers Club scenes off base, and it had turned out to be the biggest ticket item on the production designer's list. (Special effects were budgeted separately.) Scene 71 was eight pages of script and pivotal to the story, and the director planned three days for it. Badalato thought they could spend less.

The location was the Mississippi Room at the Lafayette Hotel. DeCuir estimated the scene at $14,500 ($35,571 in 2021 dollars.) It's a pittance relative to what elaborate stage sets cost to build, then and now, but the budget was tight. Even Scott hadn't anticipated spending too much on sets, because he assumed he would use more of the Navy's properties.

Badalato asked DeCuir whether the improvements amounted to a significant upgrade for the Lafayette Hotel. If so, Badalato thought they might be able to use that to make the case for a lower lease rate. DeCuir went back to his typewriter, and company letterhead, and wrote a memo that detailed the "remodel." This one factored in the "approximate market value" of the upgrades at $17,300. It listed eight things that had "permanent/potential value for the owner." It included repainting the upper area of the bar to a tan or beige color with silver and gold trim; illuminating and repairing glass block and mirror side panels, and expanding it where it was half-height to align it with a full wall; they would add six acrylic/back lit mirror floor-to-ceiling side panels in the upper bar; a decorative mirror for the back bar, and resurface the bar with a black Formica top. They also planned to add neon blue rings above the circular bar, worth $2,500, and a decorative acrylic/illuminated centerpiece.[163]

The DeCuir memo gave Badalato — and more likely Baron, the location manager — some ammunition for a better rate. The savings on the lease, if there were any, are unclear, but the art department, and assorted contractors, got the go-ahead to begin transforming the Mississippi Room into the Officer's Club.

Other things in DeCuir's budget were smaller but not without cost, like sprucing up the exterior of the Fightertown U.S.A. hangar, which included painting on the base nickname. Then they had to find places to shoot the locker room scene, the volleyball court, a dive bar and so forth.

Badalato noted the mounting expenses in a memo he sent Simpson and Bruckheimer on June 7. "There is still time to reduce this at next week's meeting with Scott and DeCuir," he wrote.[164]

Improving Navy rapport

The prop master put together a one-page budget estimating costs at $180,000. The scenes involving Goose's death alone would involve a charter boat, life rafts and helicopters. They were putting an actor in the water, which would require Scuba equipment and safety crew. They needed to depict a plane blowing up. All of that was expensive.

On the positive side, the prop master had befriended two Navy men, brothers Jim and Mark Kauber. Wade was a pro at finding what he needed and when the Navy was less than helpful, he went to outside sources. The Kaubers had been the answer on base. Having them on his side made it easier to develop other relationships at Miramar.

One issue had to do with using the Navy helicopter squadron in the rescue scenes. Some accounts indicate the squadron wasn't interested in participating in the movie. Navy helicopters normally provide support to Navy vessels. But Wade found what he needed at the U.S. Coast Guard, which was eager to participate, including with their helicopters.

Separately, Badalato and Stevens still needed official signoff from Washington, D.C., specifically Stairs' boss, RADM Jack A. Garrow. He was the head of CHINFO for the Navy, which meant he was the direct representative of the Navy secretary, as well as chief of naval operations, in all public affairs and internal relations.

On June 13, Stevens wrote a memo to Badalato and Bruckheimer. Two meetings were critical, he told them. The first needed to happen at the highest levels, so Navy operational personnel who were qualified to review and initiate all final air-to-air clearances, including resources, safety, budget and schedule, would sign off.[165]

They still didn't have Grumman's signoff on attaching cameras to the aircraft but they had moved the ball downfield. The defense contractor, working with Northrup Corp, which it would later merge with, had completed feasibility studies that it was do-able. That cost the production about $10,000. Now they needed to get costs and schedule the dates to install the cameras.

Increasing budget pressure

A lot of bills were coming in at once and many were for things that hadn't been budgeted. Scott had proven stubborn on almost all of it, mostly to his benefit. Meanwhile, Badalato kept tapping away on his typewriter. His job was to rein in expenses, and the studio was still paying close attention. It's the inherent struggle in filmmaking: The money side wants a limit, while the creative side wants carte blanche.

The expensive cowboy boots for Maverick ended up being a line of demarcation. Whether it was one thing too many or the specific sticker price, which wasn't stated, it prompted the most serious budget memo yet to Scott, despite Badalato's effort to keep it light.

The June 7 memo, cheekily addressed to "Sir Anthony Scott," hinted at the growing tensions. "As the costume department cannot give me a budget, I cannot give go-aheads on things like outrageously priced boots," he wrote. "If you'd decide on the look of our pilots et al I could find out where we have extra money for things like handmade boots!"

Entitled "Final Days," the memo included a schedule for all major pre-production activity and summarized the loose ends that remained. It covered the search for a rehearsal space, a suggestion that they cut one scene in an F-14 for actor Michael Ironside, and the hiring of an editor. It closed with a second reference to money. "BUDGET AGAIN...ALWAYS. We must have a long talk about the budget in general. I need to find out those things that are of utter importance to you as opposed to those things that you'd be willing to give up... if any of the latter exist!" wrote Badalato.[166]

The boots were ultimately purchased at Mark Fox, a popular boot store that had supplied footwear to movies for years. Tyson said the boots provide insight into Scott's style. "They were old Mexico style, hacienda green and yellow and blue," he said. "Those were the moments where you could see Tony came from commercials, where he had just 40 or 60 seconds to make a point. You didn't just go get regular cowboy boots. Tony wanted something very visual."[167]

Tyson asked the prop master if he would secure the pilot helmets, and he agreed. Given that the Navy was less than helpful, Wade decided the best way to do that was to find out where they got them. He turned to Flight Suits Unlimited in El Cajon, Calif. "I thought they used paint on them. They didn't — they use tape, so it glows at night. It's fluorescent but it has colors to it, and they make designs with that tape," he recalled.

"I sat with Tony Scott and said how are we going to know who is who?" The director said that was a good question. They decided to put the names of the characters on front. "Little funky, but for movies, you have to be able to tell who's who."[168]

Scott also decided against using the existing Navy Topgun logo, creating a ripple in the production office. "Creating new logos for helmets, aircraft, patches for uniforms, etc., will be an overage of around $20,000," Badalato wrote Simpson and Bruckheimer. He noted that the pilot's helmets were budgeted at $550 each, which included artwork. "Now, the picture has a layer of new and original design," which was more expensive.

There were 50 to 60 helmets. "I needed multiples of them for Goose, Cruise, for all of them," Wade recalled. "I probably had six of them for Cruise. I had to have doubles, and didn't know who the pilots were going to be." He needed helmets for the pilots who were actually flying and didn't know their head sizes, which made it difficult to size them. "They had to have a microphone in them. So, yes, it was costly."

By June 15, Badalato was able to send Scott another memo, noting a few things that had been resolved. The Navy had agreed to film actors in the backseat of an F-14. This would require a three-day training course scheduled for Aug. 15-17, then they could film flying scenes Aug. 12-24.[169]

At the same time, the memo dropped any niceties in asking Scott to prioritize now that principal photography was 11 days away. "As I have heard it, the locations giving us budget problems are Graduation, Hospital and Corridor, Viper's House and Locker Room," wrote Badalato. "The way we will work this is when the budget is exhausted, the work stops. If we do not proceed with caution in this department, you may end up filming sets as they exist."

PHOTO: Citation Press

Prop master Mark Wade needed multiple copies of each helmet for each actor, and estimated six just for Tom Cruise.

The TACTS Trailer, where real-life pilots reviewed their in-sky performances, brought a host of challenges. To build the set Scott wanted would cost between $100,000 and $200,000 — and was not in the budget. That meant they had to use the existing TACTS Trailer. And the production wanted the Navy to allow it to use one of their "video dog fights," which could be transferred into a video feed during filming. "The trick here is going to be to make the available technology and Navy material fit the scene," Badalato said. "We really don't have any other option."

A header in the middle of the third page stood out like an elephant on a flight deck: "Our problem with the Navy." The Navy's cooperation was fading. "The only way we are going to get back on track with the Navy is to be able to contact them on Monday with locked locations. They've had it with the agonizing process that has taken place over locations," the memo said.

It was irrelevant if the Navy was right or wrong on any particular issue, Badalato continued. "What does matter is that we are not getting their full cooperation." The memo set Monday — two days away — as the deadline for Scott to make final decisions about the ground story.

Scott, with the assistance of Kolsrud, was in the process of making some other decisions. On June 15, the same day as the memo, they had met with the captain and executive officer on board the USS Enterprise. Both moviemakers left the meeting feeling encouraged, and each wrote memos about it for different reasons.

First Assistant Director

Kolsrud's memo, sent to Stairs and copied to the director, Badalato, Simpson and Bruckheimer, was the full wish list. It referenced the meeting with the naval officers and took on a solicitous and hopeful tone, with phrases like "we wish to" and "we will want to" laced throughout.[170]

His two-page memo also covered the scene with the F-14 crashing on deck. "We want to erect the safety barrier and push or pull an F-14 into it," he explained. "Then we wish to use the regular navy crash crew to run forward, shoot C0-2 fire extinguishers on the aircraft, and to have a silver suit pull the actors out of the aircraft to simulate an emergency."

The memo was filled with other details, including the proposed schedule, which had production shooting on the USS Enterprise Aug. 7-13. It spelled out how equipment would be loaded and stored, and that the production wanted to shoot on the flight deck, the flag bridge, the signal bridge, and the pri-fly bridge. The primary flight control bridge is where the air bosses direct all aircraft activity. Communications are centered on the signal bridge.

"We anticipate needing as much time as possible on the flight deck and will alter our schedule however necessary to use all the time available when regular flight operations are not being conducted," Kolsrud wrote. A lot seemed relatively easy. They would need to wet the deck to replicate storm conditions. They needed use of a Navy helicopter as a camera platform for some shots. The memo requested permission to "put our actors in an F-14 in the catapult position," to simulate a flight crew on the ready alert position.

He also referenced the focus on magic hour, so they could get the diffused lighting Scott loved.

Scott's memo, addressed to Simpson and Bruckheimer, was different. It drilled down on the early scene where Cougar crash-landed on the aircraft carrier. The captain considered an F-14 skidding across the tarmac on one wing "impractical." They came up with a new scenario that still had Cougar landing badly, with the tire blowing out and the plane shearing off the coupling, then crashing into steel netting used on the aircraft carrier.

The director described it in dramatic fashion: "Finally the F-14 comes to rest in a cocoon of silver straps. Silver suits and medics explode from the flight deck," he wrote.[171]

A silver suit is a fire-resistant suit.

Kolsrud would remember the meeting years later, because it was going nowhere until he asked if the Navy planned a training mission on the use of its steel netting.[172] When in place it was strong enough to stop an out-of-control plane on the flight deck. There hadn't been a training in a long time, the commander said, and he could see organizing one that the moviemakers could shoot. A similar scene, where Navy crew erects the netting to stop a plane making an emergency landing, had appeared in The *Final Countdown.*

The suggestion provided some middle ground short of depicting a fiery crash. They could erect the net — which took a lot of deck crew — and incorporate that into the scene.

Landing McGillis

None of the four actresses who participated in the May 17 screen test had won the day, but higher-ups decided against bringing in another group. Scott was keen on McGillis, whose name recognition was as high, or higher, than Cruise's. "Kelly had a sense that she was collegiate, and she was smart, and she had a maturity about her, despite how young she was. And that felt right for that role and that character."[173]

At 28, she had a more mature look than some of the younger actresses up for the role. She also had an acting pedigree. McGillis attended Julliard School in New York, acting in plays by Shakespeare and Chekhov, among others. In her last year there, she landed a role in *Reuben, Rueben* (1983). Committed to finishing her studies, she had commuted from the city to the shoot in North Carolina. That performance, opposite Tom Conti, is what had led to her being cast as the widow in *Witness* (1985). The thriller, which had McGillis alongside bonafide mega star Harrison Ford, resulted in nominations for a Golden Globe and an award from British Academy of Film and Television Arts. The movie won two Academy Awards and two BAFTAs.

Her contract for the role in *Witness* required an additional, unnamed project for the studio. Next up was supposed to be a role in *The Two Jakes*, the promised sequel to *Chinatown* (1974). *Chinatown* had garnered 11 Oscar nominations, including for Jack Nicholson, Faye Dunaway, Roman Polanski and Robert Evans (best actor/actress/director/best producer). The movie took home a single statue, and that was for Robert Towne, who had penned the original screenplay.

Interest in the sequel, also penned by Towne, had cooled in the decade that had passed, Paramount still believed in *The Two Jakes*. So did Nicholson, who worked hard to bring it to life. They had landed on McGillis to play a role similar to Dunaway's. But the most Hollywood of battles had derailed it. Bob Evans, the producer, who had been an actor first, was slated to play the other Jake and Bob Towne, both writer and director on this project, didn't want him in the role. Towne felt strongly enough about it that he resisted the casting and the resulting blowup eventually shut down production. (*The Two Jakes* was ultimately made in 1990 with Towne's script, Evans producing, and Nicholson directing and on-screen with Harvey Keitel and Meg Tilly.)[174]

With *The Two Jakes* on hold in 1985, McGillis became available. When McGillis became available, Bruckheimer pounced. "Kelly McGillis had just done *Witness* and we thought she was an extraordinary actress." Bruckheimer, Simpson, and Scott went to New York to vet McGillis. "She was very engaging, and very bright, and [we] thought she was perfect to play against Tom."[175]

"I owed Paramount another film, and my agent said, 'You have to do this.'"[176] Between her two readings of the *Top Gun* script, the role of Charlie had grown more substantive, as the character shifted from an aerobics instructor to an astrophysicist military consultant.

Negotiations began in earnest in late May. It didn't take long. McGillis's contract was summarized in a June 3 internal Paramount memo. She would be paid $175,000, which improved her existing contract. It was a lot less than the $1 million Cruise would get, and $25,000 more than Edwards, except that Edwards was also to get merchandising royalties. Her non-cash perquisites were not as disparate: McGillis would receive credit not less than first position below the title and second position overall in size equal to the first star. Her dressing facilities were to be comparable to the lead star. Accommodations were a furnished first-class hotel mini suite, plus $700 per week expense allowance, or $1,250, whichever was greater.[177]

With McGillis signed, they proceeded with a screen test with her and Cruise the next day. The test reflected the producers' belief they'd found the right match. Held in Room 117 in the Dressing Room Building on the Paramount lot, it was facilitated by 19 crew, primarily from the camera, hair, make-up, and costume departments.

Tests aren't just for the actors, said gaffer Russell, who was there that day. The crew also included special effects, one person on the fan and the "smoke," a solution that thickens the air to give depth to the background. Smoke helps provide atmospheric light, which takes off hard edges and enhances an actor's look. "If you are going to shoot the movie with lots of smoke, then you would want to see that effect in a scene with the two main actors," he explained. That helps sort out lighting and special effects.

The screen test results go into the production report, or PR, the shooting document relied upon above all others for determining pay. Any time the camera works, it is documented. The one for the screen tests of the four actresses was missing, as are two of the PRs for shooting days of *Top Gun*. Regardless, with this screen test, they had found their Charlie.

Inside Casting

It was casting that set up the test. Greenberg worked from a cubicle at the front of the DeMille Building, staying busy with paperwork and other details, while Simkin worked from an office down the hall. He understood quickly why the last assistant casting person had quit. Greenberg would be working on something, say, the McGillis-Cruise screen test, then not be included. He was forbidden from taking lunch between noon and 1:30 p.m., in case someone called Simkin, although few people ever called during the lunch hour. The thing that still bugged him was that Simkin would call him at his desk and summon him to her office — to turn on her television set. Remotes were not standard in the mid '80s and she didn't want to get up. Simkin said she had an injury, and that's why she asked for help.[178]

Greenberg, who went on to great success as a casting agent, never seriously thought about quitting. "I was excited to be on the project, it was such an A picture." He knew if he endured it would be an "important credit" for him. Also, Badalato and Scott, whom he revered, were nice and helpful, he said. Sometimes Scott would roll his eyes in comradeship over something Simkin said, which Badalato confirmed.

The casting department also had the unusual task of managing the sailors volunteering as background actors in their free time. Using sailors required the go-ahead from what was then the Screen Extras Guild. (It merged with the Screen Actors Guild in 2012.)

On June 11 the guild wrote Stairs that it had "given Paramount permission to use Navy Personnel, where needed, if this practice is in keeping with your regulations."[179]

Chapter 5 - Endnotes

[144] Heatley, December 1, 2020.

[145] Badalato, January 8, 2021.

[146] Pettigrew, December 10, 2020.

[147] Semcken, November 5, 2020.

[148] Camera cost comparison, shooting requirements and budget analysis. Undated and unattributed production document, ca 1985. TGC.

[149] David B. Nowell, interview with the author, September 27, 2021.

[150] Badalato, January 26, 2020.

[151] Ibid.

[152] Ibid.

[153] Ward Russell, "Production Equipment Requirements," May 1985. TGC.

[154] Ward Russell, "Preliminary Equipment List," May 1985. TGC.

[155] "There's No Business Like Show Business and No Show Business like Costumes," Western Costume Co., undated company history.

[156] Catalaine Knell, assistant to Tony Scott for *Top Gun*, interview with the author, April 18, 2020.

[157] Tony Scott, "Getting Direct With Directors: No.33, Tony Scott," interview by Stella Papamichael, BBC, *Calling the Shots*. 24 September 2014 Transcript archived at https://www.bbc.co.uk/films/callingtheshots/tony_scott.shtml

[158] Matt Lawlor, site administrator for *Top Gun* Props and Costumes Forum, email to author, October 19, 2021.

[159] Bill Badalato to *Top Gun* department heads, budget considerations, May 30, 1985. TGC.

[160] Baron, April, 5 2021.

[161] Badalato, email to the author, October 18, 2021.

[162] DeCuir, May 12, 2020.

[163] John DeCuir, memo to Bill Badalato. TGC.

[164] Bill Badalato to Simpson and Bruckheimer, June 7, 1985. TGC.

[165] Dick Stevens, "Action Items to Expedite Navy Air-to-Air Support," June 13, 1985. TGC.

[166] Bill Badalato, "Final Days," June 7, 1985. TGC.

[167] Tyson, June 6, 2020.

[168] Wade, April 29, 2020.

[169] Bill Badalato, memo to Tony Scott, June 15, 1985. TGC.

[170] Dan Kolsrud, memo to Tony Scott and *Top Gun* executives, June 16, 1985. TGC.

[171] Tony Scott, memo to Top Gun executives, June 16, 1985. TGC.

[172] Kolsrud, January 26, 2021.

[173] Emma Brockes, "Kelly McGillis talks to Emma Brockes," Guardian, March 29, 2001.

---

[174] Jack Mathews, "The Two Jakes and the Two Bobs," *Los Angeles Times Magazine*, August 5, 1990. (https://www.newspapers.com/image/175237405).

[175] *Danger Zone: The Making of Top Gun.*

[176] Ibid.

[177] Dan Furie to Greg Gelfan, "'Top Gun' – Kelly McGillis," Paramount Inter-Communication, June 3, 1985. TGC.

[178] Greenberg, March 8, 2021.

[179] Jack R. Clinton, Screen Extras Guild, to LT Sandy Stairs, June 11, 1985. TGC.

CHAPTER 6
PHOTOGRAPHY LOOMS
JUNE 17-JUNE 25

Badalato, living and working from connecting rooms at the Travelodge, received and sent a lot of memos in the 10 days leading up to principal photography. The most important had to do with the shooting schedule. Principal photography is somewhat akin to architectural plans. In this case the movie had been on the drafting table for months, and now was taking form, with its four distinct floors.

The production planned 35 shooting days for the ground story, which would run from June 26 to Aug. 6. Documents still showed the filmmakers shooting on board the USS Enterprise from Aug. 7-13. The flight sequences, which would follow the scenes at sea, were slated to shoot at the Naval Air Weapons Station in China Lake, Calif., although an asterisk indicated that the Navy was reviewing it. Visual effects were expected to be subcontracted out, and could fall as late as the last week in September.[180]

The focus in planning the movie was on what happened first, and the ground story was a go for the Navy. It still hadn't officially signed off on the dates for the aircraft carrier, and that was becoming more pressing.

All departments, save costumes, were working out of offices at the Travelodge. The costume department wasn't far behind.

Tyson vividly recalled "the finish," one of the last things he did before he headed to San Diego. The finish is where the actor comes in to try on all the costumes prepared for a film. He had met with Cruise several times by then, and this meeting was at an office on Gower Street. It was close to the

Paramount lot so they decided to show Scott, Simpson and Bruckheimer.

"Cruise had a brand new Range Rover. I put the costumes and leather jacket in the back, got in the passenger seat and we drove to the studio," Tyson recalled. The Range Rover was just becoming a high-end ride. The British manufacturer had begun an up-market push a year earlier and its new versions featured leather trim, doors with walnut inlays, and new instrumentation.

When they got to the Paramount gate, the guard came out. "Tom said, 'We were going to Don's office.'" That prompted a blank stare, so the actor reassured them. "He said, 'It's okay. I'm Tom Cruise.' But he had on no makeup, hadn't combed his hair, wearing a T-shirt and jeans, and no wallet, no identification." Tyson sat there, taking it all in.

Cruise, even with the new Rover, wasn't a household name in mid-1985, and the guard wasn't having any of it. "Tom was getting frustrated, and he looked over at me and said, 'Tell him who I am!' The guard peered into the vehicle and looked directly at Tyson. "I said, 'I have no idea who he is!'" With that, Cruise inched the Rover forward, knocking over the wooden arm that blocked the vehicle. "The guard said, 'Buddy, you just cracked that thing!' and Tom said, 'Just send it to my office!' and sped away."[181]

"So we finally got in," Tyson laughed. "But it was a legendary moment."

With the costumes approved, Cruise and McGillis tested a second time on Monday, June 17, at Paramount, this time with 24 crew. The next few days were rehearsals, without cameras or much crew, at the Professional Artist's Group at 845 Highland.

The next two days testing involved Cruise, McGillis, Kilmer, Edwards and Tom Skerritt, who had just been signed to play Viper. Skerritt, who had more credits than all of the other actors combined, would get $100,000. Thursday, June 20, they were back, along with actors Rick Rossovich (Slider), Whip Hubley (Hollywood) and Barry Tubb (Wolfman), with each one earning $40,000. It was a light day, almost a meet-and-greet that began at 10 a.m. and ended at noon.

The next time they saw each other would be in San Diego. Cruise's deal, only now being finalized, would enable him to stay at the high-end Hyatt Islandia, where Simpson and Bruckheimer were registered. McGillis, Edwards, Kilmer and Skerritt were booked at the Bahia Hotel on Mission Bay, which was also nice, but not as expensive.

Cruise line-reviews contract

In mid-1985 the Shangri La Hotel in Santa Monica was a well-kept secret among Hollywood's elite. The art deco hotel, seven stories high with rooftop decks that overlooked the bay, was lovely and private. It lacked some common amenities — no doorman or concierge, no room service or even restaurant — but it felt removed from the mentality of Beverly Hills, even understated. It referred to its 55 apartments as "rooms."

That's where Barbara Weintraub, Bruckheimer's assistant, went to find Cruise just days before principal photography began. She had his final contract in hand and she was to have Cruise sign it, then immediately return to the office. Her expectation was that it would be quick.[182]

But instead of just signing the document, which had been through four revisions, Cruise told her to make herself comfortable, because it would take a while for him to review it. She wasn't supposed to leave without it, so she sat down in the living room while he disappeared into the back. She didn't mind. This sort of thing was typical of the kinds of things Bruckheimer needed, and she had been his assistant for several years. Weintraub assumed Cruise got on the phone with his agent, Paula Wagner, but she wasn't sure.

For six months they, or more aptly, Wagner, had played the studio and producers like a harp. The 10-page Memorandum of Agreement, now updated with a new date, June 24, 1985, was structurally similar to the original version, but the corner noted three other updates since it was first crafted in January: March 27, April 25, June 13. The changes reflected Wagner masterfully working both pedal and strings over that period.

She had taken Cruise's salary from $750,000 to $1 million ($1.94 million to $2.59 million today), and numerous other tweaks had increased his status and control. Far more important were the 5 gross points of total revenue, using a fairly broad definition in the language of the contract. High-level marketing, top-actor guarantees and control over certain details were added. Cruise would get the same living accommodations as the director and producer. And on location, he'd get a first-class trailer, though most actors were given halves.[183]

Wagner got Cruise top billing and guarantees that his face would appear on all advertisements. She'd even wrangled a $20,000 advance.

Weintraub waited for an hour and perhaps a little more before Cruise emerged. She remembers being impressed that the young actor, two weeks shy of his 23rd birthday, would take the time to read the contract. Far older and more experienced actors just let their agents handle it.

The contract reflected just one change, to Item 13, which covered MTV, or Music Television. It said the producers had to consult with the artist or his rep if the artist was to appear either partially or wholly unclothed and to give good-faith consideration to the artist's views, although the producers' decision would control. Cruise lined out "either partially or wholly unclothed." He had to be consulted on anything pertaining to the popular music channel, then just four years old.[184]

Pentagon trip, new dates

Badalato penned a memo on Sunday, June 23, to the full production. It reiterated the plan around the first two phases of photography, again with Aug. 7-13 dates for the USS Enterprise. Labeled "Top Gun Schedule & Notes," it was a broad look touching on everything from the Navy requirement that actors have three days of flight training to room checkout for crew when they wrapped the ground story.[185]

Principal photography was set for Wednesday, yet the Navy still hadn't officially signed off on the dates the production planned to be on board the aircraft carrier. To get that and other details locked in involved a trip to Washington in the final days of prep. That happened with two contingents, with only brief overlap during a meeting at the Pentagon. One of the contingents was above-the-line, and centered on a fine dining, congratulatory experience. The other involved ground-level filmmakers getting details worked out. Both parts were integral to getting what they needed.

The schmooze fest included Cruise, Simpson and Bruckheimer, who flew to Washington and checked into the Madison Hotel at 1177 15th St. It was a famous hotel, frequented by diplomats and upper-echelon business people, and considered one the best in the city. Paramount hosted a private dinner for the Navy brass and their wives to meet the Hollywood heavies, organized by John E. Horton, Paramount's representative in Washington. He was assisted by Jim Holloway, president of the Naval Historical Foundation. Holloway was a decorated veteran of World War II, the Korean War and the Vietnam War. He had established the Navy's nuclear-powered carrier program and served as chief of naval operations for four years, retiring from active duty in 1978. Other attendees were Navy Secretary Lehman, Vice CNO for Navy Air Admiral Ron Hays, and RADM Jack Garrow, head of CHINFO.[186]

At the dinner's conclusion, there was a toast to the success of *Top Gun,* followed by "accolades of Secretary Lehman and his assurance of the Navy's complete cooperation with the production," Horton wrote in his private family memoir. It included soupy praise: "What a successful affair this turned out to be and the payoff in the coming weeks with the Navy's assistance was unequaled in the unstinting cooperation and dedication of the *Top Gun* personnel to the film." It would also prove accurate.[187]

Importantly, the evening also provided grease for the second contingent, although their work in Washington would take a little longer. That group stayed at the Pentagon Quality Inn in Arlington, Va. Stevens and Tom Harmon, who had also been hired as an aerial coordinator for the movie, flew east on June 22 and stayed for five nights, according to the June 20 travel memo. Badalato, neck deep in the last days of prep, went to Washington on June 24 and returned the next day, in order to be back in time for the first day of photography June 26.

Most of the shooting schedule, which had been floating around in proposal form for almost the entire time, was approved with two significant changes. The first shortened the number of days the production would be at sea on the USS Enterprise to four nights. Below deck scenes would be shot on the USS Ranger while it was in port.

The other change was that the aerial scenes, which had been loosely planned for China Lake, would be shot in Fallon, Nev.[188]

Return to the Pentagon

The filmmakers gathered in a hallway of the Pentagon, waiting to go into the meeting with Navy brass, when producer Don Simpson emerged from the bathroom, white powder cocaine visible on his nostril. They quickly alerted him, and he hurriedly wiped it off before anyone on the military side could see it.

Cultural attitudes toward cocaine were lax in the mid-1980s, particularly in Hollywood. The vile destruction that would come with the widespread availability of crack cocaine, which helped change attitudes toward that drug, was several years away. Drug use, in general, was more accepted, cocaine was still a status drug, and there was little known about clinical aspects of addiction. Aside from general culture, and despite Simpson's coy denials, his drug use had long before gone from open secret to legendary abuse. It's difficult to find a profile of Simpson from this period that didn't openly reference his affinity for fast cars, fast women, and cocaine. But even in the context of the era, Badalato was struck by the brazenness of it. "We were in *the Pentagon,*" he said.

Simpson died of a drug overdose 10 years after the release of *Top Gun.* His exploits, including some on *Top Gun,* have been well documented. Notably, people who worked closely with him on *Top Gun* — among them Badalato and Simkin — said he was doing his job on the movie. Internet reports that Simpson took leave on the movie to go into rehab couldn't be substantiated, although several people interviewed said it would have been a good thing if he had. Treatment wasn't widespread.

"It's unfortunate that what people seem to remember about Don was his drug addiction, and not his talent as a creative producer," said Badalato, adding that he thought Simpson and Bruckheimer were deservedly credited with developing the "high concept."

"My feeling was that the studio wasn't that excited about *Top Gun,*" Badalato recalled, "but Don believed in it. And he was bigger than life."[189]

"He was brilliant," said Simkin.

The Director

Scott's schedule in the days leading up to the start of principal photography on Wednesday, June 26, were jammed with scouts and meetings and rehearsals. Once they started shooting it would be much more difficult for the director to find time to do anything else.

That Saturday was a meeting with props and costumes departments to look at helmets. The Navy required that its pilots be depicted in proper safety gear, such as regulation helmets. This had been a concern, since they would obscure the faces of the actors. The next step was to discuss stenciling the name of the characters on the helmets.

Knell organized the meeting. Working on *Top Gun* was challenging, but it was also a lot of fun. "Tony always pushed people to be better, and to do more," she said, "But he was also inspiring. You wanted to do more." When tensions mounted between Scott and Badalato it often fell to Knell, and Badalato's assistant Patti Carr, to work out details.[190]

Scott's plan to circumvent Badalato hadn't escaped Badalato's attention. "It was frustrating for Bill or anybody to wrangle Tony, because he knew how to get what he wanted," Knell said. Simpson and Bruckheimer stayed out of it, happy to let the executive producer be the bad guy to keep things on budget.

Sunday was a "reccy," short for reconnaissance, a term synonymous with scouting but preferred by U.K. filmmakers. It felt like a marathon with detours. Scott and DeCuir met that morning at the hotel and went first to North Island and a tour of the USS Ranger. Early in prep, scouting is about deciding which locations to use. This late in the game it's more typically a tech scout, to decide on specific equipment and last-minute fixes for sites already locked. But the Navy's sudden addition of a second aircraft carrier necessitated a more basic look at the USS Ranger. The focus was on seeing the places they would shoot below-deck scenes.[191]

Then they headed toward Oceanside for lunch, which put them in the vicinity of Charlie's house, where they would be shooting first. A truck was parked on the site, evidence the transportation department was getting started on base camp.

They were there to see the handiwork of the art department. The house at 102 Pacific St. in Oceanside had gotten an upgrade. The biggest change had been the addition of a back deck, where Maverick and Charlie would talk in one scene. They were staining it to give it an aged look. Inside were new carpet and some furniture. Scott liked it but wasn't sure, and suggested DeCuir bring a change of living room furniture, in case he changed his mind.

They went to the Windsock Bar & Grill, which was off the runway of Lindbergh Field. It was where they would shoot the scene where Carole and son arrive to visit Goose, who has Maverick in tow. Next was a 5 p.m. rendezvous with city officials, who joined them for a walk-through. The last stop was at the Bahia Hotel for a rehearsal with Cruise and Skerritt, who was playing Viper, the commanding officer. He was in several scenes being shot the first week of photography.

On Monday the pace was still brisk, just a lot less mileage. The main meeting was with Kolsrud, the first assistant director, and Lisa Clarkson, a casting associate. She was overseeing background actors, which had the added challenge of being exclusively Navy personnel. The meeting was to decide on the number of extras to be used for the ground story. There was also a camera test at the TACTS Trailer.

A big part of the reason it took so much time to get approvals from the Navy was concern about exposing anything classified. No one wanted responsibility for that. The production would need inserts, or individual shots of equipment, to be cut into the scene later. A list circulated in advance of the reccy included 11 scenes that required insets to capture things like the radarscope, closed-circuit landings for scenes in Stinger's cabin, MiG dog fight footage, training classes, and the simulated dogfights to be viewed in the TACTS Trailer.[192]

With approvals behind them, it fell finally to the camera and lighting departments to figure out how to shoot it. Cinematographer Kimball's core camera team was John Connor, Ken Nishino and D. Michael Wheeler, with others to be added along the way. Movie camera equipment is complicated. The main cameras take several people to operate them. Generally, the first assistant is the focus puller, keeping subjects in constant focus, with responsibility for the department and equipment. The second assistant manages the slate or clapper, which tracks film footage, and also provides care and maintenance.

Scott kept his calendar clear for Tuesday, June 25, the day before principal photography. That ensured time to rest and think before it all began.

Meanwhile, a car picked up the exhausted but happy Badalato at the San Diego airport after the trip to Washington, and delivered him to the Travelodge. They had to rework the shooting schedule to fit the USS Ranger in calendar time allotted for the ground story. The four-part plan had isolated the sea story for efficiency, but it wasn't mandatory. Badalato felt relief, because plans were locked, even if it meant more work.[193]

Excitement at the Travelodge was palpable. Crew rooms had been assigned, 67 of them at that point, and there was a steady stream of people coming in. Most were additional crew joining their respective department heads. The departments that start later in the process, like camera, grip and electric, had arrived with trucks full of equipment. The transportation department was in full motion, organizing the parking lot. The various department offices — most of them in bed-less hotel rooms — were bustling, putting the finishing touches on everything needed for the scenes at Charlie's house in Oceanside.

And then the calendar turned to June 26.

Chapter 6 - Endnotes

[180] Badalato, *Top Gun* production notes, 1985. TGC.

[181] Tyson, June 6, 2020.

[182] Barbara Weinraub, assistant to Jerry Bruckheimer for *Top Gun*. Interview with the author, May 18, 2020.

[183] "Memorandum of Agreement." Paramount Pictures Corp., January 24, 1985, rev. June 13, 1985. Contractual terms and conditions for Tom Cruise. TGC.

[184] Kenneth N. Gilpin, "Prospects," *New York Times*, July 26, 1981. 3-1. Music Television, or MTV, was launched by Warner-Amex on August 1, 1981.

[185] Bill Badalato. "Top Gun Schedule & Notes" Paramount Inter-Communication, June 23, 1985. Badalato to All Concerned. TGC.

[186] Ibid.

[187] John E. Horton, "What a Life," an unpublished family memoir. Courtesy of Horton Family.

[188] "Top Gun Shooting Schedule," June 17, 1985. TGC.

[189] Badalato, January 26, 2020.

[190] Knell, April 13, 2021.
[191] DeCuir, May 12, 2020.
[192] Bill Badalato. "11 Scenes." Paramount Inter-Communication, ca 1985. Badalato to Tony Scott. TGC.
[193] Badalato, January 26, 2020.

PART II
PRINCIPAL
PHOTOGRAPHY

June 26-Oct. 2, 1985

PHOTO: Oceanside Historical Society

Lead actress Kelly McGillis centers this photo from the first days of photography. Also pictured, left to right: Unknown, Bobbie Read, costume designer, Randy Peters, transportation and stunts, unknown, script supervisor June Samson, and prop master Mark Wade.

CHAPTER 7
SHOOTING THE GROUND STORY
JUNE 26-AUG. 2

A volleyball court filled with buff, handsome, 20-something guys. An F-14 flying close enough to the ground to shake the foundation of the control tower. A sing-along of "You've Lost That Loving Feeling" at the Officers Club and "Great Balls of Fire" at a dive bar. A line of dialogue — "I would tell you but I'd have to kill you" — that has been repeated so many times over the decades it's a cliché cliché.

The following vignettes tell the stories of those scenes, and others, many of which still live in the popular consciousness more than 35 years after the movie's release.

Most were shot during the "ground story," the first of the four segments of photography. It was the biggest block of principal photography, the idea being to get everything they needed on Miramar and on land around San Diego. Then they could send crew home and shut down operations to cut costs when they moved on to the next phase. This phase would spread over 38 calendar days, or a little more than six weeks.

Charlie's House,
Day 1, 2, 3: June 26-28
102 N. Pacific, Oceanside

There was a palpable sense of excitement among the roughly 100 crew and contractors around "Charlie's house" by the 9:30 a.m. call time. After months of prep, they would spend the first three shooting days at the Victorian cottage across the street from the Pacific Ocean.[194] The scenes had Maverick and Charlie getting to know each other better.

It looked like a movie company base camp. Peters and his Teamsters had brought in a dozen trucks and trailers of varying sizes. Craft services was there ahead of the others with gallons of coffee and snacks, while the catering company set up a cooking trailer, tent and tables to serve hot meals. They reported serving 87 lunches the first day, 89 the next, and 93 the last.

PHOTO: Oceanside Historical Society

Kelly McGillis and Tom Cruise on location at Charlie's House.

Then there were the "picture cars," any vehicle that appears on camera. The scenes at the house called for Charlie's car and Maverick's motorcycle to be parked outside.

Peters had purchased Maverick's motorcycle, a Kawasaki Ninja GPZ900R, three weeks earlier for $2,800, paying with a check written by Paramount.

They would also get some shots of the bike being driven along the beach by R. A. Rondell, the stunt coordinator, who was there that first day. He stood by, somewhat aghast, as Tony Scott took issue with the pristine condition of the Ninja. "I'm a motorcycle racing enthusiast, and Tony wants to crash it to give it a little character," said Rondell, "He starts banging on it, scraping it, basically distressing a brand new Ninja, and we're going, 'Ouch!'"

But it wasn't enough for Scott. "He started sliding the bike on its side, the left side, scraping the handle bar, the cowling. He knew how he wanted it." That included stickers, which the props department had at the ready.

Scott was hands-on with everything. Given these scenes were romantic, effort went into making the space feel intimate. The production designer worked with the set decorating department to add touches like candles, fresh flowers, and draperies that could blow in the wind. But they also came prepared to make changes. Scott had asked that extra furniture be brought so he could mix and match, and DeCuir had obliged. They all watched as the director changed out chairs or even candles.

Two animal handlers were on site for all three days to manage Charlie's pet parrot, a dog, and pigeons, and to provide bait to attract birds for the beach sunset shot. The parrot's cage was set decoration. Someone recalled doves being drugged to keep them quiet, which meant they were ill disposed to work when it came time. Wade, who as prop master oversaw the hire of the animal handlers, roundly denied birds would have been given drugs, although he did recall the pigeons failed to perform on cue. No one remembers anything about a parrot or a dog. If not for the shooting schedule and production reports, and a brief shot of a dog, the details might have been lost to history.[195]

Base camp shifted a little each day. The second day there was a reduction in trailers, from three to one. What remained was a "two-banger," two units, one for each actor. There are Internet rumors that McGillis wanted to stay in the bungalow, but paperwork shows that she, Cruise, and their respective hair and makeup people, all were provided accommodation in Oceanside for the second and third days of shooting, so they could be closer to set.

The weather over the three days was the kind tourists associated with coastal San Diego, sunny and in the 70s with a light breeze. Locals also know a phenomenon called June gloom, which was noted on a production report as "Weather: Dense fog all day – No Sun!!"

Location management

Scott had loved the house and the location but it took enormous effort to get it in shape. The owner lived in an apartment in the back, and the filmmakers didn't feel he was particularly hospitable. Managing him fell to Baron as head of the locations department.

"If anything, he did well," said Baron. "We repainted the whole thing, redid the electrical, which was a mess."

Things took a turn for the worse after Scott took issue with a tree interfering with his light. He had a grip cut it down, without getting permission. Baron had to manage the irate owner. "He got in my face and I thought I was going to get my ass kicked," he recalled. Baron was soon joined by production security and the two of them diffused the tension.

Another problem arose around the production's use of the landline. The owner had agreed to it, which was standard for the time. "He was freaked out because there was a $400 phone bill," said Baron. It was promptly reimbursed.

It would have been best if the production had finished with the location at the end of its third day on site as planned, but they would need reshoots, primarily to strengthen the on-screen connection between Charlie and Maverick, and to get better footage of McGillis. She had said privately that she wasn't looking her best in dailies, the result of too much partying, according to Badalato.

The result was that the location manager had to go back and negotiate a deal with the prickly property owner. "It was expensive," said Baron.

Buzzing the tower
Miramar Control Tower
Day 4: June 29

Flying the F-14 in the scene in which Maverick buzzes the tower would have a big impact on Lloyd "Bozo" Abel's life, making him the subject of newspaper articles for decades to come. Yet when he woke up that morning he had no idea he would be flying the scene.

Abel had orders out to another unit, so he wasn't with most of the other members of his squadron, who were at a special training on Nellis Air Force Base. That's why it was Abel who answered the phone at Hangar 3; it was Semcken, who explained what would be needed later that day.

Abel's first instinct was to resist. "I knew I was not supposed to do it. I can't pull the airplanes." So he got in touch with his CO at Nellis. He told him to handle what the movie company needed for the day. Only then did Abel call Semcken back, with Mark "Slick" Schlichter, RIO, at his side, to confirm they'd do it.[196] Semcken told the aviators that the props department would soon be there to paint a logo on the aircraft. Meanwhile, they should find the director to learn exactly what was needed of them.

Prop master Mark Wade dispatched a painter to Hangar 3 to add numbers to the F-14 they would fly, which would mark it as Maverick's. Perhaps thinking he would return to the hangar to complete the job, the painter left behind tape and blades and other tools of the trade, something that would become important later.

A graphic artist with the art department had merged elements from different squadrons to come up with the design for an imaginary squadron: a diving eagle in red with white lines of movement and a blue background over "VF1." VF designates a fighting squadron, with numbers for each squadron. While there was a real VF1 squadron, it had a wolf for its logo.

Acting the part

Abel and the RIO, and everyone on Miramar, knew where the movie base camp had been set up, so they set out for Hangar 1. They assumed that's where they would find the director, but the place seemed empty. They noticed two people and walked toward them in a scene that struck Abel as "pure Hollywood." It was actors Val Kilmer and Anthony Edwards, sunning themselves on lounge chairs outside one of the trailers.[197]

Kilmer gave them a glance through his sunglasses but didn't get up. "He said something like, 'Tony Scott is not my problem,'" Abel recalled, with a laugh. But Edwards jumped up, helpful and nice, to say he was impressed with the pilots who were going to fly the scene. The actor told them the company was already at the tower, and that's where they'd find Scott.

Abel and the RIO could see the action at the tower before they even got there, with production vehicles and limousines parked in front. They went to the stairs and began the 10-floor ascent to the tower. Somewhere in the middle they saw a senior officer "with all kinds of ribbons but wearing Levi's," hurrying down toward them. The two men stepped aside and saluted as he passed. It turned out to be actor Duke Stroud in character as the air boss. The filmmakers were shooting the interior scenes of the flyby, where the F-14 passes by with such force the air boss spills coffee on his shirt. Stroud was on his way to the costume trailer to get a fresh shirt with proper stripes for another take.

The tower was full of crew and background actors from the Navy when the duo arrived. Set documents show five flight controllers and 17 air bosses in the scene. The tower was the real thing, with props setting up the coffee station, and set decorating adding fans. Special effects were there to capture the shaking that resulted from a powerful aircraft coming that close to a structure.

Scott, between scenes, eagerly greeted them. He showed a picture book filled with storyboards. The pilots looked over the panels of individual drawings that depicted what he wanted to happen in the scene. "He wanted me to go by as fast as I can go," said Abel, noting the director's English accent as he repeated "supersonic." The pilot explained that if he flew that fast, "windows will blow out, car alarms will go off, and I'll be on screen for half a second."

PHOTO: Staff Photographer/San Diego Union-Tribune via ZUMA Wire.

John Semcken and Pete Pettigrew on a jet at NAS Miramar on July 27, 1985, Top Gun production personnel and equipment in the background.

Abel recommended he fly at a much slower pace and bring his wings back 40 degrees so it looked like he was flying faster. Scott agreed. The director also said they would fly the scene later in the afternoon when the sun was just right.

Abel and the RIO, still in a state of disbelief, talked the flight through on the way back to Hangar 3. Because the scene required he fly low, he would have to go directly over the base, as well as some adjacent neighborhoods. Abel called his wife as soon as he got to the office. "She didn't like to watch me fly, but I begged her, and she agreed."

Meanwhile, prep for the later afternoon scene continued at the tower. Scott wanted more planes for set decorating, which meant getting them towed there. Planes were kept in the hangars assigned to specific squadrons, and Semcken made calls around the base to have them brought over. There was also math involved, both on his part, and on Badalato's. They worked hard to track all costs, even that of airmen towing planes to the tower.

Telling Tony no

Semcken had a much bigger job ahead of him in reining in Scott's expectations. The director didn't seem to understand that what they were doing was outside of any reasonable norm for the base. The scene had necessitated the grounding of all regular Navy flights and required FAA approval in advance. It was also dangerous, and even highly trained pilots found it remarkable that it had been cleared. In real life, a pilot who flew his plane near the tower would never fly again, and every pilot knew it. Civilians who lived in the neighborhood were used to the normal flight pattern and would be caught unawares. Planes didn't fly low, and they didn't fly in over their homes.

As Navy liaison, Semcken wasn't involved with scenes shot off base. While he had spent a lot of time with Scott in prep, that day at the tower was his first time working with him on set. Semcken decided that when firm boundaries were needed, as was the case at the tower, he would be blunt. "Tony would push, and push, and push," Semcken recalled. "It was the only way."

Semcken, just a lieutenant but nonetheless given the responsibility, laid down the law for the scenes for the flyby early in the day. Scott would have three takes, provided he did them in rapid succession. The director argued, but there was no way around it.

"I said, 'Tony! Think about it! Pilots can't fly below 500 feet, much less close over the base, and Bozo [the pilot flying the F-14] is going to be coming in over the hangars and close

129

to the tower, which was less than 100 feet!" The Navy officer reminded him it was the first day on base. The Navy could just call it off, particularly if there were safety issues or if an order were ignored. Still Scott pushed, as Semcken continued.

"You get three because that's how long it's going to take for the admiral to shut the whole thing down," he told him. The lieutenant pointed to the phone at the bottom of the long stairs and walked him through what would happen on the Navy side. As soon as Bozo flew by once, the phone was going to start ringing. As soon as Semcken heard it, he was going to walk down the stairs and answer it. That would take a few minutes, given it was 10 flights. "As soon as I answer, they're going to tell me to knock it off, and I'm going to say, 'Yes, Sir!' And I'm going to come back up here and tell you to knock it off."

If Semcken answered the call in a reasonable time, albeit not too hurriedly, he would get to the phone at the bottom of the stairs just as the second pass of the tower was under way. By the time the lieutenant climbed back to the top floor of the tower to relay the order, the third pass would be under way. "I told him, 'That's it. That's when you have to stop.'"

The real selling point might have been something else. Semcken told him it was possible to get the whole production shut down before it ever started, particularly if there were safety issues. Three takes, and that was it. Scott "hated it," but by then he understood, and he agreed.[198]

A few hours passed and at the appointed time, Bozo and the RIO got into the aircraft and out on the tarmac. He was running up the motors as he normally would when he heard the right motor pop. That was an indication it was too hot, so he stopped to let it cool. Instead the temperature gauge stayed high, and he turned back. "Only a fool would take it up like that. I was thinking, 'Just my luck! The chance of a lifetime, and it's over with!'"

He went into the building and called Semcken with the news, and was told to get another plane. Abel and the RIO figured there wasn't time to paint it. But just that quickly, props people returned and painted the number on. It impressed Abel how quickly the movie people got it done and that it looked so good. Soon they were on their way again in the new aircraft.

Abel recalled hearing the director on the radio once during the flight, but that stopped quickly. There is a cadence to tower communication and he didn't understand what Scott had said. But Abel could see from the air that the flight was getting a lot of attention on the ground. "I was crossing over the highway, flying over the cul-de-sac, there were cars pulling over, all of these people looking up at me." One friend from the base told him later that he assumed "some pilot had gone berserk and was having his last flight."

Enough people knew beforehand about the flight that a good-sized group, including Abel's wife, collected by the tower for the impromptu air show. Cruise was in the crowd, and when he heard her say the pilot was her husband, he came over to say hi. She didn't know who he was and, already unnerved, told the actor to "take a hike." Later, at an event with cast and Navy personnel, she was introduced to Cruise. He recognized her right away and responded with his famous grin, saying, "I think we've met."

The three-fly-by-limit Semcken described for Scott is "exactly what happened," said Semcken. One thing he hadn't anticipated was how upset the adjacent neighborhood would be. Because they never saw planes flying low, they naturally assumed something was wrong. Calls flooded the switchboards, which hadn't been advised in advance what to tell people.

When Abel landed he was told to report to the admiral's office. "I looked at my RIO and said, 'You're a witness! We were ordered to do it.'" They weren't in trouble. The only drama was that no one had told the media, so no one had told the public.

The flight was "the most bitchin' thing I'd ever seen," Semcken said.

Willard and props

That wasn't the end of it for everyone. The prop master soon found himself summoned to Willard's official office, at the real Topgun school. "He had the most iron blue eyes I've ever seen on a guy," recalled Wade, "and he said, 'SIT. DOWN.'" Wade took a seat like an enlisted man.

Willard wanted to know if it was Wade's job to oversee the painting of the F-14s. Wade said it was, and that he had hired someone with experience painting aircraft. Well, Willard said, the painter had made a mess, leaving food, razor blades and tape behind.[199]

"He said something like, 'If we suck something into one of the motors of these planes, it's millions and millions of dollars. You better get a different painter, or talk to the guy,'" recalled Wade. He assured Willard he would and they agreed to communicate more in the future, since the props department would re-logo planes whenever they were switched out. After that, Willard "became kind of friends with me, kind of okay."

Being the pilot who buzzed the tower stayed with Abel, even during his years flying for Northwest Airlines. People would ask him about it and the other scenes he flew in the movie well into his retirement.

Work hard, play hard, '80s style July 4

Movie production is organized as a condensed work cycle, generally five days a week with long hours, unless on location, in which union rules permit six-day workweeks. The cast and crew on *Top Gun* worked 12-hour days and six-day weeks, and when they went over, crew was compensated under union rules. Production reports show it wasn't unusual for assistant directors, in particular, to work 14 or 15 hours.

The crew also lived together at the Travelodge, and when the workday was done, it was time to relax. The hotel had a good-sized bar, which became a regular stop. Outside was a large triangular pool. One side of the area was established early in prep as the domain of producer Don Simpson. Two phone lines were installed for him. When they weren't in use, they were locked inside the bar, a process overseen by Billy Badalato, then 19. He was officially assigned to the transportation office, but also stood in on occasion as an assistant to Simpson. The young PA had taped off the area, which was centered around a large, circular patio table shielded by a blue umbrella. Simpson would sit at the table and talk on the phone. On occasion he talked on two calls at once, a phone in each hand, itself something out of a movie script.[200]

"Wrap" is common usage for finishing something; wrap parties on most movie and television productions are associated with the end of a project. On *Top Gun*, there were weekly wrap parties, and on occasion, daily parties. Then there were bigger parties, the first one on the 4th of July, a union holiday. Parties were generally organized by Randy Peters, head of the transportation department.

The production had leased the entire hotel and had the room to do what it wanted, but there were limits. "One time we filled the Jacuzzi with soap. We thought it would be kind of funny," recalled the younger Badalato. "Then it just exploded. I didn't know you could make that many suds. It took over half the pool and the manager freaked out at us." He said the incident stifled further pranks.

As Navy liaison to the movie, Semcken worked on base but also spent time at the Travelodge. "There were a lot of parties," he said. Cast and crew also went to local bars. Wednesdays featured "Animal Night" at the Officer's Club on Miramar. It was open to all women as well as members of the other branches of the military with credentials.

"There was a line going out the gate at the base to get in," recalled Peters. "That's where the line in the movie, 'a target-rich environment,' came from." Semcken agreed. "It was really popular."

McGillis, interviewed for the reissue of the movie in 2013, acknowledged "a lot of partying going on after work." The legacy of the movie surprised her, she said, but making it had been a good experience. "We just had a good time. ... That movie was like being at camp. It was fun."

Frank Whiteley, who worked for the production as an uncredited bodyguard to Tom Cruise, recalled being at the hotel to deliver sides, which are pages of the script to be shot the next day. He heard laughter behind one door as he knocked on it. One of the male actors opened it about two inches, until he recognized Whiteley, at which point he opened it all the way. The young man smelled marijuana.

"Hi Franky," said the actor, reaching for the paperwork. "Look, everyone, homework," he said, tossing it over his shoulder into what was a small party. "Let me guess ... Cruise has rewritten the scenes?" The actor gestured for him to join them, but by now the young man could see he was wearing a pink negligee with a furry collar. Behind him were other actors in a state of undress, and alcohol.

"I was a young Mormon boy, and I was sure the gates of hell had opened up," said Whiteley, who said he nervously backed away, drawing more laughter.

Cruise was much more serious, just in general, Whiteley continued. The actor only occasionally went out with cast and crew, which often hung out together. "Any time we met someone with authority, a pilot or whoever, Cruise would engage in conversation with them. Otherwise, he was standoffish." Whitely said the actor was sensitive about who signed autographs. "Tom was the star of the show, and he wanted everyone to know it."

The production avoided trouble, but there was one close call. After shooting the scenes at Kansas City Barbeque, Tony Scott was picked up for drinking and driving. Badalato and Peters got calls about it, and someone called Whiteley, "San Diego has a lot of one way streets and Tony was going the wrong way on one of them. That's why the police pulled him over," recalled Whiteley. He got the call because his father was an attorney. "They hoped he could pull strings, and he did."

Introducing instructor Charlie
Shooting in the hangar
Day 8: July 5

It took several days to shoot the classroom scene in Hangar 1, with the bulk done before July 4, the rest concluding on July 8. The famous scene has Maverick and Goose discovering that Charlie, who Maverick met the night before at the Officer's Club, was a Ph.D. and their instructor, Charlotte Blackwood.

PHOTO: PH1 Harold J. Gerwien, U.S. Navy, courtesy of National Archives.

The camera crew preps a shot for a scene in the hangar. Pointing and on the left is Ward Russell, gaffer, and on the right, in hat and glasses, is cinematographer Jeff Kimball. Center, far side of the Panavision, is camera operator John J. Conner. The man in the shorts is Tony Scott. The lens on the Panaflex camera is affixed with a filter holder and graduated filters favored by Scott to add color or otherwise enhance the images.

It contains one of the most famous lines from the movie.

The scene featured a lot of the cast, including Val Kilmer (Iceman), Rick Rossovich (Slider), Whip Hubley (Hollywood), Barry Tubb (Wolfman), Clarence Gilyard (Sundown), Adrian Pasdar (Chipper), Tom Skerritt (Viper) and Michael Ironside (Jester). Background actors included two Topgun pilots, two RIOs, five "Top Gun adversaries," two aircraft maintenance officers, and eight crew.

One of the pilot background actors was Heatley. He'd met Scott in prep, but his first turn in front of the camera — one of several — had nothing to do with the director. An extras casting person had seen Heatley on base, got his contact information, and then followed up. Scott was surprised when he saw the operations officer on set, and shouted out a greeting by name. After the take, Tom Cruise came over to introduce himself to the pilot. Heatley said the actor told him Scott had regularly held up Heatley's photos, developed into oversized images, as the look and feel of *Top Gun*. He appreciated it, and said he was genuinely impressed by Cruise. "I was 39 and he was 22 or 23 and carrying this big movie all by himself. I thought that was pretty cool."

"It was supposed to be a classroom and the blackboard was blank." The former Topgun instructor drew a Venn diagram, a pictorial design with overlapping elements, of something that might really have been in a Topgun classroom. "No one told me, I just did it, and Tony liked it." There were other finishing touches such as aircraft maintenance equipment, tools, flight gear, and coffee.

Navy props on the list included an A-4 aircraft made up in "communist colors," three nondescript F-14s, one aircraft-towing vehicle, and a Jeep. What ended up in the background were four aircraft that had been towed and placed behind the back of the classroom. Two of the high-powered jets had canopies up.

The scene, nearly four pages of script, has some of the most memorable lines in the film. One — "I could tell you but then I'd have to kill you" — is a topic on Reddit and the subject of a YouTube mash-up. There are claims that the line appeared elsewhere first, but none of the identified places either contain the phrase or predate 1985. It appears in the script exactly as said by Cruise.

PHOTO: PH1 Harold J. Gerwien, U.S. Navy, courtesy of National Archives.

Film crew on the tarmac at Miramar Naval Air Station on July 27, 1985, Charles Starr/San Diego Union-Tribune/ZUMA Wire)

The script doesn't include Iceman's line, "bullshit." That was ad-libbed by Val Kilmer.

"I have a need for speed" is a Cash and Epps original. Skaaren edited it slightly, after being directed by Simpson and Bruckheimer to go back and incorporate more details and dialogue from the early draft.[201] Cruise and Edwards delivery of the line as a two-parter, where Maverick says, "I feel the need," and they both say, "the need for speed," made it that much more memorable. The line is on the American Film Institute's list of 100 greatest movie quotes of all time.[202]

Launching Meg Ryan
Day 11, 27, 28: July 9, July 26, 27

Actress Meg Ryan, then 24 and largely unknown, wowed everyone she met associated with the movie, starting with the interview process. She was hired for the role of Goose's wife just a week before her first day on set.

Jeff Greenberg, casting assistant, said he put Ryan on a list of 10 names he gave to Simkin. He had seen the actress in a television show called "Charles in Charge." "She was sort of outstanding on a mediocre show, and she fit the description of what they were looking for to a T."

Simkin recalled Ryan coming in to audition for Charlie. "When she came in, she was wearing hippie clothes, and did her reading. She was completely wrong for the part." When the role of Carole Bradshaw, Goose's wife, was subsequently expanded, Ryan auditioned again and this time, Simkin said, "She did a fantastic reading."[203]

"I remember when Meg came on, we looked at her test," Tom Cruise told an interviewer for a Paramount documentary. "She was just a light bulb. She just, poof, burst in the room with that smile and glow."[204]

Ryan had studied journalism at New York University and acted on the side to earn money. She left college after being offered a contract to play Betsy on the television soap opera "As the World Turns." "For two years [1982-1984] I made that show an intensive training ground," she once told a writer. "My character cried more than any person on television."[205]

Her ability to conjure tears was noteworthy during the scenes where the newly widowed Carole picks up Goose's things from Maverick. It was an intense scene, and she was called upon to cry repeatedly. "She was the cutest thing you'd ever seen in your life, beautiful and bubbly and adorable," said Semcken, who watched from the sidelines. "But what an actress! When they said 'Rolling!' she could start crying, the real thing. I got emotional just looking at her."

The scene was shot multiple times, as is typical, and virtually everyone was awestruck by her performance. Each time, Ryan cried on cue until she couldn't do it anymore. "Eventually she ran out of water," said Semcken. The tearful parts of the scenes didn't end up in the movie. "If America had seen her cry, she would have been bigger, sooner," said Semcken. "How she could recall whatever she recalled to have that amount of sadness, it was amazing."

The scene also required a large prop. The commercial jet in the background was flown in, one of two times the movie production required special clearance. The other was a visit from Steel, who came in on the Paramount corporate jet on July 27.

Volleyball and hot, young actors
Day 15: July 13
Miramar

Nobody above the line gave the volleyball scene much credence ahead of time. Scott had pushed in prep for more than a day to do the scene, and they'd told him he had a half day to shoot the half-page scene.

Scott hadn't liked any of the locations they found off base with volleyball courts, including on the beach. While there were basketball courts and other recreational facilities on Miramar, there wasn't a volleyball court, so they had to build one. Once they identified a location, DeCuir and his team designed a regulation court with surrounding low-level stadium seating. They dug it out, poured braces for the net-poles, and brought in dump trucks full of sand.

The production designer was in downtown San Diego having dinner and called to check on things. The construction manager told him there was a problem, so DeCuir cut the meal short and headed to Miramar. "All the sand was seriously damp, even wet, like they'd literally taken it from the beach that morning," he said. "They'd spread it all out to dry it but when I tried to walk around, it stuck to my shoes."

There was a sense of excitement about the scene. "All these guys were buffing up to look so good, and here we were," recalled DeCuir, "with wet sand. It was one of those, 'You'll never work in Hollywood again' moments." With the call time 10 hours away they came up with a solution without knowing it would work.

"We brought in big hot-air machines, Bunsen-type burners to heat it up and dry it," he said. "My guys were out there all night with rakes, the big machines blowing." DeCuir returned to base before daybreak. "When the sun came up it seemed a lot better," he said.

He was still worried when the young man they hired to be a technical consultant on the scene approached. "He said, 'Are you in charge of putting the sand down?' I probably blinked back at him," recalled DeCuir. "He said it was the best sand he had ever played on!"

The young man was Terry Nolan, a college student and serious competitive volleyball player. Nolan had been competing at a doubles volleyball tournament when he met Tony Scott. The director was there with a small entourage taking it all in. They told Nolan they were looking for someone to train the actors, most of whom didn't know how to play volleyball. They also wanted to hire competent volleyball players as stand-ins or even to do stunts for the actors.

Later Nolan went to Scott's penthouse quarters on Mission Bay to help storyboard the scenes. "He wanted Maverick and Iceman in competition, all kinds of swing on the net," he recalled. Scott was irritated when the younger man told him it didn't happen that way. "He said, 'I'm not making a feckin' documentary!' so I said, 'Well, you can do it that way, but you'll look foolish.' That got his attention. He wanted just enough net swinging-type action that it wasn't ridiculous."[206]

Part of Nolan's job was to recruit the volleyball player doubles, one each for Maverick, Iceman, Slider and Goose. "I did a decent job of finding guys I thought would look good," he said, but all credit for making them match went to costumes, hair and makeup. He still remembers being impressed by the degree to which hair and makeup could make them look like the actors. "It was amazing," he said.

"The first time we went somewhere, a practice or maybe to go shoot it, we got into vans," carting all the actors except Tom Cruise, who took his own limousine. That didn't seem to sit well with the other actors, he said. It was downhill from there for Nolan, when it came to Cruise. "We nearly got into a fight," he explained.

It happened during the rehearsal for the volleyball game. Once they were on base Nolan started with a demonstration. "I set the players up, put that guy on the right, that guy on the left, showed them how to pass and hit." The skilled players rallied back and forth, and the actors watched, then played with them. Cruise wasn't a volleyball player, so of course he wasn't very good at it, said Nolan.

"We were rallying back and forth, hitting the ball back and forth," he recalled. He would hit the ball at him, and as the pace quickened, Cruise charged Nolan from the other side of the net "like he was going to hit me." He took the reaction to mean the actor thought he was trying to show him up.

He said Cruise stopped inches from his face, as the people in the stands — people from the Navy there as background actors — leapt to their feet. They started shouting and "trying to egg on a fight." Nolan wasn't sure how it broke up, but it stuck with him. He thought Cruise was "cocky," and had a huge "chip on his shoulder," but also allowed that Cruise might have just been in character. "He's really into his craft, so he went to a different level in the scenes," he said. "But he was half a second from throwing a punch."

Scott, for his part, wanted tension between the characters caught on camera. It certainly fit for the scene headed, "Vicious Volley Ball Game – Miramar Base."[207] Someone recalled another scuffle, this one between actors, although that was the locker room scene. Scott said not to break it up.

The volleyball scenes were scheduled for half of one day. Scott would say, 'Okay, I got the idea, move around to get the shot.' Coverage, where the cameras are moved around to get each actor, was a big effort. The net would come down to shoot the action on the other side. "That's what seemed to take forever," Nolan said. As the day progressed, he started working out hand signals and other moves that intrigued Scott. Then the director saw one of the actor's doubles spinning the volleyball on his finger.

141

"He said, "Oh, we've gotta film that!" So, that's where the scene started. The director also observed a player picking up a volleyball with one hand, and wanted that. "Almost everyone else could palm it, but not Cruise. He's not a big guy, and his hand wasn't big enough to pick it up with one hand." But the actor wouldn't give up, and time passed as he tried to sort it out. "He was so determined to do it," he recalled. Eventually they let air out of the ball, Nolan said, and that made the difference.

The Officers Club
Day 17, 18, 19: July 16-18
Lafayette Hotel

The call time that Tuesday was 7:30, earlier than normal for the production. Generally they had started at 9:30, which meant they were there later in the day to capture the sunset light. But today they'd be indoors so they weren't worried about magic hour. Background actors filled the bar — 30 Navy officers or people dressed like officers — along with nine Marine officers, filled in. Catering served 209 hot lunches the first day, then 199 and 197 hot lunches on the subsequent days. Music was playing as they got the set ready, when McGillis came out. She sat at the bar listening to a Walkman, bobbing her head to a different tune and getting into character. She was into the music enough that she didn't know when things grew quiet on the set. All eyes were on the actress, who was quietly singing along, oblivious to the crowd. It was a light moment.

Cruise also listened to music to prepare for scenes. He had a boom box and at one point invited people into his trailer to hear new music he really liked. The tape was "Little Creatures" by Talking Heads.

The scene is also known for a noted face in the crowd. Pete Pettigrew, the real life "Viper," hired as a technical consultant on *Top Gun*, appeared as Charlie's date at the officer's club. The retired Navy pilot and Topgun instructor, known for shooting down a lot of enemy planes during the Vietnam War, is also known as Charlie's "older man" date.

In terms of producer happenings, Badalato observed an exchange between Simpson and Bruckheimer that provides insight into their relationship. Shooting the scenes at the makeshift O Club made for long days, particularly around singing the same song over and again. At one point Simpson announced he was leaving, which prompted Bruckheimer to chime in that he would, too. Badalato said Simpson told him no, he wouldn't. The executive producer recalled that Simpson told Bruckheimer, "I pay you to stay."[208]

Day 28: July 29
Kansas City Barbeque
600 West Harbor Drive, San Diego

Shooting the bar scenes at Kansas City Barbeque, one of the most famous locations associated with *Top Gun*, wasn't the original plan. Even better, what ended up on screen of Maverick, Charlie, Goose and Carole's visit to the dive bar only vaguely reflects what was in the original script. It was a night scene, and it didn't feature the piano or a rendition of "Great Balls of Fire."

At first Scott had been intent on a cowboy bar for the night out, but once convinced there weren't any in San Diego, he agreed to a beach bar. That led to negotiations with Jake's Restaurant in Del Mar, but when the owners thought more about the need to shut down for an entire day, they changed their mind. That left Baron with less than a week to find an alternative.

He had one possibility, Barnacle Bill's on Harbor Island, but no location manager likes to go to a director with a single option. Something caught his eye on his way to pick up a signed lease at Seaport Village in what was then the warehouse district of San Diego. That lease was for the scenes on the pier when Maverick would take Charlie for a sunset ride on his bike.

That accomplished, Baron went back to the spot he'd noticed, the Kansas City Barbeque across the street. It had easy parking and was next to the railroad tracks. It wasn't a beach bar but the door was wide open and it had a good, dive-bar feel to it. The waitress, who remembered all the details, noted that Baron didn't seem to be in a hurry. He had lunch, then ordered a beer and started shooting pool, getting a good look at the place. Only after time had passed did he tell her he was with the movie company. Baron asked the waitress if she thought the owners would be interested in having the movie shoot a scene there.[209]

Martin and Cindy Blair had opened Kansas City Barbecue three years earlier, shortly after relocating from the Midwest. The restaurant wasn't a big moneymaker and they had other jobs, so they hadn't been there when Baron visited. They had seen *Witness* and knew who Kelly McGillis was, but had never heard of Tom Cruise. "Hollywood" was completely foreign to them, but they happily agreed to meet with Baron the next day.

"He asked us how much we would normally make in one day," recalled Martin Blair, "and we told him about $1,000."[210] That's what they agreed on — if they moved forward. Baron told them the director would have to sign off, but if he agreed, it would happen quickly. The location manager went back to production offices and wrote a memo to Scott, handing it off to his assistant. It was dated July 23.

The Blairs said that during Scott's visit to look at the location, he honed in on the upright piano stored in a side room. It had been part of Cindy Blair's childhood in Kansas City. They brought the piano across the country with them but didn't have room for it at the house. "He loved it," said Martin Blair, and Scott said he would write a scene around it.

Things like that were the reason the producers had put screenwriter Warren Skaaren on payroll and often on-set. He was nimble and could fix whatever came up or work with Scott's ideas. This scene developed as they were shooting it, solving problems along the way. For instance, Edwards, aka

Goose, hadn't been given much notice and didn't know the words to "Great Balls of Fire." So they wrote the lyrics on a piece of paper, which can be seen atop the piano in the scene.

There's also a child in the singalong, like both Aaron and Adam Weiss, the twins who played "Bradley," Goose and Carole's son.[211] They came to the movie via an open casting call. A neighbor in Point Loma had seen the ad and urged Martha Weis to take her boys. It was a crowded casting call, but two days later they were called back to meet with Scott. That appointment had involved some awkward time in the waiting room, where she and her kids sat with two other parents with sets of twins.

The Blairs said Edwards and Ryan went out of their way to connect with the kids to prepare them for the scenes. Cruise also came out to say hi and have his picture taken with them. It was a memorable and fun time for the Weis family, and both boys, who were switched out in the scenes. Neither of them ever acted again.

Another change from the original screenplay was the switch from night to day. Grip and electric set up carbon arc lights directly outside the windows so that it remained a sunny day inside even when the sun moved in the sky. Other things stayed in or shifted slightly. The original script notes that Maverick and Goose "ARE NOT DRUNK." While they don't appear drunk in the scenes, they aren't established as being sober, either. Most noteworthy may be one shift in dialogue. Carole, Ryan's character, ended up with a line that Skaaren had originally written for Charlie to say to Maverick: "You big stud! Take me to bed or lose me forever."

It had been a long day for all the actors, but longest for Cruise and McGillis. The call time that Monday morning was 8:30 a.m. Edwards and Ryan were at makeup by 8:50, McGillis at 9:20 and Cruise at 9:30. Edwards and Ryan were wrapped and on their way back to the hotel by 7:15 p.m.

Cruise and McGillis still had the motorcycle scenes across the street on the pier, as did R.A. Rondell. It was magic hour, so there was a finite time to capture it. "At the time, also, Tom wasn't really a rider," Rondell recalled. "I'd take the bike, do a little riding around, get him comfortable doing pull-ups and rideaways."

To get the shot on the pier that he wanted, Scott summoned Peters, who was in a production vehicle. The director wanted him to drive, pacing Cruise and McGillis, while Scott did the camera work himself. Peters opened the rear door of the station wagon so it sat flat, and Scott climbed in, and they drove down the pier. They got footage of Cruise and McGillis, as well as Rondell and McGillis.

"Tony would hang out the side, yelling," said Peters. "He was like that, technical, but also pretty old school, 'Let's make it real.' He knew exactly what he wanted."

Rondell also credited Peters with making the shot work. "Randy is very hands on," he said. "He's a transportation coordinator and captain, but he's a stuntman in his own right." Peters has credits for both in the movie.

Pulling the plug
Day 32: Aug. 2
Int. Goose's Room, Int. Mav's Room

In advance of the shooting day Badalato sent Scott a memo about a scheduled carrier meeting. It would fall at the end of the shooting day Aug. 2 to prepare for the big company move to the USS Enterprise on Aug. 3. That meeting, with Milligan of Grumman, was important, because the defense contractor had finalized its engineering plan on how it would attach cameras to the F-14s. Horton's initial thought that costs were rolled in with the daily fee with Grumman, hadn't turned out to be true. A months-long battle, where Badalato balked at its first bill, was finally playing out, and not a moment too soon.

The primary scene to capture was Goose coming to talk to Maverick about buzzing the tower. It required work on the part of the actors but it wasn't complicated. The memo stressed the need to wrap early to prepare for the big company move to USS Enterprise. They had lost time because Kelly McGillis had a sore throat, he wrote, asking the director to help get the carrier sequence off and running on time.

"Even though the scenes you're doing are 'emotional,' etc., the fact is you only have one and a half pages of work. Please don't spend hours redressing the set!"

There was a lot to move, including cameras that had to be packed for safe transport to the aircraft carrier, already at sea. "They will have an early call on Saturday and cannot be packing their gear at 10 p.m." That would be late, given the 8:30 general call time, and a full crew, and the fact they worked 12-hour days.

The two scenes they were shooting, 139 and 140, included Cruise, McGillis, and Skerritt, as well as Michael Ironside, as Jester, who was added to the scene just the day before. They also had actor Ron Clark, as the inquiry commander, along with 10 background actors dressed as officers, sailors, a court reporter, a Navy chief, and Maverick's lawyer. It was full crew, with some 133 lunches served by the catering department.

Badalato's focus was the USS Enterprise. Late in the afternoon on Aug. 2 he drove to Miramar to make sure the shooting day was winding down as requested. Instead he found cameras rolling, so he borrowed a walkie from crew. As soon as the action stopped, Badalato radioed Scott that it was time to wrap it up. The director replied enthusiastically: "Yes, yes, Bill! Will do!" The executive producer kept the walkie and moved toward the generator while Scott did another take. Then he radioed the director again, which prompted a similar response. "Hi Bill! Just one more!"

Badalato had a different idea. He unplugged the electric cord, turning off all but the carbon arc lights.

"Cut!" shouted Scott, to uproarious laughter.

Chapter 7 - Endnotes

[194] "Call Sheet – Jun 26." June 26, 1985. TGC.

[195] Wade, April 29, 2020.

[196] Lloyd "Bozo" Abel, LCDR USN (Ret.), F-14 aerial coordinator for Top Gun. Interview with the author, November 27, 2020.

[197] Ibid.

[198] Semcken, November 5, 2020.

[199] Willard, December 2, 2020.

[200] Badalato Jr, July 15, 2020.

[201] Proser, "Top Gun," 46.

[202] "AFI's 100 YEARS...100 MOVIE QUOTES: The 100 greatest movie quotes of all time," American Film Institute, accessed November 27, 2021, https://www.afi.com/afis-100-years-100-movie-quotes/

[203] "Behind Closed Doors: Top Gun," REELZ TV, produced by Lauren Selmon Roberts, released Jun 21, 2020.

[204] *Top Gun* 30th Anniversary DVD Extras.

[205] Vernon Scott. "Meg Ryan's world turns from soap to Spielberg." United Press International/*Tampa Bay Times*, August 11, 1986. 2D.

[206] Terry Nolan, consultant to *Top Gun*, interview with the author, November 9, 2020.

[207] Call Sheet, July 13, 1985. TGC.

208 Bill Badalato, Interview with the author, December 2, 2020

[209] Baron, April 5, 2021.

[210] Martin Blair, co-owner of Kansas City Barbecue, interview with the author, June 26, 2020.

[211] Diane Bell, "Tom Cruise movie sequel takes off without San Diego's 'Top Gun' twins," *San Diego Tribune*, July 6, 2018. In the 2018 interview, Adam Weis revealed the twins were paid $384 apiece for each of their three days' work on *Top Gun*. https://www.sandiegouniontribune.com/news/columnists/diane-bell/sd-me-bell-20180707-story.html

Chapter 8
Telling the Sea Story

USS Ranger: July 23-25 — Day 23, 24, 25
USS Enterprise: Aug. 3-6 — Day 33, 34, 35, 36
The War Cloud: Aug. 8-9 — Day 38, 38 (Sea
Rescue Scenes)

San Diego — Aug. 2

The Travelodge had been home to the full crew for nearly six weeks, and it now took on a very different feel. The original plan had been to shut down operations in San Diego as they shifted to the next phases of photography. The sea story was up next, then air-to-air photography, and finally, special effects. Those things happened in different places with different shooting requirements. There was a slight wrinkle to the plan, because they needed to factor in retakes.[212]

Retakes are a normal part of filming, and different from "additional photography." The former happens when they know they haven't captured what they need — generally discovered in reviewing dailies — while additional photography happens later, after they've pieced together the movie and realize a new scene or element is needed to tie it together.

The alteration in the schedule made by the Navy had also contributed to the time crunch. Splitting the movie production's access between two aircraft carriers, and the dates in which the Navy would accommodate it, meant fitting the three days on the USS Ranger into the time frame allotted for the ground story. It also made sense to schedule the ocean rescue scenes during that time.

That said, it was more work for everyone, starting with the production department. They are the center of any movie, providing organization and support to all other departments. Their job was even more critical on *Top Gun*, as they had to plan for each of the four distinct segments. The department was getting pulled in different directions — which now included planning for as much as a week of reshoots — with one immediate priority. They needed to make sure everything was lined up for the 35 people going out on the USS Enterprise.

Equipment, cast and crew had to be airlifted to the carrier. There were six shipping pallets in all, two for electric and one each for camera, grip, props, and costumes. Each department secured their gear to pallets and created shipping manifests. The transportation department would get it to Miramar, where Navy personnel would review the contents and clear it for the aircraft carrier. Crew would carry their duffel bags and personal items. The Navy would move personnel and equipment to the USS Enterprise on Aug. 3 and manage the return trip Aug. 7.[213]

In the meantime, production staff at the Travelodge was overseeing the checkout of the larger crew, which had occupied about 80 hotel rooms. Most people had been there for at least a month, some much longer. The reshoots meant they would be in San Diego a little longer, only with a smaller number of rooms and secure storage space. Department managers who weren't going out on the USS Enterprise were still working, getting the spaces where the remaining segments would be shot ready, or prepping the remaining scenes.

And, a party was in the offing.

Kamikazes in the water cooler

Aug. 2 was to be the last of the Travelodge parties, and the best to date. It started early for some and grew in momentum as more crew returned from set, or from securing equipment for the move to the USS Enterprise.

Peters, who oversaw transportation, was in charge of the party. "Tony gave me $1,000 and said to go for it," he recalled. The sum would translate to about $2,591 today. He made vodka kamikazes in a five-gallon glass jug, which was hoisted atop the water cooler. The Travelodge parking lot turned into a large boisterous tailgate party. The show wasn't over, so the moment was bittersweet for members of the crew going home, since many wanted to be going out on the USS Enterprise.

That was especially true of Sharon Mann, the 2nd AD who had injured her leg the day they filmed scenes at The Plunge, the giant saltwater pool in San Diego. She was on her way to get Tom Cruise for his scenes when she was injured. Mann stepped onto one of the steel steps of the makeup trailer, which normally set with the weight, but instead swung back on her. "It was like stepping on a shovel, and it flies up and hits you," she recalled.[214]

The step sliced into her right kneecap, sending blood everywhere as she collapsed back onto the steel deck. Cruise, who was in makeup, heard her screaming and rushed out to help. "He was the first person to me," Mann recalled. "He scoops me up in his arms and carries me to the nearby shade of a building." Her knee was throbbing, and Cruise stayed with her until the crew arrived a short time later. The accident required a 20-minute shutdown of all work to clear the set while transport came to help her. She was taken inland and hospitalized overnight.

She returned to the office after a couple of days. "It was a terrible contusion, and I couldn't bend it," she said. Her limited mobility meant she couldn't work on board the USS Enterprise. Mann had been one of three women approved for the trip, which had made it an especially exciting proposition. Women weren't allowed in combat at that point and until recently, hadn't had roles on aircraft carriers, which meant there weren't sleeping quarters or bathrooms for them. Script supervisor June Samson was replaced by Lloyd Nelson, who worked continuity on second units for *Top Gun* when needed, although it isn't clear why, in this case. In the end, Lt. Sandy Stairs, public relations liaison for the Navy, would be the only woman on board and would sleep in the infirmary. She was also part of reshoots aboard the USS Carl Vinson.

There was still plenty of work for Mann to do while the others were at sea. "I remember a lot of ice packs, doing paperwork and prep and planning." And she remembers the disappointment. Her consolation prize was that she's been able to tell the story of how a chivalrous Mr. Cruise scooped her up in his arms.

As for the party at the Travelodge, it went on late into the night. "It was a lot of fun, and a lot of people weren't feeling great the next day when they had to go out to sea," said Peters.

Location, location, location

When Scott and the rest of the movie production set out for the first night aboard the USS Enterprise, they had had the benefit of having worked for three days on the USS Ranger when it was home-ported on North Island. At the same time, the two ships were very different.

The technical designation of the USS Ranger was CV/CVA-61, meaning aircraft carrier/attack aircraft carrier, while the USS Enterprise was CVN-65, meaning aircraft carrier nuclear propulsion, with the Ranger the 61st carrier commissioned by the country, and the Enterprise the 65th.

The USS Ranger was 1,046 feet long, while the USS Enterprise, at 1,123 feet, was the longest naval vessel ever built.[215] It was big enough to require two autonomous operations when it came to living accommodations. Sailors lived and worked one side or the other, bow or stern, to shorten the amount of time it took to get around. Each side of the ship had its own mess hall and entertainment areas.

The USS Enterprise CVN-65 — there are other vessels named Enterprise — still has the distinction of being the longest naval vessel ever built, and it was decommissioned in

2017. The Ranger, launched in 1956, was decommissioned in 1993.

USS Rangeer
North Island
Day 23, 24, 25: July 23-25

If you want an illustration of why movies aren't shot in chronological order, the range of scenes shot on board the USS Ranger 10 days earlier provides it. These were pivotal parts of the story from the beginning, middle and near the end of the script.

The range included Cougar relinquishing his spot on the Topgun roster, and Maverick and Goose finding out there is a spot for them. They also shot the scenes from the Ready Room, where the pilots plan for their mission, and from the operations side, the side of the conversation coming from people on the ship communicating with pilots in the air. They also shot the scene where Maverick takes Goose's name off his locker in the Ready Room after he is killed. The pilots' sides of the dialogue would be shot a month later.

The art department created a nameplate for the commander's office, along with papers, books, pen, coffee mug, glasses, and even booze. The props department came up with gold wings, which Cougar turned in, along with the photograph of his family he uses to explain himself. That image would be used again for the action scenes depicting Cougar losing focus in the aircraft, where he grips the image. All the shots weren't inside. They got shots of the hook pulling out of the airplane, part of the scene where Cougar loses control in the landing. That's one of the scenes they shot that didn't make it into the movie, and there were a lot of those.

The USS Enterprise, which was launched in 1960, was also the first nuclear-powered aircraft carrier, and later the first to have more than two nuclear reactors. In 1974, it gained the distinction of being the first Navy carrier to launch the F-14 Tomcat after its development by Grumman.[216]

Shooting on the Ranger hadn't been that much different than other location work. Sure, it was unusual to be working on a naval ship, but the work involved shooting scenes with the full production crew, access to all equipment, and the ability to go on and off the ship to get anything that was forgotten, and to go back to the hotels at night.

The production set up base camp nearby where the Ranger was docked with the usual number of trucks, including for camera, set dressing and construction departments. There were two makeup trailers and three honey wagons, and a large area for catering. Each day, catering provided about 30 breakfasts and between 140 and 150 hot lunches for crew.[217]

Even maneuvering around on the USS Ranger wasn't too challenging, as it was home-ported, which meant it was operating with about 60 to 70 percent of personnel. The only inconvenience came the first day. when they had to clear the set for 20 minutes so the Navy could "transport caustic materials via pipes on board."

Working on board the USS Enterprise was something entirely different, as was being offshore on maneuvers.

On board the USS Enterprise Offshore, Pacific Ocean Day 33, 34, 35, 36: Aug. 3-6

Of the 35 sleeping spaces allotted to the movie production by the Navy, 21 went to crew. That included the DP, two camera operators, four camera assistants, two electrici ans, three grips, one "propman" and one "wardrobe," the script supervisor, two sound techs, one makeup, one hair, and two PAs. Scott had 1st AD Kolsrud and 2nd AD Patrick Cosgrove, who replaced Mann, to manage the set and plan for the next day. There were three Navy liaisons, Semcken, Stairs and Richard Milligan from Grumman. The remaining slots were filled by Scott, producers Bruckheimer and Badalato, and cast members Cruise, Kilmer, Rossovich, Edwards, Whip Hubley, Barry Tubb, James Tolkan, Duke Stroud, and Tim Robbins.[218]

The movie production was coming along on a training mission, and it needed to fit in.

A July 31 memo "Carrier Instructions" laid out process and rules. No alcoholic beverages were allowed on the carrier. "Violation of this strictly enforced rule will result in serious consequences for the production."[219]

The Navy had requested Paramount provide duffel bags for individual gear, which was easier for transport. Crew was given those and instructed to pick up soap and shower footwear from the production office in advance. Clothing requirements included long-sleeve shirts, windbreakers, warm jackets, jeans but no shorts, dress slacks and shirts for "informal dinner with Navy personnel." Work shoes were recommended but sneakers were "permissible."

Peters, who hadn't imbibed much at the wrap party, was up at 5 a.m. to oversee the transporting of cast, crew, and equipment to Miramar, where they would be flown out to the aircraft carrier. The camera, grip, and electric departments, as well as props, had a 6:15 a.m. call time on Aug. 3, and the general call time was 8 a.m. Cruise and Edwards had 8:30 a.m. call times. Cruise had a driver, who picked him up from the house he had rented in La Jolla.[220] A van went to get the actors, including Edwards, for the 8 a.m. call time, while other production vans shuttled crew to the helicopter squadron.[221]

The Navy took it from there, starting with the first of several safety briefings, the first covering the flights to the USS Enterprise offshore. Cast and crew flew in one helicopter while their duffel bags were stowed in helicopters designed for freight, along with the pallets.

Memories fray as to the duration of the flight, but no one thought it was short. All they knew about their destination was that it was in the Pacific Ocean, but precisely where was classified. Paperwork shows they arrived on location by 11 a.m. Landing was more memorable because Navy personnel quickly arrived at the aircraft and hurriedly led them away from the helipad to their gear, which was already offloaded. Cast and crew were told to stow it in their respective quarters. Lower-level crew were led to the floor just under the flight deck and shown to a large narrow bunk room, three bunks high with perhaps a hundred berths in total. About half a dozen movie crew were assigned to bunks.

The rest were shown to better accommodations, individual staterooms, but not necessarily private. The aircraft carrier had private staterooms for commanders and XOs, while the next rank shared a double, with a bunk bed and one desk and closet space. "Officers got staterooms, so the actors got staterooms," Semcken said. The most junior officers, ensigns and lieutenants and junior lieutenants, were typically assigned to a four- or six-man stateroom, which was a suite with two or three double-bunks along with a separate room with a desk and seating. The one woman went to the infirmary.[222]

As soon as personal gear was stowed crew went immediately to set, which was the flight deck. There they were given another safety briefing that put them on alert. Flight deck crew provided support for planes taking off and landing under all circumstances. The planes were extremely hot, with powerful engine intakes strong enough to suck in a person under certain circumstances. Propellers and rotors and other moving equipment and machinery could crush limbs. The crew worked amid dangerous fumes from fueling the planes to the exhaust they put out when in operation. Just dealing with the elements in the open ocean was taxing, with both extreme heat and cold and wind, which could blow a sailor off the deck.

After the briefing they went to lunch, then returned to set. A lighter workload had been planned for the shortened workday, and the effort focused on capturing the Navy at work. They shot scenes 2 through 5, which included deck operations, like F-14s landing, the hooks catching the planes when they landed on deck. Another shot was of a landing signal officer holding a "pickle," a handheld switch box that controlled lights. There were limitations in equipment. They weren't able to use a crane, so they would use a forklift and a scissor lift for shots that required height. In general, sea conditions made it harder to protect the equipment.

Kimball's core camera team had remained Connor, Nishino and Wheeler from the start of principal photography, and the cadre of camera crew expanded on the USS Enterprise with additional equipment. They added a Steadicam as well as a Panaflex Platinum camera. Additional crew included Tony Rivetti and Joseph Valentine.[223]

The camera, grip, and electric departments set up the equipment to capture the light available at magic hour, with the first shot at 5:12 p.m. While paperwork noted that Valentine was there to manage the Steadicam, it wasn't a Steadicam but a Panaglide, which was Panavision's version of a Steadicam, meaning it could get steady shots from a moving platform.[224] People often used the two names interchangeably.

His real contribution to the movie, Valentine said, are the shots of Navy crew on the flight deck. "I shot the opening sequence with a Panaflex with a 10/1 long lens on sticks at the crotch of the ship," he said. The crotch of the flight deck is between the angled deck and the portside bow of the ship.

It was about five feet deep, and he and Rivetti, who was the assistant, climbed into it to set up the production camera. The 10/1 lens, which was eye level with the deck, enabled the wide angle shots of Navy crew running around on the deck.[225]

They were done shooting by 7:18. Hair, makeup, property, and wardrobe had been wrapped for dinner by 7 p.m. while the camera and grip departments stayed to secure flight deck equipment and had a later dinner. Some people ate in the mess hall, getting their trays of food alongside sailors, while others ate in the officers' wardroom.

Everyone was exhausted by day's end. Kimball described a feeling of sensory overload just from being on the flight deck. The safety gear was cumbersome; just getting used to the motion of the vessel in the steady 30 knots of wind offshore took adjustment, and that was before the first jet roared in at 180 miles per hour. The engines were deafening, and the jets rushed in and out, one after the next, the equipment grinding and straining as the aircraft jerked to a stop. He felt like his senses were "muffled" by the end of the day.[226]

The dange of it was recognized by the movie production. Two hazard-pay adjustments were added for camera, sound and grip departments working during flight operations the first day, a change that would be applied for each of their days on board.[227]

Meanwhile, the ship kept working.

Filming aboard
Day 34: Aug. 4

The first full day on the ship was the most ambitious. Scott set out to tackle Maverick's triumphant return to the ship as a hero, where he has performed courageously, regaining his self-confidence as well as that of the other pilots. "He cuts his engines, and the ground crew swarms."[228]

The crew had a 5 a.m. call time on Aug. 4, and used the time making the Navy props shiny, and getting the cameras and lights set up. Cruise, Kilmer, Rossovich, Hubley, Tubb, and Robbins were due to wardrobe to be fitted in flight suits by 6 a.m., then to makeup, and due on set by 7 a.m. Notably, Edwards — whose character, Goose, was dead before these specific scenes — was marked "home," which in this case was his stateroom.[229] He would be needed in other scenes.

This took the most background actors yet, although there would be one scene even bigger before they left the ship. This one required around 100 Navy personnel to stand in as background actors, many of them dressed in flight suits by the costume designer despite the fact they weren't pilots. They were unpaid, in keeping with Navy policy in place throughout the production. The group, composed of deck crew and four officers, needed little coaching in how to cheer and applaud Maverick's success.

The camera crew set up a Panaglide — marked as Steadicam on paperwork — for 45 minutes, which was used to capture the pilots running toward their planes. Valentine knew the still-new technology well, having assisted in its development by working with Garrett Brown, considered the inventor of the Steadicam. "You can count the number of Steadicam operators on one hand through the early 80s and still have fingers left over," said Valentine.[230]

The day also included work on the scene where Iceman tells Maverick he can be his wingman any day, which happens in the same milieu, with the same lighting. Neither scene was finished that day, but other elements were.

The twilight time was used to get striking aerial sunset shots of the aircraft carrier. Those shots were taken from a Sikorsky SH 3 Sea King, which had taken them to the carrier. The Seahawk, a Navy version of the Blackhawk, was combat-ready but used for many things, including moving personnel and equipment. It went up from 4 p.m. through wrap at 4:52.

Steadicam

The Steadicam, which had a significant impact on cinema, was an innovative handheld movie camera introduced in the mid-1970s. The technology enabled a level, steady shot that hadn't been possible before in a hand-held, by isolating the movement of the camera operator from what they were shooting. Before, most shots were limited to the tripod and the dolly. The Steadicam offered a very different look. The industry took note of it right away, while public awareness of it grew in specific films, like the Depression-era *Bound for Glory* (1976), which featured a tracking shot through a migrant camp. Real attention came after director Stanley Kubrick, who saw a Steadicam demo and recognized the technology as "revolutionary," decided to use it extensively in *The Shining* (1980.) The technology has continued to improve over the years, but it still takes a trained operator strong enough to carry heavy weight on their back, often while running to capture actors in front of them in motion.

On the flight deck
Day 35: Aug. 5

The next morning had the same 5:30 a.m. call for crew, but actors were due in earlier than they had been the day before for makeup and wardrobe at 5:45 a.m. They resumed work on the flight deck on the scene depicting the hero's return, and the now familiar competitive rivalry between Maverick and Iceman. Again they used the 100 background actors but in place of the officers were 10 air operations personnel.[231]

The production crew broke for lunch from 11:30 to 12:30, and when they returned it was something very different. The rest of the shooting day was on the "pri-fly," or primary flight control area, which was in the tower on the deck.

It was up to the camera, grip, and electric departments to get the equipment to the upper level of the ship. Movie lights and cameras and various grip equipment always takes effort, but here they had to navigate 12 flights of narrow stairs. They lucked into using a private elevator until someone with ribbons tried to get on it and found there wasn't room. "That was the last time that happened," said Kimball.

The scenes on the pri-fly included the ship-to-air communications with Maverick and the other pilots in flight. Capturing the sound had been challenging. Bill Kaplan set up the sound cart in a restricted room. His main issue was with the sound of the radar system. It permeated the room, getting into every mic. It became clear to Kaplan it had to be shut off, but the Naval officer in charge wouldn't authorize that. "Then he got another guy involved, and he said, 'We have other systems,'" said Kaplan. "And they shut it down."

The coverage included the airboss, and Maverick's request for a flyby of the ship. They tried variations of the shooting script as they went. The script has the livid airboss telling him "negat…!" until the admiral "pipes up."

"Don't be an asshole. Give the man his flyby."

That unrealistic dialogue didn't make it into the movie, but a lot of the dialogue rewritten on the ship did.

Actors Kilmer, Rossovich, Hubley, Tubb and Shroud left on a Seahawk helicopter around 4 p.m., and once back in San Diego, they traveled to Los Angeles. It marked the end of work for those actors "until further notice," according to the production report.[232]

One that got away
Day 36: Aug. 6

The biggest scene in terms of background actors kicked off the last full day. Scenes 47, 48 and 49 depicted Cougar's ill-fated flight, which creates Maverick and Goose's opportunity to go to the Topgun school. None of it ended up on screen.

In the early stages of the script, Cougar's flight ended with a more violent crash than the one that ultimately got on screen. The Navy had resisted the scenes, but Scott pushed. In prep he and Kolsrud got them to agree to a compromise. They could get imagery that would depict a jet going into a steel net. It would still be a crash, but no fire and nothing in the air. Some back and forth with the Navy had followed, Kolsrud said, but they ended up with a plan to shoot the scene with 150 Navy crew while they were out at sea. The idea was to taxi an F-14 down the runway and stop it at the barrier — which required caution, since it was only for emergencies and damaged the jets in real life — and speed it up in post-production.[233]

The Navy agreed to it, in part because it involved training it needed to conduct for sailors. "They have to put up a steel net that will catch an airplane doing 100 miles per hour," the former 1st AD explained. Called a "barrier drill," it took about 90 seconds for the throng of sailors to get it stretched out, which was about how much notice they had that a plane was coming in for a rough landing.

For a real emergency, the net was contained under a hatch on the flight deck, and an engine-operated baggage train would pull it out and drive it across the flight deck. "They erect the barrier, jump on the mule and drive across the flight deck, stretching it out," said Kolsrud. Then sailors run and grab pieces of the barrier, pylons, and get it up there fast and efficiently." The practice drill was a little different, using a backup steel barrier. It was hard, physical work, and the production needed to shoot it several ways, which meant repeating the task.

A deck chief oversaw the Navy crew. "He didn't really like having us there. He had his regular routine, and we were gumming up the works," recalled Kolsrud. He helped them, but he "was not a friend."

There's a huge amount of noise on the flight deck, and everyone was wearing ear protection. That meant that the speaker, where instructions were broadcast, was incredibly loud. Kolsrud thought they had done maybe a half-dozen takes when real strain started to show. The captain of the ship had given them a time limit because jets would be landing, "at a certain time, maybe 1 p.m., so we could shoot to 12, and then get off the flight deck." As the morning progressed, time got tighter and the stress level rose.

"The sailors hated doing it. It was a practice barrier, and it can't be put back perfectly. It gets covered with grease, it's a mess, there's a time limit, we're going fast," Kolsrud recalled. "It was not one of the fun parts of being out there." The worst part was that they weren't getting what they needed, which was a shot of the plane they could manipulate into looking like it hit the barrier.

They tried one more time, and clearly failed. "I'm feeling the burning eyes of the guy who would like us off his deck," recalled Kolsrud. "I told Tony, 'Pull the plug. We should go now,' and then there's the voice of God, loud, on the PA." Apparently, he'd softened up in the time they'd been there, because the voice said for them to try one more time. "It was the Navy guy, whose life we were mucking up, and he knew we had to get off the flight deck." In the end, "he *was* our friend."

They got the extra take. "We got amazing film, but taxiing into the barrier — we couldn't get it to work. That's why it didn't get in the movie."

"Turn the ship around!"

That day also delivered the most famous behind-the-scenes story from *Top Gun*. Scott demanded, and ultimately succeeded, in getting the captain of the USS Enterprise to turn the ship back so he could shoot the sunset. Over time the exchange with the Navy has taken on the feel of a fish tale, growing more elaborate — and more expensive — than it actually was, according to numerous interviews.

The version of the story most often told — that Scott physically pulled out a checkbook and wrote a check for $25,000 so he could keep shooting — "never happened," according to Semcken.

The director did agree to write a check to Paramount for $10,000, and later gave it to Badalato, according to the producer.

How they got there is the interesting part, which means revisiting the agreement between the Navy and the production. The movie crew was to fit into the training operations of the ship, not the other way around. They'd had the full support of Navy personnel over previous days. The job of 1st AD Kolsrud was to manage the set and whatever else the director needed, which in this case included being the primary contact with the navigator on the bridge.

Each night, Kolsrud met with him to go over what they planned to shoot the next day. A lot of effort went into that plan, such as where the sun would be at the necessary time and the turns they needed to make. "The navigator would plot things backwards, and create the course the ship would have to take to accommodate them." There were a lot of things being factored in separately on the bridge, lines of demarcation, points the ship wasn't supposed to go beyond, and maneuvers it needed to run as part of its training mission.

Kolsrud learned something about those constraints on his trips to the bridge. "A sub can disappear, but a carrier doesn't have anything to protect itself with besides airplanes," he said.[234]

Scott was focused on shooting the scenes, and hence was less aware of the constraints they were under from the bridge, or the layers of effort it took to accommodate the movie production. Some of that was by design. Good crew, from department heads to the assistant directors, try to solve problems before they get to the director to keep them free from distraction so they can focus on storytelling.

At the same time, Scott discovered the utility of manipulating light with a turn of the ship.

He discovered on the first day that he could point, "and boom, the ship turns and faces that way," recalled Kolsrud. In the process, the subject, say a group of F-14s on the flight deck, was backlit. The USS Enterprise was able to turn relatively fast, which might have made it seem easier than it was to shift the direction of the longest aircraft carriers ever made. "We keep shooting, point us that way, the ship turns."

That was pretty much how it had gone until late that last afternoon, when Scott was focused on capturing his last sunset. It was going to be a beauty until the ship started to move away. The director commanded that the ship be turned back, and someone radioed the bridge.

"We get to that point and this time the word comes back, 'No we can't — we're not going to.' Tony wasn't used to that," recalled Kolsrud.

Scott was perhaps 20 feet up in the air on a scissor lift with the camera, looking down at Kolsrud, when he was told the bridge had said no. He saw Scott go "…pale. Tony looked at the bridge and looked back. He said, 'What's happening? Turn it back!' Because he can't talk to me, since he's up in the air, he starts shouting," recalled Kolsrud, "turn the blankity-blank ship!"

So, the 1st AD, working with Semcken, checked again, only to get the same answer. "We don't know why, but the tenor of it was, 'It's my ship, and we're not turning it.'" Scott came down off the lift, and by then Badalato, who wasn't far away to start with, was also there. The executive producer had been communicating with the Navy on other matters. He could see the perspective of the bridge, but he also wanted to help Scott and the movie. "It was a dramatic situation," said Kolsrud.

Another interaction with the bridge ensued, this one involving Badalato, and a comment came back from the bridge along the lines of, "Do you have any idea what it costs to run this ship?' Badalato doesn't recall how the exchange led to a $10,000 guesstimate, but allows it was probably his idea.

Wherever it came from, Badalato wasn't going to approve it. The budget constraints hadn't changed, and potentially had grown worse. The production was there to capture what the Navy was doing on its training mission, and the Navy had more than worked with them. Production paperwork had notations like "2 F-14s, 1 SH3 helicopter" to try to keep up with the special services they were using, which presumably would have an associated cost. Badalato didn't want to upset the delicate balance, and it was entirely possible at that point for there to be a much bigger bill.[235]

He told Scott the production wasn't paying to turn the ship, and Scott said he would pay out of pocket. "Tony did that several times with various things," Kolsrud said. "He had the reputation for saying things like, 'I'll pay for the overtime.' And he did." But $10,000 was likely a record.

With the sum agreed, another radio exchange took place. The production would compensate the Navy for departing from its planned schedule. "And then the ship turns, and I am summoned to the bridge," said Kolsrud. The camera crew returned to getting the shot.

The 1st AD knew his way because of his meetings with the navigation officer but this time he climbed the stairs with a degree of trepidation. To that point, he hadn't even seen the captain, and there he was, sitting in his chair on the bridge. "He was a dignified guy, an enormous guy," recalled Kolsrud. "I was never in the military, but I stood at attention."

The captain wasn't happy, and Kolsrud listened as he explained why, nodding and feeling small. It was a humbling experience for the 1st AD, who agreed with the captain, although he didn't say it. "The captain was more flexible than he should have been," he said.

Semcken, who was on deck for the whole exchange, said he thought the captain of the ship got tired of this movie guy barking commands at him and wanted to smack him down.

Whether Scott's check was actually cashed is unclear, but he didn't end up paying out of pocket for it in the long run. Scott often told people the check bounced. The incident quickly took on legendary proportion and was something people on the movie side of the equation laughed about. "The Navy side didn't think it was that funny," said Semcken.

Tom Cruise's near fatal first stunt
Day 38, 39: Aug. 8-9

PHOTO: PH2 Michael D.P. Flynn, U.S. Navy, Public domain, via Wikimedia Commons.

The production of Top Gun went out for two very eventful days aboard the supply tug, War Cloud.

Shooting the rescue scenes in the water off Point Loma in San Diego might have proved fatal for Tom Cruise, if not for Navy Seals. The actor was in the water in heavy equipment, surrounded by his parachute prop, when the strong current took hold of it. The cords wrapped around him, pulling the actor out of the prop life raft and under water, dragging him down.[236]

The production had chartered the War Cloud, a supply tug, to shoot the rescue scenes. It was a 150-foot ship, 90 feet of its deck flat, open at the stern. It was a licensed, working vessel designed to haul supplies to offshore oil rigs and provide other commercial marine services, like towing lumber barges. It was also comfortable. Its 34-foot beam made for roomy living quarters for up to a dozen people, a well-equipped galley, and a pilothouse with more appointments than were required by the U.S. Coast Guard.

The docks where the vessel was berthed were on the east side of the bay, north of the Coronado bridge and next to the Chart House restaurant, and owned by R.E. Staite, a general engineering contractor specializing in marine construction. A crane on the dock helped load the vessel for the movie company, which planned two full days aboard. But the majority of prep had happened over several months. The props department had acquired properly sized safety straps and helmets and other gear to go with the flight suits and other costumes accumulated by the costume departments. It made for a heavy costume, difficult to maneuver around in, particularly in water.

Wade acquired a Navy-issued raft and dye used in real-life water rescues, along with parachutes and rescue bags. The most significant part for the prop master had been safety preparations, including a 15-foot rigid inflatable raft. It was nimble enough to move easily from the larger ship to the authentic Navy life raft. The production hired professional safety divers, with full scuba equipment, as the first line of protection. The water, even in August, was in the neighborhood of 68 degrees, which meant if there was trouble they'd want to get them out fast.[237]

Wade also brought the Kauber brothers along with two other active-duty Navy rescue swimmers. The prop master had gotten to know the brothers, thanks to their help with procuring some harder-to-find props. They were Navy Seals. Jim Kauber ran the safety school attended by Cruise and Edwards, as part of flight training required by the Navy. All four men came out on their own time, without compensation, in keeping with Navy protocols. All of them were in wet suits with safety equipment that included knives in sheaths strapped to their bodies.[238]

Wade likewise wore a wetsuit since he was in and out of the water all day. "The life raft is a prop," he recalled. "Who else is going to work it? Most of the time, I just moved the raft around with Cruise in it. He was in full gear, so it was a little tricky. I made sure my two Seal guys were in the water with me, so I had help!"

The conditions were rough, something reflected in the scene itself. "It was a weird spot off Point Loma," said Kauber. "I even got a little queasy." It felt dangerous, even before the incident. "It was the only time I ever feared for my life, with choppers coming in, I couldn't breathe from the spray they were drawing up."

They shot various scenes over the course of the day. Anthony Edwards was there playing the role of the newly deceased Goose when needed. One scene had Maverick cradling his lifeless body. Another shot had them hauling a body up to the helicopter, which actually was Edwards.

Things went awry when the wind took hold of the parachute, somewhat like the script had imagined. Only instead of Cruise skipping across the top of the water, it sucked him under. "A parachute will inflate in the water, just like in the air, and that's what happened," explained Kauber, who was about 40 feet away and saw it happen. The lines of the parachute hooked onto equipment Cruise was wearing. "It pulled him out of the raft, and under water, and the boy was on his way down." It didn't help that he was weighed down by the wet flight suit and safety equipment.

Danger, well-scripted

The plan, going back to prep, had been to make the sequence as realistic as possible. A June 5 memo, "SAR Goose's Death," listed 48 consecutive shots that begins with Maverick ejecting from the F-14 and ends with a "wide shot of Goose's forlorn body floating – the raft whipped by spray and wind from the helo downdraft."[239]

Scott's vision was to have dramatic underwater footage of both Maverick struggling with his harness and Goose's lifeless body being encased in the parachute. The idea was to have Cruise pull himself into the lifeboat, exhausted, and see Goose's parachute in the wreckage. Maverick begins calling and paddling to him, and when he gets to the cords of the parachute he begins to pull at the cords, then more frantically, until a "dark shape appears mummified in the chute."

News Coverage

The accident involving Cruise appeared in press accounts about a year after *Top Gun* came out, after Navy rescue swimmers received a commendation for it, and went public. This account is based on interviews with six people who were there, along with those press accounts and the Navy commendations. Some details, like how many movie crew members were on board, couldn't be determined because the production reports summarizing the work for each of those two days was missing from an otherwise complete set of PRs.

Here's how it was laid out in the memo:

"31. Mav. slashes the chute and harness away from the body.

32. Wide as he pulls Goose into the raft alongside him - where is Goose's raft

33. BCU Mav. as he unwinds the mummified head.

34. BCU Goose's head is revealed as chute is pulled away – a large dark hole penetrates the side of his skull

35. 2 shot Mav. broken cradles Goose's body in his arms.

36. Wide top shot ocean – a tiny island raft amongst smoke oil and debris- dissolve to black.

37. Sound of helicopter overhead – screen illuminates with red titanium flare."

The goal of a shot list is to detail what will happen in a sequence, blow by blow. The list lets crew know exactly what the director is planning for a scene or scenes, which ensures everyone is at the same line on the same page. Shot lists aren't facts, and they can change. In this case, it largely played out as scripted, according to cameramen who were there, Navy swimmers, and others.

Jack Cooperman was among the most experienced cameramen there, with more than 20 years in the business. He was on *Top Gun* only a few days, during which he did both helicopter and underwater work. While the PRs for the shooting days weren't available, the names of both Cooperman and the assistant cameraman he worked with, Wayne Baker, appeared on the prior and following days' PRs, as traveling to and from location. Their names were also on a Travelodge room assignment list.[240]

Cooperman, who worked a lot with Scott over the years, said the director took time to describe the previous scenes that set up the water rescue. That included how Maverick and Goose ejected from the plane and how they parachuted to the water, detail that ensured he understood why what they were portraying in the water was happening.[241]

"In real life, [ejecting pilots] can hit the water and sink and get wrapped up in the shroud lines of the parachute. Based on that, we did the aerials." Cooperman recalled the helicopter rotating up and down to get a circular pattern in the waves, which ended up in the movie. The more elaborate scene, which the cameraman remembered vividly, didn't make the cut.

Cooperman and Baker worked as operator and assistant, Cooperman said. In this kind of scenario, it would have been Cooperman in the water with the camera and Baker in the boat getting the cameras ready. Baker would hand the camera to Cooperman, who would shoot scenes until the camera ran out of film. He'd hand it back to Baker, who had another one ready and waiting. "That way we were always ready to go," recalled Cooperman. That was true with SCUBA tanks or whatever else was needed.

Crew readies the mannequin that will double as Goose in the shot.

PHOTO: PH2 Michael D.P. Flynn, U.S. Navy, Courtesy National Archives.

The goal here was to capture the rescue of Goose's body from the water. "Once they put that mannequin in the water, they would lower it down to a depth to set it up. I would have to give a visual hand signal when I was ready, to show the camera was rolling." The crew added some lead to make it sink a little lower. Once Cooperman gave the signal, the crew started pulling the entombed mannequin forward, which was toward the cameraman underwater.[242]

The shot had been set up so the sun was behind Cruise in the recovery raft, creating a silhouette. The hardest part was the last few seconds, because Cooperman had to lift the camera out of the water to capture Cruise's face as he took the facsimile of Goose's body. Cooperman recalled that the camera was incredibly heavy to lift out of the water, enough that it took serious exertion. He could still see Cruise's tormented face, as he acted out receiving Goose's body.

"It was a really nice sequence that Tony designed, and we executed, and it didn't get into the film."

Robert G. Willard, who worked on special effects, said the dummy made to look like Goose helped pull Cruise underwater. "They just got a dummy, and stuffed a picture in the face card, behind the glass, and it was enough to look like Goose." It was made of foam, and when he saw them adding water to make it sink lower in the raft, and even weights, he said he warned them. "I told them, too much weight and you will lose it. I was overruled." He saw what happened from the ship. "All of a sudden the dummy starts to sink, waterlogged, and Cruise's leg is wrapped around one of the shrouds of the parachute."

Kauber saw it happen but was too far away to react. Two other Navy rescue swimmers, Daryl Silva and John Butler, were closer. "They free-dove down there and cut Cruise loose. It's lucky they got to him in time." They had knives as part of safety gear, which they used to cut him free.

In the roughly 40 seconds it took to bring him back up, Kauber had swum closer to the life raft, and was there when they surfaced. "Cruise had inhaled a lot of salt water and we threw him up into the Zodiac. "He looked like he was unconscious, but he came to. I think he landed either on his stomach or his chest, because once he hit the side of the rubber boat, it was like a self-induced CPR, and it forced all that water out."

They got Cruise to the ship and out of the costume. The actor was still struggling to regain his strength when Scott — unaware of the severity of what had occurred — yelled that he wanted to get another take. Cruise began yelling at the director that he wasn't going to do it, using some "choice words" for Scott. "It's the only time I saw Cruise lose it with Tony Scott," said Wade. "He was pissed."

"I remember Cruise being adamantly opposed," said Kauber, with a degree of understatement. "He was raising his voice to Tony Scott. As far as the actual conversation, it revolved around whether he'd get back in the water," said Kauber. "It scared the heck out of Cruise. He was that close to being crab bait in San Diego Bay."

"Cruise came as close to dying as anybody on a set I've ever seen" is how actor Barry Tubb described it to the New York Post.[243]

Kauber was under the impression that divers with oxygen tanks had been hired in case of emergency. He recalled seeing one of the men yelling that Cruise was going down. "They weren't really part of the rescue," he said. "I don't think they wanted to get entangled with the parachute either." Without the PRs that summarize the day's work, it's impossible to verify that there were other rescue swimmers.

But Cruise did return to work on camera, which included getting back in the water. The one demand he made was that the Navy Seals be there with him, Kauber said.

Not everyone on the ship was aware of the incident. The former owner of Latitudes Marine Inc., who was on board the War Cloud that day, doubted it was that big of a deal. He never knew about it, he said, and he was there both days. The captain, who wasn't working that day and asked that his name not be used, spent half of one afternoon chatting with Edwards, who he said was approachable and nice. Cruise was polite, he said, but "more of a loner." It was a memorable day for the novelty of it, but not because there was any drama. "It's the only time we did movie work," he said.

Cooperman also said he had no knowledge of an accident involving Cruise.

All these years later, Kauber regrets that he didn't demand they cut the top out of the parachute before shooting. The danger of it being drawn under water was predictable, so much so that he warned the director. Scott didn't think that it would look authentic if the lines were cut. Kauber let it go, in part because he believed they had professional safety divers there.

Silva and Butler were later awarded Navy Commendation medals for their rescue efforts.[244]

Kauber also picked up a Navy Commendation, although that one was for another incident that occurred later in the same trip. They were just getting to the dock when Tom Prophet, the key grip, stepped off the ship and missed the dock. At that point the ship was pulling into the pier, and he was caught between it and the pilings. Kauber jumped in to get him out. Peters, who was on the dock, was also there to help lift him out before he was crushed or drowned or both. Prophet was still experiencing discomfort a day later and went to Sharp Cabrillo Hospital for X-rays.[245]

PHOTO: U.S. Navy All Hands magazine, May 1986.

The official magazine of the U.S. Navy ran this image with a caption that said Tom Cruise had been "entangled in his parachute and almost drowned before he was rescued by U.S. Navy divers."

Credit snafu for Skaaren

Landing the job of fixing the *Top Gun* script was big for Skaaren, and it put him on a national stage. But it had been stressful from the outset, when he'd sequestered himself away to do the first rewrite. The intensity had let up but never fully abated. He'd spent time traveling back and forth to San Diego, when he'd asserted early in the process he wanted to work from his home in Austin. It was taxing to manage the various players, alternatively Simpson and/or Bruckheimer, Scott, and Cruise.

"Sometimes it was dual, Tom Cruise and Tony Scott," said Alison Macor, author of a biography of Skaaren, "Rewrite Man." Sometimes the scriptwriter would have reworked something over many hours only to find out one person or another wanted different changes.

He wasn't impressed with Scott but it was a different story for Skaaren with Cruise, who provided a lot of input for the character of Maverick. "Tony Scott wasn't an organized thinker, and Cruise was, which is probably why he and Cruise related well," explained Macor.

As they were finishing photography for the ground story Skaaren received news as stressful as anything else he'd experienced in the previous months: The legal department at Paramount wasn't going to include him in proposed writing credits. Based on Writers Guild of America guidelines, studio officials believed the credit should go to Cash and Epps. Skaaren was "dumbfounded" by the news, wrote Macor,[246] who since 2019 has served on the advisory board of The Warren Skaaren Charitable Trust.[247]

The WGA paperwork was happening slightly ahead of schedule, because the studio wanted to get credits managed ahead of another process, which was the planned novelization of the movie. Derivative books based on movies or television shows were a focused profit center for studios in those days.

Skaaren had just 10 days to respond to the WGA filing. He prepared an elaborate rebuttal that documented his extensive changes to the script. In the meantime, he was less available to the production.

Chapter 8 - Endnotes

[212] Bill Badalato, "Balance of Schedule Notes Carrier Schedule," Paramount Inter-Communication, July 26, 1985. Re: 'To All Concerned, Ground Story complete per REVISED SCHEDULE of 7/21/85.' TGC.

[213] "Cast going to the USS Enterprise," Production Report, August 3, 1985. TGC.

[214] Sharon Mann, second assistant director (AD) on *Top Gun*, interview with the author, August 9, 2020.

[215] USS Enterprise (CVN-65) Westpac/Medcruise 1986 25th Anniversary. https://www.youtube.com/watch?v=f-9Aw2FYEjc

[216] United States Navy, "F-14 Tomcat fighter fact file," July 5, 2003. Archived from the original on 2 April 2006. https://web.archive.org/web/20060402215910/https://www.navy.mil/navydata/fact_display.asp?cid=1100&tid=1100&ct=1

[217] Production notes, August 4 – August 6, 1985. TGC.

[218] *Top Gun* production notes, ca 1985. TGC.

[219] "Carrier Instructions." Paramount Inter-Communication, July 31, 1985. TGC.

[220] Peters, August 3, 2021.

[221] Call Sheet, August 3, 1985. TGC.

[222] Semcken, November 5, 2020.

[223] Badalato, production notes, ca 1985. TGC.

[224] "The Shining and the Steadicam, An Interview With Garrett Brown," US Patent and Trademark Office. https://www.youtube.com/watch?v=YpcP-6nBi5c

[225] Joseph Valentine Panaflex® operator for *Top Gun*. Interview with the author, August 21, 2021.

[226] Les Paul Robley, "Flying High With Top Gun," *American Cinematographer*, May 1986. Reprinted online June 10 2021. https://ascmag.com/articles/flying-high-with-top-gun

[227] "Hazard pay," Daily Production Report, August 3, 1985 and "Hazard pay, Steadicam." Daily Production Report, August 4, 1985. TGC.

[228] Director's notes, August 4, 1985. TGC.

[229] Call Sheet, August 4. TGC.

[230] Valentine, August 21, 2021.

[231] Call Sheet, August 5, 1985. TGC.

[232] Daily Production Report, August 5, 1985. TGC.

[233] Kolsrud, January 26, 2021.

234 Kolsrud, January 26, 2021

[235] Daily Production Report – Aug. 6, 1985. TGC.

[236] Chuck Conconi, "Personalities." The Washington Post, May 22, 1986. https://www.washingtonpost.com/archive/lifestyle/1986/05/22/personalities/267b6ffc-e2b1-4322-80c8-9608d03bd23c/

[237] Wade, July 20, 2021.

[238] Kauber, March 17, 2021.

[239] Tony Scott. "SAR Goose's Death." Scene summary and shot list, June 5, 1985. TGC.

[240] Daily Production Reports, August 3- August 7, 1985. TGC.

[241] Jack Cooperman, cameral operator for *Top Gun*. Interview with the author, September 4, 2021.

[242] Daily Production Report, "Special Notes," August 10, 1985. TGC.

243 Larry Getlen. "Tom Cruise's Danger Zone" *New York Post*, Aug. 28, 2011.
https://nypost.com/2011/08/28/tom-cruises-danger-zone/
244 "Real-life drama highlighted filming of movie 'Top Gun." *Daily Press*
(Victorville, California), May 23, 1986, C1.
245 Kauber, March 17, 2021.
246 Macor, Rewrite Man: The Life and Career of Screenwriter Warren Skaaren., 98.
247 Alison Macor, interview with the author, January 10, 2021

CHAPTER 9
AERIAL SCENES
MIRAMAR: DAY 40, 41, 42, AUG. 12-14
FALLON, NEV.: DAY 43-53, AUG. 16-25

Day 40: Aug. 12

Capturing the jets in flight was always referred to as "air-to-air" in paperwork, but in actuality it was also ship-to-air and ground-to-air. Air-to-air imagery was far less developed in 1985 than it is today and they were trying to get as much footage as they could from as many places as possible.[248]

There were four primary scenes in the air they needed to capture for the screen. Two happen early in the movie during the training exercises and the competition to be "Top Gun," where Maverick beats Jester and is beaten by Viper. The third was Goose's death — the priority in terms of mentions in production documents — and the fourth was the climactic dogfight. They had 13 shooting days to get the scenes.

The call time on the first day, Aug. 12, was 5:45 a.m. The briefing began promptly at 6 a.m. and it was clear right away how different this would be from the other stages of photography. The actors were gone, and in their places were Navy pilots and RIOs. The stars here were the F-14 Tomcats, F-5 Tigers and A-4 Skyhawks. Scott was inclined to direct them, too, but it became clear at the first briefing that the Navy should be in the pilot seat for these scenes.[249]

It was Bob "Rat" Willard, both operations officer and executive officer of the Navy Fighter Weapons School, who would run things in Fallon. Willard always had final responsibility for the Navy's side of the movie production, but aside from the occasional intervention, he tended to stay on the sidelines. Semcken, despite his lower rank, held authority to make decisions about the movie, and it had worked. Scott would argue with Semcken on points of disagreement, but didn't challenge his authority. Semcken was there that morning, too, but it was Willard's show.[250]

Willard was as shining an example of an all-American as could be found in the 1980s. Athletic, with blond hair and penetrating blue eyes, he had played football at the Naval Academy and after graduating had become an aviator. He was a true master of the F-14, and was deployed multiple times to both the Western Pacific and North Arabian Sea before being tapped to lead the school that trained fighter pilots. He had a presence that engendered confidence and trust beyond the regard that came with his title. Part of it was that he genuinely listened to what people had to say, whether superiors, sailors, or movie crew, before he made a decision.

Willard talked of "Missions," rather than scenes, and how each one would be worked out in advance. Safety was key, as was following all Navy regulations. Then he turned the floor over to Clay Lacy, a pilot who had arrived at Miramar in his Learjet 25 outfitted with a rare camera system. He was hired to get footage of the F-14 and other jets in the air. Lacy had filmmaking experience, including as aerial coordinator on the James Bond movie *Octopussy* (1983). The commander was aware of that, but he also knew what he didn't know. "There was a learning curve to the flying," explained Willard. "We were being asked to fly into the frame of a camera, which we weren't accustomed to."[251]

Lacy was happy to share how it would work from his perspective. "This was military, and those guys are all formation pilots," he said. "It's not just getting out there to dogfight. You have to plan so we can film it." Lacy gave the example of one plane flying around another to get a shot. "Everyone knows how and when you're going to do that."[252] They would keep in close contact via radio.

The briefing lasted more than two hours. The pilots were in the air by 8:30 and back by 10:30, with a debriefing at 11. They broke for lunch and did it all again. This time the pilots were in the air from 5:30 or 6 p.m. to 7 or 7:30, depending on when they first took off. The briefings took on a pattern they would have for the rest of aerial photography.

After the first briefing it was decided that Scott and Willard would meet privately beforehand to go over the day. "I would tell him what I wanted, and he would tell me what the planes could do," Scott told an interviewer for a Paramount documentary on the movie.[253]

Willard, or another pilot, would take the storyboards drawn by Scott and the shot list provided by an aerial coordinator and diagram what could be done on the board. They also used miniature F-14s on long sticks for things that couldn't be effectively shown in two dimensions.[254]

Cameras were rolling that first day — they used about half the film of a typical day — but they didn't focus on any specific scenes. The most important thing was establishing a routine — a feel — for how shooting would work that made sense to everyone on the project.

Willard's assignment explicitly required that all Navy rules be followed, one of which was that all aircraft stay at least 500 feet apart in the air. But the filmmakers shot a head-on pass with an F-14 and F-5 and the dailies showed they couldn't follow the rule and get what they needed. "It was this great big screen — film, no sound — and way up in the corner of the screen, a little flicker of a plane," said Willard. It wasn't something a clever adjustment could fix. "Not even close."[255]

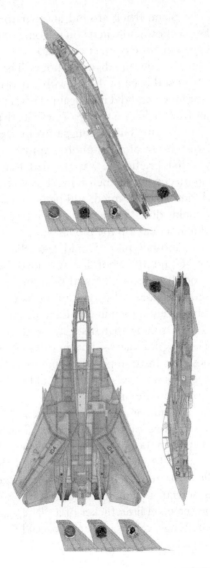

CREDIT: Matt Lawlor

Only one F-14 was equipped with externally mounted cameras, as shown here. Tail markings and canopy names were changed, depending on the scene.

Heatley had been one of the pilots in the air, and at the dailies. "It took a split second, and we were barely doing 300 knots, half of what you would normally do."[256] He said they knew they would have to reshoot it if they wanted to meaningfully get footage of the planes, which they did the following day.

In the interim, Willard went to see the admiral. Cassidy had kept a reasonable distance from the movie production, something that provided a degree of safety should things go awry, but he had received briefings. On this day Willard brought props — models that could demonstrate the issue — and told the admiral he believed he could safely conduct the close passes to get the movie production the shots it wanted.

"His instruction was direct: 'You do it,'" recalled Willard, "'but touch one plane to another and it's over.'"

Air-to-air
Day 41, 42: Aug. 13-14

The prep for the air-to-air shots had been incredibly time-consuming. Grumman, the defense contractor that designed the F-14, had signed off. It had taken a lot of time and effort to work out the technical and financial details of attaching cameras, but they'd done it.

A lot of people involved in the production were referred to as "aerial coordinators" in different ways and at different times. Two of them, Tom Harmon and Dick Stevens, were technical consultants and liaisons with Grumman, with Harmon focused on the mounts. Anything attached to the jets had to withstand the same forces as the jets, so they rigged specialized cameras instead of the Panavisions being used on the ground.

Bozo Abel was one of those named an aerial coordinator in the credits. Since helming the flyby at Miramar, he had been assigned responsibility for the F-14s used in the movie. In addition to flying, which he did a lot, it was his job to select, schedule and manage the aircraft. The plane he flew for the flyby — #104 — was the main one modified by Grumman to carry cameras. He called it the "camera bird."[257]

Lacy's Learjet 25 with its Astrovision system was called the "camera ship." The camera system dominated the aircraft. It was bolted at the centerline of the plane and filled the middle of it. While Lacy flew the jet, Nowell operated the camera system from a console set up in the back of the aircraft. It faced the camera system, which had periscopes that extended out several inches from the top and bottom of the aircraft. In addition to controlling the lenses in the periscopes, the operator had to control the movement of the system. It was able to get a 360-degree shot and could be panned left or right, or tilted up and down as much as 46 degrees, all by remote control. It also had a monitor, a major innovation at that time.[258]

"I don't remember a lot of the people [from *Top Gun*], but I remember Scott," said Lacy. "He rode along with us" in the Learjet. The pilot recalled the director having some suggestions in the air, "and I'd have to tell him to be quiet. It's not a deal where you make last-minute changes," he said. But it went smoothly. "Tony Scott was a very successful guy, but as far as aerial shots, he didn't have any experience with it. He understood that. He was a good guy."[259]

Kimball sat in the jump seat near Lacy, who piloted the plane. Scott sat next to Nowell so he could see the monitor, which showed what the camera captured. Greg Schmidt, the camera assistant, changed seats depending on whether they were shooting from the periscope on the top of the aircraft or below it. They couldn't operate both at once, and the equipment had to be shifted based on vantage point.

The only downside to Lacy, as far as the production was concerned, was that he was expensive — a prime example of the law of supply and demand. "Nobody had ever seen this camera system," said Nowell. "We were the only ones who could do this kind of thing."[260] But it didn't change the budget limitations of *Top Gun*. The only way to manage it was to use the Astrovision system as little as possible. That meant two days at Miramar and a similar period in Fallon.

The technology wasn't a secret to the industry. Lacy worked closely with Continental Cameras Systems, which had won two special Oscars from the Academy of Motion Picture Arts and Sciences for the technology. The first was in 1977 for the Periscope Aerial Camera System, and the other was in 1982 for the development of a pitching lens for motion picture photography.[261] But the system wasn't available for commercial use in 1985.

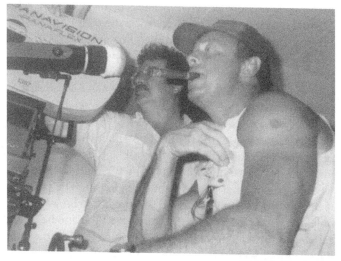

PHOTO: Greg Schmidt

Tony Scott and Jeff Kimball inside Lacy's Learjet with Astrovision system.

The high-performance Learjet — Lacy built the Astrovision system in it in 1975 and Nowell had been working with him since — was an outstanding delivery system. The plane could comfortably travel at 250 knots, or 287 miles an hour, which made it a favorite with the business class. Its stability also translated to smooth camera shots and the ability to pace F-14s at up to 250 knots.

The record speed of an F-14 is 1,544 miles per hour and they were typically flying half that, but it was still a blur. "We generally flew lower, closer and slower than we were comfortable with, or used to, in order to capture some of what Tony wanted on film," Willard said.[262]

The last two days of flying at Miramar looked like the opposite of the first. This time they shot cuts — pieces of film used by editors in post-production to transition between sequences — that covered a lot of material. They continued to refer to the organized efforts to get footage as missions. Mission 3 broadly covered Scenes 1 through 46B while Mission 4 captured cuts for Scenes 158 through 172. Missions 5 and 6, the following day, had the same purpose.[263]

In the mix was capturing an F-14 flying upside down. An important scene early on has Maverick and Goose flying inverted in an encounter with a MiG, which Goose snaps a picture of with a Polaroid. It shows the characters are rebels and stellar aviators.

It was also out of the realm of possibility, which irked the Navy guys. Technically it was possible for an F-14 to fly inverted, but it wasn't something they would do and they would never be that close to another aircraft. The pilots — increasingly comfortable around the director, who was in *their* milieu — told him as much. Scott revived the line he'd used earlier in production: He wasn't making a documentary. Pilots would sometimes restate it to each other: "He isn't making a documentary."

At the same time, their biggest booster was Scott. "Tony loved the pilots — loved them," Badalato said. "Authenticity was a big part of what he was after, and these were the guys."[264]

The dominant feeling was camaraderie. Sharon Mann, who was bumped up to 1st AD for the air-to-air sequences after having to sit out the carrier work, noted a mutual respect. "They were impressed with us, and we were impressed with them," she said.[265]

186

"Most of the crew hadn't been exposed to the military," explained Badalato, "and vice versa." Initially there was novelty to it, but they got to know each other, and how they worked, quickly with the intensity of the shooting schedule. "There was a mutual admiration society between the crew and Navy."

"I was impressed with the movie production," said Abel. "They were very well prepared."

On to Fallon
Day 43-53: Aug. 15-25

In 1985, Fallon was a distinctly Nevadan town. It featured the Nugget Casino and Stockman's Bar, Restaurant and Casino, along with smaller stores and a Dairy Queen, Bob's Root Beer Drive In, and Kent's Supply Center, the oldest retailer in Nevada. The town lies 60 miles east of Reno and at that time had a population of 4,680, while Churchill County had 15,029, according to numbers provided by the town library.[266]

Fallon Naval Air Station provided the lion's share of opportunity. The total on-base population in 1985 was 1,345, with 780 of them military personnel, according to a spokesman.

Things had been well-prepped for the crew. Peters had overseen the delivery of production vehicles to Fallon; a camera truck, a station wagon, two crew cabs, and two maxis, which were trailers that could pull whatever they needed.[267] The Navy brought additional equipment, which would vary day to day in terms of what was on the production report. The first day the Navy had three vans and a station wagon, two helicopters, two F-14s, and three F-5s.[268]

Baron found a hotel for them that had space for dailies, hired set security, and found some rental cars. "I had my hands in everything," he said. That included some props work in Fallon. "They needed to paint the names on the jet of the pilots, their call signs," Baron said, "but we couldn't find the painter." So Baron and Wade, with approval from

Badalato, broke into the painter's box. "We got spray paint and decals, got onto the flight range, and painted the jets ourselves."[269] Wade had brought the decals prepared by the art department.

There are always surprises in shooting on location, and every movie is a little different for a 1st AD, but this was a lot different. Mann, the only woman there, wasn't working with typical locations or sets or scenes. It was heavy on camera, grip and electric, and much lighter in other departments, but it was still up to her to manage Scott, the crew and the paperwork. Here, she also had to operate within the dynamic presented by the Navy. While the Navy had largely blended into the movie production during the ground story, it dominated the work in Fallon, as it had on the aircraft carrier. "Was it a boy's club in Fallon? Sure, but it was actually a lot of fun. I kept my head down."[270]

Something else emerged when they got to Fallon. The Air Force had loaned its Cine-Sextant tracking system to their efforts.[271] Although a memo had circulated about it in prep, no one on the camera side seemed to know much about it. The new technology was potentially a big boost for the production. It contained a rack of six to eight cameras with powerful telephoto lenses and a recording system. The console and operator station were contained in the mount, which would tilt with the lenses so far the operator could be almost parallel to the horizon. They just had to sort out how to use the system.

Overall they had settled into Fallon quickly, thanks to the three-day warm up at Miramar. There was no morning mission Aug. 15, which meant the first briefing wasn't until 2 p.m.[272] When they returned to the skies, the routine was re-established.

Throughout photography, Scott had awoken early, well ahead of the call time, to work on storyboards. He got up even earlier in Fallon to be prepared for his meeting with Willard, according to his assistant.[273] It was a series of back-and-forth exchanges between them. "Tony was a visualist, a good one," said Willard. "He liked things back-lit, early morning or late in the afternoon. There were certain sun angles he wanted. So, we would have to shift the directions we were coming from to get those lighting angles he became so famous for."[274] Lighting was something easily accomplished, but there were things he wanted that just couldn't be done.

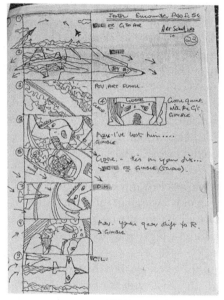

Tony Scott was a prolific storyboard artist. With these drawings he was showing what he wanted to capture with the death of Goose.

PHOTO: Chelsey Schaffeld

Included in the mix was a flight plan and shot list done by Stevens. He had been introduced to the movie through his ties to Grumman, but had taken on a much more active role with the production office. His flight plan was based on Scott's storyboards with an eye toward making the aerial photography also reflect an efficient use of resources. Stevens wasn't a pilot, but as an engineer he had a deep understanding of what the equipment could do in concert with the jets, and he had experience working with the military.[275]

His efforts aligned with those of Badalato in terms of staying on budget. He complained that cuts for Scenes 158-172 had been shot over several days instead of one. He made the point that broadly shooting dozens of scenes wasn't the same thing as getting down what was needed for four key scenes. He also wanted them to use the Cine-Sextant tracking system more.

Stevens' grumbling about redundancy and repetition didn't endear him to Scott, and increasingly the director listened less. Crew picked up on things like that. They liked and admired the director, and followed him easily.

All of that was happening in the background of the briefings with the larger group. "The meetings were very professional," said Mann. They would break everything down, in detail. "They'd talk about which planes and what angles, and where the cameras would be, and how fast they would go, and who would do what," she said.[276]

"It was show time," said Badalato, who would pop into briefings, although he didn't necessarily sit through them. "I just remember their hands were in the air showing maneuvers. One hand would be a plane flying, and the other a chase plane. "The pilots brought their best to the table, wanting to help."[277]

There was energy to the briefings, but they were serious, recalled Larry Blanford, an aerial camera operator who had taken leave from the U.S. Air Force to work on the movie. "They were run by Rat Willard, and they were set up like a military briefing, with military instructions."[278] The exception was the last briefing of the day, which was more relaxed.

The meetings weren't necessarily small, said Blanford, who was on his first film and would go on to a career as a director of photography. "There would be as many as 30, 40 people, movie crew and pilots, camera assistants, camera operators, flight crew — four planes, and two for every one of those." There were also pilot briefings, which were smaller.

Blanford was part of a second camera unit that also included Gary Tolbert, George Leahy, Nick Alvarado, and

William Kelly. "We came on the movie way late, non-union. That was the delineation."[279] Scott sought them out expressly for their military camera experience.

But even with military training there were limitations to what anyone could do with a heavy circa-1985 film camera under the influence of G-force. A human on a walk is operating at 1-G, or a force equal to their weight. Get in a vehicle and drive fast and that increases. An extreme example would be a Formula 1 race car driver moving at an extremely high speed who brakes suddenly and might experience 5-Gs, or a force equal to five times their weight. That was a normal experience for a fighter pilot, and not just for a few seconds. That's what they mean when they say they are "pulling Gs."

"My very first mission, I am sitting in the back of a plane and they hand me a 35mm camera with a 6x6 graduation filter taped over it," said Blanford, "I shoot 16mm." As a member of the Air Force, he was acutely aware of the eject lever in the backseat, which wouldn't be accessible with the equipment. When pulling Gs there was a physical pressure powerful enough that it became difficult to move an arm to pull a lever, much less shoot film.

"I went, 'Sir? It can be so violent in the back of a fighter jet. These guys aren't photo pilots. They'll break to your right at three Gs and your head will bounce off the canopy." All the same, Blanford said he'd do it, but he also warned them: "I don't think the camera's coming back."

He got one shot with it using the graduated filter, which he thought was a shot of the faux MiG. "Then the camera broke away. They had to pull the seat to get every piece of glass," he said.[280]

"To that point, movies about aviation had all been done a certain way," Scott told an interviewer later. "I was trying to do something different."[281]

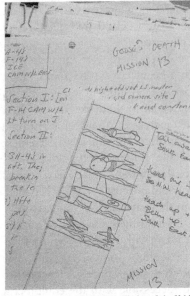

Production reports during aerial photography often had attachments that included Tony Scott's storyboards for the day and planning notes of aerial consultant Dick Stevens.

PHOTO: Chelsey Schaffeld

Ground-to-air

Despite all the effort to capture scenes air-to-air, it was good, old-fashioned camera work on the ground that was getting the best footage.

Sorting out where to put the cameras took considerable effort given the terrain of the northern Nevada desert, Mann related. The production used two helicopters but for the most part transported crew and equipment in vans. The helicopters weren't military; they were noted in production reports as the "Llama Hilo" and the "Hughes Hilo," based on the makers, Lama and Hughes.[282] "The jets could fly 100 miles in a half a minute, so there were huge distances we had to travel to get the cameras set up," said Mann. "By Jeep it could be a couple of hours — and there were no roads. It was just wilderness."[283]

The main purpose of the helicopter was to scout locations and transport crew. "It was a crazy helicopter, flown by, like, a bush pilot with a wild mustache," recalled

Mann. "They would fly ahead and the crew would follow on the ground, bouncing all over on Jeeps. We would find them." They could usually manage issues that arose, as when the Lama helicopter had an oil blowout. It was only down an hour before they had it fixed.

Sometimes it took hours to get to the new location. Mann remembered one day when they stopped after a few hours for a meeting. "There were two or three vans. It was a lot of camera people and me." She had to go to the bathroom and looked around for somewhere appropriate. "There wasn't a tree anywhere, just a lot of tumbleweeds." She had her pants down when she heard the helicopter. "I'm peeing, and the helicopter is overhead!" Mann figured the best thing to do was to stand up, pants at her ankles. "I gave them a big wave," she said. "With Tony you were balls out. That's the way it was."

The best location was a 4,000-foot precipice in the northwest portion of the range, which Scott and Kimball discovered while scouting in the helicopter. It was stunning, huge rock pinnacles above the Carson Dry Sink, all of it with wide-open sky. The best part was there were places to set up cameras where they could be eye level with the jets, at least for a few seconds as they roared by. The intrepid crew transported all the equipment up the mountain.

"You really don't achieve a true sense of how fast they fly when you're moving alongside them air-to-air," Kimball told American Cinematographer magazine. "But when you're static shooting with a 1600mm lens, and the object comes straight at you, you get an incredible sense of how fast they really travel."[284]

Once they got the traditional cameras in place and ready, they would sit and talk and wait for the planes. Scott was incredibly enthusiastic, and imaginative, and it was inspiring to the camera crew, said Nowell, who would go on to work with Scott on almost every project he did.[285]

One conversation with the director on the mountain stands out most to Nowell. The director described his vision for the dogfight scene, where the planes are in combat. He described a sort of choreography. It might be that the A-4 Skyhawk made up as the bad guy would be on the tail of the F-14 Tomcat, and the Navy pilot would make a brilliant maneuver. "He wanted it to be like the *Rocky* fight sequence, with music to drive it," he said. The *Rocky* (1976) sequence was famously written out, blow by blow. For *Top Gun*, the visuals, with the music — which Scott told him Bruckheimer was getting — would be enough to tell the story.

The Cine-Sextant camera tracking system on loan from the Air Force was an impressive piece of technology, particularly for 1985. It had the look of military equipment; two giant white cannon telescopes, parallel-mounted on a rotating turret, sitting atop an industrial mobile trailer, sprung on four motorized jacks. Stable, powerful and nimble, it was state of the art. Unfortunately, its weight of over six tons made it difficult to get it to the more remote shooting locations. It wasn't turning out to be much use to the production, a source of frustration for Stevens.

They were kept busy enough shooting the movie the way they knew how to do it. There were four cameras on the ground working constantly, usually together, Nowell said. As the days went by, the footage got better and more usable, according to the editors who were reviewing it.

Then an incident brought new importance to Stevens' perspective.

A dangerously close call

The camera crew was atop one of the highest perches they had found on Aug. 17 when there was a near miss.

"We went up on top of the mountain and split up so they could do rolls," said Semcken, who was with the camera crew. His job was on the radio to communicate with pilots, who were used to flying at high altitudes and didn't have a lot of visibility below. It was out of the norm so even instrumentation wasn't helpful.

"I was telling them, start the maneuvers, full power, afterburner, pull back," and the pilots did what he said, until one didn't. "I was saying pull back, pull back, PULL BACK!" The pilot did it just in time, clearing the mountain by only 30 feet. "Yes, it was that close," Semcken said.

They could see the afterburners, and the jet blast was so powerful it knocked everything over, equipment crashing to the ground. If they had been closer to the edge of the precipice, "it would have blown us over the side," Semcken said.[286]

"In the movie you see it kind of stall, like it's standing there in the air," said cameraman Greg Schmidt, who was there. "Then the afterburners hit. What you don't see at 120 frames is all the beach chairs and cameras and water coolers flying up in the air when the plane leaves."[287]

It had scared everyone, including Semcken. Then he got mad. "Everything we did was by the book. One thing like that, we have an airplane crash, and a bunch of people die? That's the end of the movie, which is the least of it."

The incident made it onto Stevens' handwritten memo dated Aug. 19.[288] Stevens noted that Scott had changed all the briefed headings for the morning mission on Aug. 17, so pilots prepared for one thing but ended up doing something different. It "even put the pilots over high hills, often flying blind into the camera," wrote Stevens. "One near miss was noted by Cmd. Willard."

Willard had been in the air when it happened, but on the radio, and he shut the shoot down. They had been "continuously driving the airplanes where they had to maneuver to miss a hill. There came a point when an airplane came too close. It just wasn't safe, so that was it." The pilot was sent home, but wasn't written up, because it hadn't happened as part of his Naval duties.[289]

The production report for Aug. 17 noted that the day's second mission was scrubbed, too, "due to storm conditions."[290]

The Aug. 18 production report included a note about a dead battery on the Hughes helicopter, the crew transport vehicle, which required that a second helicopter fly out to charge the battery.[291] But the helicopter was still having battery problems the next day, and this time it stranded crew. They called the Navy, which sent out a search-and-rescue helicopter. It picked up the main group by 8 p.m., and got to the crew farther up the mountain about 25 minutes later.

"The Hughes Hilo started but was unable to airlift the last two people from the mountain due to complete darkness," according to the PR. A four-wheel-drive vehicle was "dispatched up the trail and met the stranded crew. All arrived at the hotel safely at 11:30 p.m."[292]

They didn't fly on Aug. 20.

Stevens delivered a memo Aug. 20 with a list of things that should be done going forward. Some of it reiterated what had been agreed upon the first day, others addressed what had happened without stating it explicitly. He wrote that the director and aerial coordinator needed to arrive at "absolute agreement about the mission details," and that those details then be worked out with "Rat, Bozo, Clay Lacy, and Dk Stv" before the pilot briefing, the latter an abbreviation for himself. He also noted that the radio operator should be "thoroughly rehearsed on comms + flying sequences before launch." The memo was put in a file for safekeeping and doesn't appear to have been distributed.[293] Stevens died in 2019.

No one needed to tell Willard that Scott's ideas had to be managed. He'd already had an encounter with the director to straighten things out. One day they were trying to shadow and capture an A4 passing overhead. "That had to be done at very low altitudes," said Willard. "The F-14 had a radar altimeter. The A4 did not."[294]

Willard knew the jet wash from the F-14 was "the real thing" from experience. He had flown into the F-14's jet wash. It turned his A4 sideways "and spit me out several hundred feet, very abrupt and unexpected." He also knew what it was like to fly at low altitude and feel the exhaust under his jet.

"Tony Scott was radioing me to go closer and lower. I said, no. Stay safe. I was as close to that jet wash as I could safely get and shoot his scene."

Willard summed up the experience by referencing a call he received from a military coordinator on another movie. They wanted to know how to liaise with Hollywood. The aviator, who became an admiral and led the Pacific command before he retired, said he was candid. "I told him there is a tension between what the director is going to want and what the aviators can give," and that he had personally bumped up against it.[295]

"You have to say, "No, move the set. No, we won't go any closer to that.""

Although it's not clear if Stevens' memo was circulated, his concerns were shared. The near catastrophe vindicated Stevens, whose safety cautions up to this point had been casually ignored by Scott when they ran contrary to the director's "vision." From this point forward, when Stevens expressed safety concerns, either at the briefing with the pilots or after the briefing at the ground-to-air shoots, Scott listened.

Critical air sequence
Day 49-51: Aug. 21-23

Clay Lacy came to Fallon for several days starting Aug. 21. That day he was intent on capturing footage to illustrate the accident that kills Goose. Maverick loses control of the F-14 as the result of backwash created by Iceman's F-14.[296]

Mission 13 is a good example of how they prepped for the scenes in flight. Scott's drawings of it showed two aircraft flying next to each other, one plane shown from the front heading northwest and another from the rear heading southeast. A fourth frame showed two planes flying with slightly different headings.

Stevens' shot list incorporated three A-4s and two F-14s and detailed what Lacy and Nowell would capture in the Learjet. Years later, a cameraman would assume it was Scott's list, because his recollection was that Stevens, persona non grata to some on the crew, since he bugged Scott, didn't know enough to have penned it. The handwriting, however, clearly matches that other notes handwritten by Stevens.

The shot list broke the shoot into three sections. Section 1 was en route to the new ground camera site. Lacy was to shoot high to get an offset, long-shot master. That is the shot that forms the basis for the larger scene, in this case, capturing all the planes in the air. There was an F-14 with a camera mount that would fly and turn left to capture Ice's aircraft next to an A4.

Section 2 was over the ground site. That had the three A4s in tactical formation with the two F-14s chasing behind. "They fly head-on to site with 2 A4s breaking up and out while the F4 chase the lead directly over the site." Another said the "A-4 chased by F-14s fly 360s in front of camera site."

One thing they weren't trying to get was a flat spin. Maverick loses control after jet wash from Ice's F-14 cuts off air to one engine. With it stalled, and the other engine going full throttle, the plane pulls sharply in that direction. It's so sudden it sends the aircraft into a flat spin, like a plate. The story was based on a real problem that happened with the aircraft. It was so dangerous that it had to be depicted using mock-ups, special effects, and plate footage.

Separately, Lacy recommended a pilot they could hire to get the plate footage.[297] Art Scholl Aviation was already well known in the industry. Scholl was hired and would work independently.

Last days in Fallon
Day 52, 53: Aug. 24-25

Chris Lebenzon had joined Weber in the editing offices at Paramount at the end of the ground story. They worked in

Building 10, each in their own office hunched over KEM editing machines, scanning for the best footage and manually splicing it together. The flatbed editing machine, invented in Germany 50 years earlier, had improved over the years to meet the evolving demands of film editors. It could manage and synchronize film and sound reels at the same time, handle more film, and do it faster than the once ubiquitous Moviola, which was rapidly headed toward retirement.[298]

The film editing software that would revolutionize the process was still years away. "In film you had to remember [the best takes], and roll down manually on a flatbed to find the shot," said Lebenzon. "It was a lot of leaning over and threading, but it allowed you time to think about what you were going to do."[299]

Once the movie wrapped, they would be at the head of the creative organizational chart, with direction from Scott and the producers. By now they'd had a good look at the aerial photography coming in, and they were concerned. While there was great stuff, there wasn't enough of it. One thing they knew they needed was another shot of the flyby, which they relayed to producers.

"They came to me in a panic and said they had to have it," recalled pilot Abel, who had flown the first tower flyby at Miramar. He was in Fallon both flying and overseeing the F-14s. The shots that were usable included the approach to the tower but not a long view, they told him. As fancy as the close-to-the-ground flying looked, Abel said, "any fighter pilot was capable of flying that scene."[300]

At the time of the request, he had in the air an F-14 piloted by Lt. Scott "Dancing Bear" Altman, a future NASA space shuttle astronaut. Abel coordinated the shot between the tower chief and Altman, then called Scott on the UHF radio. The director was up on the mountain with the crew. Nowell remembers gathering up equipment. "We got a tripod, cables, battery, and a completely rigged camera," he said. He and Scott got in the helicopter and flew back to Fallon "as fast as we could," Nowell cradling the camera in his lap. As soon as they got to the base they unloaded, "Tony set up the camera" and got the shot.[301]

Willard recalled the last day in Fallon, as they were making plans to leave. He was starting to think about his regular job on base, and some instruction work ahead. "Bozo was sending the F-14s back to Miramar," and it was all winding down.

They set the cameras up on the hill beside the cliff for the last time. "There was an almost vertical drop several thousand feet into the desert, and to the east were the rock formations. But the plateau terminated into that drop." The cameras were set up at the edge of the dropoff, where they could see the planes flying up through the canyon. "I had to fly at low altitude near the camera, and spill out over several thousand feet of airspace past the cliff."

Willard was in the brown A-4 and Bozo was flying the F-14 with the camera mounts. Ben Schneider was flying the third aircraft. "Tony finally ran out of storyboards," Willard said, and he asked the pilots if they had anything they wanted to show them.[302]

"We spent the final day flying, doing a lot of things: verticals, loops, scissors, rolls, and we were flying low passes over the cameras." That's when they did the pitch pulse with the F-14. That's where the pilot is flying at a fixed speed and suddenly pulls the stick back toward his lap, sending the jet skyward. The jet would roar at full power, which meant they were pulling 6.5Gs, "the training limit," Willard said.

"It was the first time Tony had seen it," he said. "He wanted that to be the flagship maneuver of Maverick."

Expensive

All of it was costing money. Movie production accounting is unlike almost any other business. Most companies take in money, and deduct expenses, to determine profit. A movie budget starts with a number and subtracts as money is spent. Cost reports are regularly prepared.

The original memo estimating hourly costs of operating various aircraft, sent in May by the Comptroller of the Navy, had formed the basis for the budget for air-to-air photography. The initial memo hadn't included the F-14, but it had since determined the hourly cost of its operation at $7,600. After totaling that, along with other figures like the fees they would pay Lacy, the budget was set at $900,000.[303]

Every day the production worked, Badalato prepared a cost report that incorporated which aircraft went up, for how long. The Navy did the same thing. Both were thorough, and on the Navy side, with forethought that it could easily withstand an audit. Then Badalato deducted that figure from the total budget. A copy went to the studio.

Maguire hadn't come with them to Fallon or to San Diego or on the carriers. But he was paying attention from his office at Paramount.

Lacy's Learjet

The contract for Lacy's "Learjet Model 25 Photo Aircraft" reflected a charge of $1,250 per hour, with a four-hour minimum per day, or $5,000. That didn't cover his personal services, which were based on the SAG rate for a daily stunt pilot, or overnight expenses, or per diem. The contract also increased Lacy's insurance from $25 million to $100 million, at Paramount's expense.

Camera ship

Clay Lacy was known to the movie industry for several reasons. He had launched the first jet charter operation on the West Coast and by 1981 was the world's first all-jet, fixed-base operator, or FBO. His service assured both safety and comfort for a clientele that included movie stars, producers and studio executives. It enabled them to move around for business or whim with ease, which contributed to the growth of the company. Clay Lacy Aviation would double its footprint at Van Nuys Airport by 1984.

Another was his connection to the development of aerial camera systems.

Consumers had been seeing footage of airliners soaring through the sky in television ads for years without understanding what it took to get those shots or how dangerous it was.

Pan Am World Airways was among the first, with a 1969 advertisement promoting the brand-new 747.

The spot featured a plane with the Pan Am logo moving across the screen, accompanied by a calming male voiceover. "Chances are you've heard about the plane with the spiral staircase in First Class, the plane with the two wide aisles and three wide-screen movies and the eight-foot ceilings in economy," the melodic voice says with just a trace of pride. "And chances are you've wondered: Who's going to get this incredible bird off the ground? Now you know, Pan Am will bring you the world's first 747."

John Carroll and Ernst "Bob" Nettmann, both from England, were behind shots like that, generally from older planes with open fuselage. They worked to get footage for British Airways, which was in fierce competition with Pan Am and wanted to promote its own fleet of 747s. Sometime in 1971 they were flying in a B-25 to get footage of 747s on the ground when things went awry. The World War II-era aircraft "lost one of its two engines, had an on-board fire, missed hitting the hangar housing the 747 by 15 feet, and then forced another 747 off the runway in its emergency landing."

Carroll relayed the story, which had happened about six years prior, to the Los Angeles Times in 1977. "We knew then that there had to be a better way, a safer way to film this stuff than out of the bomb bay of a B-25," he said.

They formed a company called Continental Camera Systems in 1972 to build a camera mount for helicopters. In 1974 they began working on technology the industry was using called Astro-Vision, now widely known as Astrovision. "We used Clay Lacy's Learjet exclusively and 95 percent of the time he is the one flying it because the work requires a lot of formation experience."

"We really revolutionized air-to-air photography," Lacy said.

In the same Los Angeles Times story in 1977, Carroll had praised Lacy's skill beyond his knowledge of formation flying. He was a former air racer, a military fighter pilot, and a United Airlines captain. "If the pilot were anyone other than Clay, I'd say there were risks, chances involved, but not with him."

Nowell, camera crew working with Kimball on *Top Gun*, is also quoted in the then eight-year-old story. He said flying with Lacy was akin to "walking down the street with your best friend. You're certainly not afraid they're going to push you in front of a car."

Chapter 9 - Endnotes

[248] Daily Production Reports, August 12-26, 1985. TGC.

[249] Call Sheet, August 12, 1985. TGC.

[250] Semcken, November 5, 2020.

[251] Willard, December 2, 2020.

[252] Clay Lacy, aviation consultant for *Top Gun*. Interview with author, April 22, 2021

[253] *Danger Zone: The Making of Top Gun.*

[254] Ibid.

[255] Willard, December 2, 2020.

[256] Heatley, December 1, 2020.

[257] Abel, November 27, 2020.

[258] Lacy, April 22, 2021.

[259] Ibid.

[260] Nowell, September 27, 2021.

[261] Nettmann Systems International website. History, Awards, and Memberships. http://nettmannsystems.com/about-nsi/history-awards-and-memberships/

[262] Willard, December 2, 2020.

[263] Daily Production Reports, August 13-14, 1985. TGC.

[264] Badalato, January 26, 2020.

[265] Mann, August 9, 2020.

[266] Research assistance provided by Carol Lloyd, Director, Churchill County Library. Interview with the author, August 5, 2020.

[267] Peters, August 3, 2021.

[268] Daily Production Report, "First Day in Fallon." August 15, 1985. TGC.

[269] Baron, April 5, 2021.

[270] Mann, August 9, 2020.

[271] "The Cine-Sextant serves as a support system mounting of cameras or any electro-optical devices used in target tracking and data acquisition." Cine-Sextant Mobile Tracking System, Photo-Sonics. Inc. website, accessed October 19, 2021.https://www.photosonics.com/cine-sextant.htm

[272] Call Sheet, August 15, 1985. TGC.

[273] Knell, April 18, 2020.

[274] Willard, December 2, 2020.

[275] Badalato, January 26, 2020.

[276] Mann, August 9, 2020.

[277] Badalato, January 26, 2020.

[278] Larry Blanford, aerial camera operator for *Top Gun*. Interview with author, August 12, 2020.

[279] Ibid.

[280] Ibid.

[281] Daily Production Reports, August 15-25, 1985. TGC

[282] Daily Production Reports, August 15-25, 1985. TGC.

[283] Mann, August 9, 2020.

[284] Robley, "Flying High With Top Gun."

[285] Nowell, September 27, 2021.

[286] Semcken, November 5, 2020.

[287] Greg Schmidt, first assistant camera operator for *Top Gun*. Interview with the author, May 13, 2020.

[288] Richard Stevens. Incident memo, August 19, 1985. TGC.

[289] Willard, December 2, 2020.

[290] Daily Production Report, August 17, 1985. TGC.

[291] Daily Production Report, August 18, 1985. TGC.

[292] Ibid.

[293] Richard Stevens. Memo to file, procedures for remaining aerial cinematography. August 20, 1985.

[294] Willard, December 2, 2020.

[295] Ibid.

[296] Daily Production Reports and in some cases, attached Shot Lists, August 21-23, 1985.

[297] Lacy, April 22, 2021.

[298] Steven Ascher and Edward Pincus. *The Filmmaker's Handbook* (New York: Penguin, 2007). From an excerpt of the 3rd Edition, Chapter 15. https://westcityfilms.com/wp-content/uploads/2015/03/Filmmakers_Handbook-3rd-Ed_editing_film-plus.pdf.

[299] Chris Lebenzon, film editor for *Top Gun*. Interview with the author, March 20, 2021.

[300] Abel, November 27, 2020.

[301] Nowell, September 27, 2021.

[302] Willard, December 2, 2020.

[303] Badalato, January 26, 2020.

CHAPTER 10
RESHOOTS, DANGER, EFX
SEPT. 6-MID OCTOBER

Day 53-59: Sept. 6-16

Throughout photography, the daily production report — the summary of everything that happened that day along with an overview of consolidated info for all shooting days — had left a void under a section on the form that read, "Est. Finish Date." It read "1985." After Labor Day weekend it got more specific.

That weekend, while the rest of the production company was shut down, Scott, Weber and Lebenzon went to work at their offices in Building 10, known at the time as the Scoring Stage. It was home to Studio M, for music, and ADR, or audio dialogue replacement, along with editing offices. By now the *Top Gun* production had five offices there, and neighbors that included editors at work on the television shows "Cheers" and then brand-new "MacGyver."[304]

None of them were working that end-of-summer holiday weekend, and the Paramount lot was quiet as they settled in. The director and the editors huddled in front of a KEM flatbed editing machine. What they were looking through that weekend didn't include sound. Their focus was making sense of the footage captured in Fallon. Screens on the equipment were relatively small, perhaps 12 by 18 inches. There hadn't been a script supervisor in Fallon, but even the information on the PRs was meaningless to them. For that matter, their previous planning was irrelevant.

Most of the footage was "unusable," said Weber, and with more than 114,000 feet, there was a lot of it. "We'd see a shot and say 'okay, that's for this scene,' and set it aside," he recalled. They spent the entire holiday weekend culling through it, noting where the usable clips were in the reels. They pieced together what story could be told with the material at hand. They would build from there.[305]

Reshoots, retakes, pickups

The production company shut down from Aug. 27 to Sept. 3, but when the crew resumed work that Tuesday, there was a plan in place for what scenes needed to be revisited in San Diego. At the end of the day, the paperwork named an estimated finish date of Sept. 27. It was the first precise date on the PR.[306]

They had three days to prepare for seven days of photography, during which more than a dozen scenes would be revisited, and two added. The crew was smaller than it had been before, the catering department serving just 45 lunches a day, but it was an intensive effort. Most of the days were at Miramar, but they also returned to Charlie's house for a full day and to Kansas City Barbeque.

While paperwork referred to the work as "reshoots," Weber said it was more accurately retakes, where they would improve on dialogue or some aspect of a scene, rather than reshooting entire scenes, or pickups, where they added shots to fill out the story, including for a montage, where short pieces of film are edited together to expand and advance the story.[307]

Each day they covered a lot of ground. The day they resumed shooting, the first of two Fridays, was a return to the locker room at Miramar, including the famous scene where Iceman tells Maverick he's dangerous, and another where Iceman tells him he was sorry about Goose, and that everyone had liked him.

One scene just required Cruise and Edwards. They returned to the airport set where Carole and her son arrived to visit Goose, but the part they redid didn't require Meg Ryan. The focus was on the lead-in and the dialogue between Maverick and Goose as she approaches.[308]

A number of the scenes or portions of scenes they filmed never made it into the film, as is typical. One clip that didn't make the cut had Maverick walking around a jet and seeing Iceman's name. Meanwhile, away from the plane, Viper and Stinger are watching, and Viper tells Stinger to keep sending Maverick up, which did get in. Most of the cast came in at some time during the week. Several days included Rossovich, Edwards, Hubley and Tubb.[309]

A group returned to Kansas City Barbeque midweek. Scott had told the Blairs the day they shot the dive bar scenes that he wanted to return, and Baron followed up. "They told us they were going to film the last scene at the original officers club but liked our place. We closed the restaurant for half a day this time," said Blair.[310] Shooting the scene took a couple of hours, and it was just Cruise, McGillis, and a bartender on camera.

The Ninja and the F-14

Thursday they captured the scene where Maverick drag races the F-14, one of the most famous scenes in the movie.

R. A. Rondell had worked on the movie off and on throughout the run of photography. He also was working on a television show in Los Angeles, and would come down on the weekends or as needed to coordinate and participate in stunts. He had coordinated the scene where Charlie chases Maverick, also driving in it. This time he was on the schedule for 3-7 p.m., the block of time that included Scott's magic hour.

The Navy made an F-14, and a pilot, available and blocked out airtime for the scene. The movie production set up a base on a dirt road near the fence of the runways, while the cameras were closer. One vehicle was set up as a pace car so a camera operator could get footage of the motorcycle and F-14. They all waited for the magic hour.[311]

"We worked it out with the pilot going the other way, where he'd bank a turn, and I would take off, grabbing gears, all the flashing marker lights on my left," recalled Rondell. He needed a running start, and a PA set up more than a mile at the top of an embankment next to the tarmac. The stuntman drove up there to wait. "It definitely wasn't flat," he recalled. "It was a dirt road with a bunch of mounds, rollers and hoop-de-doos." One crew, with Scott and the cameras, coordinated with them using walkie-talkies. Another crew coordinated with the pilot.

When he was given the cue, Rondell started down the road on the Ninja. It took the full mile to build speed. "Tony was cuing me, and I would get through all that, to get onto the runway." He had done motocross, so he was skilled in off-road motorcycle racing.

It was exhilarating for the young stuntman. "I remember hearing that jet coming from behind me. He would go right over the top of me, doing touch-and-goes." Rondell spoke of the feel of the jet wash from behind, hitting his back and blowing him forward on the bike. "Then he would touch down and it would blast me from the other way."

He was still catching his breath when it was time to go again. "Then Tony was, 'Cut! Cut! Back to one!' And I would race back as quickly as I could get there." Scott was revved up, too. "He wanted two to three rounds, fast. He wanted it just right. Tony was all fired up, 'Go, man, go!' Not yelling at you but the intensity was pretty high." It all happened in a condensed period, perhaps 30 minutes, although with his heart pounding it felt like 15. Drag racing the F-14 was "thrilling."

"How fun is it to drag race fighter jets down the runway at Miramar, and to have permission to go fast? Electric! With Tony Scott and Tom, and all the stuff going on?" he said. "Very electric." A long career of movies and television later, Rondell still remembers *Top Gun* as one of his favorite gigs.

The final major effort in terms of set rebuilds was the last day, a Friday, when they returned to Charlie's house. It was a smaller crew than had been there the first time, but still nearly four dozen people. They redid portions of the dinner date, where Maverick apologizes for being late and Charlie insists it isn't necessary. McGillis was wrapped by midafternoon, her work on the movie finished.

Cruise stayed, and when the lighting was right, Scott and the crew went to the beach to get shots of him riding the motorcycle. In the months since his first lessons on a bike, he'd learned a lot, and he loved it. They got him riding in the sunset.

Famous flyer

Scholl gets the Chipmunk up to peak altitude… and stalls the engine. With red, white and blue smoke pouring from the wings, he starts a free fall toward earth—rolling, sliding, twisting and looping his way down. So far, he's always pulled out to fly and teach another day.[312]

— John Hall, Sports Columnist, Los Angeles Times, Oct. 25, 1968

Art Scholl began prepping his lightweight aerobatic biplane for work on *Top Gun* on Sept. 9 at his hangar at the Rialto Airport. His job for *Top Gun* was to get footage that would go behind the actors seated in cockpit sets for a process called rear screen projection. The moving clouds and blue sky would make the scenes that much more realistic.

Prep that day had involved readying the Pitts S-2 plane for movie work. The main task was fixing the camera to the backseat and connecting a remote control device to the pilot's seat. The placement was key because the camera lens had to have a clear view of the sky. That was more complicated than it sounded, given the tail of the aircraft.

In addition to motion picture flying, Art Scholl Aviation, which he ran with wife Judy Scholl, also did aerobatic shows and ran an FBO. Their "fixed base operator" was a private terminal that offered aircraft maintenance, rentals, fuel, hangars, education, and an air taxi service. The training was primarily in aerobatics, advanced stunt flying. It was time- intensive so he had just a few students.

PHOTO: Citation Press

Judy Scholl, also a skilled pilot, has continued to run Art Scholl Aviation and to honor the legacy of her husband. This photo was taken inside the company hangar at San Bernadino Airport in 2021.

Over the next few days, Scholl and his team went out to get plate shots, the term used for what he was collecting. There were always two planes, Scholl in his Pitts and a chase plane, which was occupied by a pilot and mechanic, which provided a degree of safety. The Pitts Special had made a name for itself over the decades, winning pilots numerous aerial competitions with its versatility and reliability. They'd get what they could for the day and return to the hangar at Rialto Airport. Judy Scholl would be there waiting to help offload the plane.[313]

Art Scholl was well known around the country, and not just for his extensive movie and television work. He was getting more of that than ever, some of it high profile, like *The Right Stuff* (1983) and *Indiana Jones and the Temple of Doom* (1984). He was admired for his daring performances at air shows. His name appeared in newspapers thousands of times. That was generally as a performer, but he also made for a great story. Feature writers regularly tracked him down to give readers or viewers a closer look at the guy in the sky doing loop-de-loops.[314]

Depending on which aircraft he had with him, he would invite reporters to go up, or, even better, to load their film in a camera fixed to the wing. It was understood the film belonged to the paper or reporter, even though it was Scholl pulling the string.[315] It was great marketing, because they were guaranteed to get some amazing shots. That meant he ended up on a lot of front pages, which, in turn, helped promote the air show, pleasing organizers and assuring future bookings.

He was also a hero to a lot of military pilots because of the flying he did in international competition. "He was an aerobatic champion for the United States," said Bozo Abel, referring to Scholl's place on the aerobatic team that represented the country from 1963 through 1972, competing all over the world, including in Moscow and East Germany. Scholl won the U.S. National Aerobatic Championship in 1974, also in a Pitts Special. Abel read flying-related trade magazines as a youngster, and Scholl "was always in there."[316]

Flat, inverted spin

On Sept. 16, the two planes headed to the Carlsbad area, Scholl in the lead. They flew most of the afternoon keeping in contact via radio. The goal was to capture footage for the scene where Goose dies after the jet goes into a flat spin.

The two people in the chase plane told investigators they were nearly done for the day. They watched as he did an upright spin over the ocean.[317] That's where the plane is put into an intentional idle or stall and goes into a roll and yaw in the same direction. In aviation, roll is rotation around the axis of the fuselage, where a yaw is left-right motion around the axis perpendicular to the wings. The footage would reflect air, water, air, water, and so forth as it spun toward the ground. That was different from what Maverick and Goose would have experienced with a flat spin.

Scholl recovered from the maneuver and returned to about 4,000 feet. Then he entered into a flat, inverted spin.[318] That maneuver starts similarly to an upright spin, by going into a stall, but in this case the plane spins upside down, with the roll in the opposite direction of the yaw. The chase plane watched as his plane plummeted through the recovery altitude. For the first time in his life, Scholl wasn't able to right the aircraft. His last words on the radio were: "I have a problem. I have a real problem." It was 5:45 p.m.

They radioed for help, and the U.S. Coast Guard sent out an 82-foot cutter and a helicopter to search. They found debris from the plane that night,[319] and covered roughly 25 square miles before calling off the search the next day. Neither his body nor the aircraft were ever recovered.

Scholl's death was national news. There were a lot of people in the movie business who knew him and had worked with him. The production, which had forged the contract with his company, handed everything over to the studio. Paramount handled the awful details.

The people who knew Scholl best, and his skill as an aviator, were shocked. "I saw him the day before," said Lacy, who had recommended Scholl for the plate work. "They were calling it quits, and he said, 'let me try one more time'," said Lacy. "It was just a point-of-view shot."[320]

Pilots have speculated on what happened out there for years, whether it was equipment failure or operator error.[321] The four-page report from the National Transportation Safety Board, which investigated the incident but didn't have the benefit of a recovered aircraft, simply recorded it as "loss of control."[322]

"He was trying too hard to give them what he thought they wanted," Lacy said. He added that he would have done a forward spin and turned the camera upside down.

Scholl obviously took more risks than many pilots, and there had been close calls. He was known to make changes to the structure of aircraft, as in trimming wings, but he had an advanced degree in aeronautics, and it had always worked.

At the same time, modifications to his Pitts Special were already well-established before the accident.[323]

"It was puzzling because we had an aerobatics school and he specialized in teaching flat spins both upright and inverted and so I don't know what went wrong," Judy Scholl told a journalist in 2015. "There was a lot of thought given to the performance of the airplane when it gets into a certain flat spin maneuver because there had been some problems with pilots being unable to recover from that. But Art taught that and how to recover — it was a recoverable event. Except in this case, for some reason, it wasn't."[324]

Joe Cooperman, a cameraman who had at an earlier point helped Scholl rig cameras in aircraft, offered other insight. "Because of the way the camera was rigged to the aircraft, it was on an angle. To get a 90-degree perspective of the background with the clouds and the sky spinning, which was to be used in the rear projection, if you did a spin upright, not inverted, the camera would sit on an angle... By inverting it he was able to keep it 90 degrees to the horizon, so the tail rudders would not be visible."[325]

That's why Scholl would have been doing it that way, Cooperman said. But more than that, he knew how to do a flat spin and come out of it. It was an incredibly dangerous maneuver for F-14s and other jets, but less so in a relatively lightweight plane like the Pitts. Cooperman believes it had to be equipment failure.

Pete Fusco, author of "The Crowd Pleasers: A History of Airshow Misfortunes from 1910 to the Present," posits "that the weight of the rear-mounted camera moved the aircraft's center of gravity too far aft, a situation that can make spin recovery problematic, if not impossible."

Abel had been deeply saddened by the death of his childhood hero. "It was a very tragic loss of a great, great pilot," he said.[326]

Scholl had vast experience. At the time of his accident he had the equivalent of nearly two years in the air, based on his logged flying hours, according to the NTSB. He'd also been recognized for his knowledge of safety. The Screen Actors Guild had put him on the Safety Investigating Team in the wake of the helicopter accident that claimed three lives during the filming of a scene for the *Twilight Zone: The Movie* (1982.) He was well educated, having earned a Ph.D. in aeronautics in 1976.[327] He served as head of the Aeronautics Department at San Bernardino Valley College from 1958 to 1974, before turning to his businesses full-time. At the time of his death he held four FAA certificates.[328]

He was 53.

Art Scholl
Dec. 24, 1931 – Sept. 16, 1985

Special Effects
Hangar 34, Burbank Airport
Day 60-70: Sept. 18-Oct. 2

Hangar 34 at the Burbank Airport was a Quonset-style building that had gone up in the late 1940s. The semicircular structures had proliferated during World War II, thanks to their relative ease of construction and sheer functionality. Set upon a concrete foundation of about 5,000 square feet, its tall walls were jacketed with metal sheeting and topped with twin hinge trusses that held up the arched roof. Thanks to its sturdy design, and various updates, it remains in use today.[329]

The main requirement for the space for this last stage of photography was that it be big enough to accommodate special effects, and rear-screen projection on this scale needed a lot of real estate. "It was a big, empty hanger, more for private jets, but big enough for a real jet and rear projection," said Baron, who had been in Fallon and returned to help set up the hangar. "I literally swept it out myself."[330]

Rear-screen projection, also known as process photography, was the primary method used to show scenes with moving backgrounds in film over many decades. It's most easily recognized in driving scenes, where actors are talking as the pre-filmed background moves and trees or buildings or other cars appear to go by. It's not used today, thanks to bluescreen and other less expensive technological advances. In 1985 it was state of the art.

The production department had moved into the offices on one end of Hangar 34 well ahead of the others. They added new phone lines and furniture, and gradually more crew returned to work. Some were in the offices but most worked on the sound stages. Jimmy Tyson, the costume designer, organized flight suits for the actors, craft services set up its kitchen to feed at least 60 people each day, and the transportation department moved cast trailers into the parking lot.

The biggest addition to the crew as they prepped the space was the Special Effects department, six people overseen by Allen Hall. Over the previous weeks they had built and installed an elaborate stage set that was a mockup of an F-14 cockpit. The grip and electric departments also grew significantly.

The Hansard Co. was hired to do the process photography. They put in two screens. The one behind the cockpit was the larger one. The projector was on the far side, so the images came through from behind it. The screen in the front of the cockpit was off camera. It was maneuverable and there to match the sky, which would be seen in the reflection of the cockpit glass.

Dave Baranek knew who Semcken was, but he didn't know him well when Willard called to say he and the other lieutenant were going to Paramount. Willard picked Baranek, a RIO, because he was a communications instructor at the Topgun school. They wanted them to review aerial footage and go over pilot dialogue. In fairly short order, Baranek and Semcken flew to Burbank. They felt like longtime friends before the plane even took off, he said.[331]

A pretty young woman driving a white station wagon emblazoned with the Paramount logo greeted them at the airport. It was just the start of what would be a memorable day on a date easy to remember.

The driver took them to the other side of the airport and the hangar where crews were finishing up prep for the special-effects segment of photography. They saw the cockpit mockup and a special effects guy asked the flyers what the different dials did. Eventually the driver took them to the Paramount lot, where Tony Scott greeted them. They hadn't been there long when a call came in about Art Scholl. His plane had crashed into the ocean and he was presumed dead.

Everyone had watched Scott take the call, and knew something was up. "He hung up and told us what happened," said Baranek. "It was surreal. Here, a guy who was working on the film is killed, it just takes the air out of the room." Scott stood looking at them for a second, then said he needed to call his wife. He sat down by the phone and made a very quiet, personal call. "That was his priority, and it was heartfelt," Baranek said. They couldn't make out the words, but it was "very consoling, calm and slow."[332]

Everyone was in shock, and it was decided they needed to get out of the room, "to change our setting." They ended up in a large screening room, where there were already pockets of people including some of the actors. Everyone was shown aerial clips, without sound, including film shot of the actors when they flew in the F-14s. G-force had not been kind to them, and the shots documented a fair amount of airsickness. Baranek said he could hear the young men in the room cajoling each other. When one of the images showed a particular actor vomiting, another called out, "That's some of your best work, right there."

Most of what they saw was raw footage of the planes flying the aerial scenes, which was the reason they'd called the pilots there. The producers, Scott, and the editing department knew there were key issues to be sorted out. They had siloed the material they had, and needed ideas about whether what they had put together worked, and most of all, they needed dialogue for the new scenes they were creating. While the script had some dialogue for the scenes, it didn't match up with what had actually come in.

Semcken and Baranek went with Lebenzon to an editing room. "He showed us how to work the editing machine. I remember it had an engraved plate, *Flashdance* 1983 and *Beverly Hills Cop*, 1984." They spent a few hours talking it through. Scott was also around, and he ordered pizza for everyone. Then the aviators went to their hotel for the night. The next day a driver picked them up and returned them to the studio to record cockpit chatter that would be the basis for dialogue in the aerial scenes.

"This time they were going for the gold," said Baranek. A small projector was set up in a room with a big couch, and the film they'd worked on the night before had been recut. A number of people were there, including Lebenzon. They had three ways to record the aviators, a scriptwriter, someone taking dictation, and it was all being taped, and several other people stood around in the room.

They watched footage and talked as if they were flying the airplanes. "It was stuff like 'Check 12' and 'Watch the guy on the tail,'" recalled Semcken.[333]

Baranek, who wrote a chapter about the movie in his book about being an RIO called "Topgun Days," said he thought it had taken about 25 minutes. "Then the film stopped, and I guess we were done." They met Simpson and Bruckheimer before they left. "It's the only time I personally met those guys," he said. Then they got back in the Paramount station wagon to begin their return to San Diego.

The full crew began work on special effects that Monday, Sept. 18, less than two days after Scholl's death. He had worked independently, so most of the crew didn't know him, but he was still part of the movie. "There were a couple of really sad days," said Ward Russell, chief lighting technician. "It really affected Tony. Even though he wasn't responsible for it, he was still the head of the production and it was one of his guys."[334]

A faux F-14

Creating the mockup of the F-14 had been a long process. Wade had begun it in May, after Badalato heard about an F-14 "mothballed" at Davis Monthan Air Force Base near Tucson. The prop master flew out to the military aircraft boneyard to have a look. "There were planes as far as the eye could see, but the production didn't want a whole airplane. The lot overseers led him to a jet the Navy thought would work. They stood there looking at the retired F-14 and asked Wade what the filmmakers wanted to do with it. He replied that they were thinking of "sectioning" it. "They said, 'Do you know how heavy that is! We aren't going to cut one of these apart to do that."[335]

When Wade relayed the news that recreating an F-14 as a set would require building one he also began collecting parts, like seat harnesses. The real coup was getting a canopy, the piece that covers the cockpit.

Building the faux fuselage was the work of a master carpenter, similar in complexity to constructing a wooden ship, Willard said. The wood had to be joined and shaped to match the canopy, which took a great deal of time and patience. "We had pictures of the cockpit, and we borrowed all the dials from the Navy." They might not have given them everything, but the angles they were shooting from didn't require perfect instrumentation.[336]

A radio system was installed to connect the actors to the director. Movement was provided by a gimbal attached to the base of the mock-up. "It was a mechanical device that allowed you to put something on it, rotate it back and forth and side to side," he said.

Lights, camera, roll plate!

The camera department remained the same, but the lighting and grip departments grew dramatically.

Russell, the gaffer, had nine people working under him. That included two ACLTs, or assistant lighting techs, three lamp operators, two generator operators, and two light ring techs. The grip department was also beefed up, with two best boys, two extra grips, and grip to operate the crab dolly,[337] which got its name from its ability to move in any direction, including sideways.

The light ring they built was about 25 feet in diameter, with two 10 kilowatt lights mounted at the 180 degree marks, Russell said. The producers had seen something like it in a rock and roll show and recommended it to them. He and Kimball liked it because it enhanced the sense of movement and created shadows like those from clouds. "It made it look like the plane would start going up in the air or dip down like it was going down or that it was turning," he said.[338]

Meanwhile, something had gone awry with the gimbal, which controlled the cockpit set. They had designed it to operate hydraulically, Willard said, "but we bent something the first day." That didn't change the fact that the heavy cockpit set had to be moved, and with an actor inside. "We ended up doing it all by manpower," Willard said. The faux cockpit was held up mechanically but shifting it was hard physical work.[339]

"There were six guys jockeying Cruise and Edwards around like Egyptian pharaohs," recalled Heatley, who was there to help work on dialogue. "There was a circular light around them and Art Scholl's photography in the background. It was incredible."[340]

Earlier in the day Heatley and Skaaren met in one of the hangar offices to go over dialogue. The scriptwriter took notes on a yellow legal pad while the pilot talked through what Maverick and Goose would be saying, the same kind of jargon as Semcken and Baranek contributed a few days earlier.

Heatley recalled Skaaren grumbling about being there, and complaining about $37,000 in pay. It was just part of what the writer was actually being paid, but it irked the Navy man, who wasn't being paid anything for his time. The scriptwriter apparently didn't share that he was in arbitration over whether he'd be included in the credits and the impact that had on his pay. The studio, led by Dawn Steel, believed Skaaren played an integral role in the movie, and submitted additional paperwork to WGA in support of his efforts to receive screen credit. The arbitration was forced when Cash and Epps objected. The duo would go on to pen *Legal Eagles* (1986), *The Secret of My Success* (1987), and *Turner & Hooch* (1989).

Heatley said Skaaren handed the three pages of notes to Scott, who looked at them for all of "15 seconds." The pilot was outfitted with a headset and mic that connected him to Cruise and Edwards, and went up on the platform. Heatley said he would read the lines to the actors, who repeated them on camera.

Over the next few days all the actors came in to do their parts. Their dialogue was also polished to match up better with previous scenes. It was detailed work although it wasn't hard. The actors had to climb into the contraption, and wait while a crane lowered the canopy over them. "It took 10 minutes to put it on, and another 10 minutes to take it back off," Willard explained.

He was up on the platform that served as the entry and exit point to the mockup. A water spray bottle was used to make the actors look sweaty during intense scenes. A mole fogger operated by a finger pump put smoke into the cockpit for scenes that required it.

Given the difficulty in getting the canopy on, the actors often had to stay in there for long periods, and it wasn't comfortable. There was a lot of complaining. "We put air conditioning into it so the poor little pilot actors didn't get overheated," said Willard.

He had reason to be peeved. As the days went by, the actors turned the squirt bottle on him. Kilmer and Rossovich were the main culprits, especially Kilmer. "They were all kind of arrogant, except Edwards. He was alright. They'd shoot me with the squirt bottle, and I'd tell them — I don't think that's a good idea." But they just laughed.

The last time they were on the schedule, Willard waited until they called wrap. Instead of getting the canopy off to let Kilmer out, Willard got the mole fogger and put a couple of puffs of smoke into the cockpit. Soon Kilmer was obscured from view and pounding on the two-inch-thick canopy glass. They soon lifted the canopy off, and smoke billowed out. "He really meekly stepped out and walked away."

The best part was that Anthony Edwards made reference to the prank when he was a guest on Johnny Carson's show. "He said something like, 'We learned one thing. You don't mess with the arts guys.'"

Adding shooting days

There had been a battle around the actors wearing the helmets in the background. The studio wanted to see the actors' faces, particularly Cruise's. The Navy didn't want to depict its pilots flying without helmets, which were essential gear. Semcken said he did his best to drive home that point: depicting pilots in the air without oxygen masks was unrealistic. F-14s flew at high altitudes where there wasn't enough air to breathe.

Paramount wasn't making a documentary. "The studio was paying a lot of money for Tom Cruise and the cast, and they wanted to see their faces," Knell said.[341] Scott's assistant recalled him getting creative shots, like clouds reflecting in the face shields of the actors. Things like that didn't sit well with the studio, which was closely reviewing dailies. The studio threatened to fire Scott over the masks, Weber said, one of several times it happened in the course of making *Top Gun*. Knell said that didn't deter Scott from shooting what he wanted, although he did hold back a reel at one point, rather than sending it promptly to the studio for development, in order to dodge drama.

They had begun the week thinking the end date was that Friday, Sept. 27.[342] Toward the end of the week they realized they needed more time and added one shooting day, which pushed the finish date to Sept. 30.[343] That was a Monday, when they subsequently added two more days. Over those days nearly every male actor who portrayed a pilot or RIO returned again.

By the end they had footage of the actors with both the face shield and the oxygen masks on, and off, but the favorite configuration was a compromise. The masks would be attached but down, hanging next to their faces, as if the pilots had unhooked them for a break.

Top Gun wrapped principal photography on Oct. 2.[344] Mostly.

Chapter 10 - Endnotes

[304] Billy Weber, film editor for *Top Gun*. Interview with the author. April 10, 2020.
[305] Ibid.
[306] Daily Production Report, September 3, 1985. TGC.
[307] Daily shot lists, September 6-16, 1985. TGC.

308 Call Sheets, September 6-16, 1985. TGC.

309 Ibid.

310 Blair, June 26, 2020.

311 Rondell, February 28, 2021.

312 John Hall, "Ballet in the Blue," *Los Angeles Times*, October 25, 1968, III-3. https://www.newspapers.com/image/383000738

313 Emma Foster, "My husband, the real Goose," *Daily Mail* (London), November 27, 2015. Accessed online. https://www.dailymail.co.uk/news/article-3335091/My-husband-real-Goose-died-daring-stunt-filmed-Gun-d-glad-Navy-heroes-taking-air-again.html

314 "Scholl's career spans 25 years," *Herald* (Jasper, Indiana), July 5, 1977, 9. https://www.newspapers.com/image/541138447/

315 Hall, "Ballet in the Blue."

316 Abel, November 27, 2020.

317 "Dangerous aircraft maneuver was last stunt for famed pilot," Associated Press/*Santa Cruz Sentinel* (Santa Cruz, California), September 18, 1985, D-1. https://www.newspapers.com/image/62898824/

318 Jack Jones, "Famed Stunt Pilot Scholl Believed Killed as Biplane Falls Into Sea During Filming," *Los Angeles Times*, September 18, 1985, R4. https://www.newspapers.com/image/402341241/

319 "Famed Stunt Pilot Crashes Off Coast," *Los Angeles Times*, September 17, 1985, I-2. https://www.newspapers.com/image/402417913/

320 Lacy, April 22, 2021.

321 Pete Fusco, *The Crowd Pleasers: A History of Airshow Misfortunes from 1910 to the Present*, (New York: Skyhorse, 2018).

322 National Transportation Safety Board Aviation Accident Final Report, Accident Number: LAX85LA393, September 16, 1985. https://app.ntsb.gov/pdfgenerator/ReportGeneratorFile.ashx?EventID=20001214X37820&AKey=1&RType=Final&IType=LA..

323 Hall, "Ballet in the Blue." and "Scholl's career spans 25 years."

324 Foster, "My husband, the real Goose"

325 Cooperman, September 4, 2021.

326 Abel, November 27, 2020.

327 David Gustafson, "Hall of Fame '90," *Sport Aerobatics*, February 8, 1991. https://www.iac.org/hall-fame-1990-art-scholl.

328 "Art Scholl Film Collection," Smithsonian National Air and Space Museum website. https://airandspace.si.edu/collection-archive/art-scholl-film-collection/sova-nasm-2013-0006.

329 "Bob Hope "Hollywood Burbank" Airport Terminal Replacement Project Burbank, California" Historical Resources Assessment. Prepared for March 2020, revised draft. https://bobhopeairporteis.com/wp-content/uploads/27.-Appendix-H-Historical-Architectural-Archaeological-and-Cultural-Resources-Volume-2.pdf.

330 Baron, April 5, 2021.

331 Dave "Bio" Baranek LT USN (Ret.), Topgun instructor and "MiG" pilot for *Top Gun*. Interviews with the author, August 27, 2021 and August 30, 2021.

332 Ibid.

333 Semcken, November 5, 2020.

334 Ward Russell, chief lighting technician (gaffer) for Top Gun. Interview with the author, September 27, 2020.

335 Wade, April 29, 2020.

336 Willard, December 2, 2020.

---

337 For more information on the specialized job titles of filmmaking, see: https://www.nfi.edu/best-bo

338 Russell, September 27, 2020.

339 Willard, December 2, 2020.

340 Heatley, December 1, 2020.

341 Knell, April 18, 2020 and September 12, 2021.

342 Production Report, Monday, September. 23, 1985. TGC.

343 Production Report, Tuesday, September. 24, 1985. TGC.

344 Production Report, October 2, 1985. TGC.

PART III
WRAP, POST-PRODUCTION, LAUNCH, LIFESPAN

Producers Don Simpson and Jerry Bruckheimer stand in front of the movie poster at the West Coast premiere of the movie on May 15, 1986 at Mann's Cinema 21 in Mission Valley.

PHOTO: Bob Redding/San Diego Union-Tribune via ZUMA Wire.

CHAPTER 11
USS CARL VINSON, MISSILES, WRAP
OCTOBER ... SOMETHING

More reshoots and pickups

Internet sleuths have a hard time nailing down an official last day of principal photography for good reason. It shows up in Internet databases loosely as "October, 1995." Internal Paramount financial documents show an end date of Oct. 2, which is when they completed special effects. A set of production reports that encompass nearly all days of principal photography also stop at Oct. 2.[345]

But they weren't actually done with photography yet. They still needed reshoots on an aircraft carrier, and shots of a missile or missiles being fired. On Oct. 9, a *Top Gun* shooting crew took a third trip to an aircraft carrier, this one the USS Carl Vinson. It was an overnight trip, which provided two days to get pick up shots. "My recollection is that it was a continuation of the work," said cameraman Greg Schmidt. "We didn't come back later to do it. It was part of the same project."[346]

The nuclear-powered carrier was on par with the USS Enterprise in size, and it too was out on a training mission. It was newer — its maiden voyage had been just two years before — but that wasn't what made the trip feel different, and it felt *very* different. First, there were just 11 people in the group, seven of them filmmakers. Navy handlers Semcken and Stairs also were there, as were aerial consultants Stevens and Harmon.

The camera crew, again led by Kimball, consisted of Schmidt, John Gilbert and William Kelley, and Bill Coss as an assistant cameraman. Coss said it was Schmidt who got him on board. His job involved moving equipment and loading film magazines in a medical office at the base of the command center.[347]

Badalato was also on the list as an "assistant cameraman," presumably because it was easier for him to fit onto the manifest that way than to explain the role of an executive producer. He said he couldn't recall how that happened, but he knew *why* he was there. "I was always present when the shooting company was on a Navy asset or property," he said. "It was the watchdog aspect of the job," having to do with liability for Paramount in the event something went wrong.[348]

PHOTO: Department of the Navy

This photo of the aircraft carrier USS Carl Vinson was distributed by the Navy to movie crew in a media package that also included a detailed schedule for their stay on the vessel.

More significantly, the Navy exerted a lot more control with this contingent, something evident from the instant the helicopter landed on the flight deck. The group was greeted by Stairs, and their equipment and duffel bags offloaded to be "staged abreast island structure," the giant 10-plus story operations center of the carrier, where a guard also was posted.[349]

The filmmakers were shown to Ready Room 9 where they were greeted and briefed by additional Navy personnel. Ready Room 9 resembled the set in the scene in *Top Gun* where the actors are in a classroom setting, briefed before their first real mission. These visitors were also briefed and given off-white folders emblazoned with a gold leaf USS Carl Vinson insignia. It contained pages of information about it and its leadership complete with photographs and the official printed magazine style brochure about the new vessel. Ready Room 9 would serve as their de facto production office for the less than 30 hours they were aboard.

The packet included a schedule prepared for them by the Navy, based on what the production told them it still needed. It had the filmmakers' time managed to the quarter hour. The Navy schedule gave them 30 minutes to "scout locations from 0-10 level," like the shortest reccy the director had ever been on. Next up they were to meet escort officers for lunch in Wardroom 3, although camera crew could take longer to set up equipment. The tight scheduling continued from there: "(4)1300 – Cameras and production personnel in place on flight deck for 1315 overhead of VF-51 ("Hollywood") aircraft. (5) 1500 – VF-51 aircraft completes cycle, returns to NAS Miramar. Additional F-14 opportunities until 1630." VF-51 was a fighter squadron.

The Navy schedule reflected free time for the filmmakers from 4:30 and 5:30 p.m. whereby they could get a quick snack or relax in Ready Room 9. The better bet is that camera crew was prepping on the flight deck by 4:30 p.m. in order to be in place and ready for the 5:45 p.m. scheduled flyby of VF-51 jets. The Navy saw the movie crew wrapping up its filming by 6:45 p.m., dinner shortly thereafter, and either retiring to state rooms or "enjoying free time" in Ready Room 9 at 8 p.m.

Breakfast the next day, again in Wardroom 3, began at 6:15 a.m. Planes would be flying overhead starting at 7:45 a.m. F-14s would fly until 9:45, then other aircraft. "Back-up" photography was allotted for after lunch from 12:30 to 2:30, with other aircraft scheduled to fly. But all gear was to be "packed and staged" at the island structure in time for the pre-flight brief for the return of any equipment at 3 p.m., which would include "final remarks by CO/XO." The only flexibility evident on the Navy's schedule was the 3:30 p.m. departure, which was noted as "Approx."

It had all been crisp and controlled. "The equipment had to stay out of the tower on the deck," said Schmidt. "They didn't want us bringing it inside, which was actually easier for us." He thinks the main thing they shot on the trip was a flyby, to get a shot of an F-14 buzzing the ship, given their limited movement.[350]

Coss recalled the added challenge of moving equipment around on the ship. Most of his time was spent in the office, loading magazines with film or organizing what came in. That meant he didn't see too much, "planes taking off, touch and goes, close ups of wheels, that kind of thing." A Navy runner would pick up the camera magazines for delivery to movie crew, so fewer non-Navy personnel were on the deck. But Coss loved the experience. Working on the USS Carl Vinson was "the experience of a lifetime."[351]

Coss said they took off on the same style two-rotor helicopter they flew, either an F-46 or H-53, according to paperwork. Only instead of returning them to Miramar they were taken to the Bay Area, and returned south via different transportation because the helicopter had somewhere else to go. The cameraman wasn't sure if they were returned south via bus or plane.

It's unclear whether the tightening was a reaction to Scott's earlier battle of wills with the commander of the USS Enterprise or just a different commander's operation. But

Navy personnel, both enlisted and officers, say the branch never makes the same mistake twice. When a mistake is identified — as with the flat spin that killed one of its pilots — there is intense review and procedures are changed.

Missiles ready for close up

The producers had included filming a missile with their request for everything else, but it was also the most complicated ask. The question wasn't if Navy leadership would allow a non-cleared film crew to record its weapons systems — they wouldn't. Weapons systems are highly classified so at a minimum, there had to be a workaround. A secondary deterrent, from the perspective of the production company, was the expense, because they didn't have the budget to pay for a special missile firing.[352]

The solution was to glom onto a planned missile training, with the assumption that film crew — including Scott — *wouldn't* be the ones to shoot it. "I think Tony just said, can Heater do it?" said Heatley, whose recollection was that Badalato and Scott actually knew about a scheduled missile shoot before he did. Navy procedure required the presence of a safety officer. He had the training and the top security clearance needed. More importantly to the production, he was a skilled aerial photographer.[353]

Heatley was well known to crew on the production by then. He'd been a cameraman when they were shooting the air-to-air scenes in Miramar, a consultant working on dialogue with the scriptwriter, and a background actor in numerous scenes. This was something different.

Being a safety officer — overseeing the firing of the missiles during a training exercise — wasn't part of Heatley's regular job. He said it was fairly simple to get approved once they identified the mission. "I was qualified, and they said, okay you do it." The use of a movie camera leased to the production, and permission to give the footage he shot to the editing department, also was approved.

Internet reports that one or two missiles were photographed, or that just one missile was fired because that's all Paramount wanted to pay for, are false. "All they did was let me have a Panaflex while I was the safety observer for the shoot," he said. It is possible that they reversed footage on screen so they could use a particular image twice, but he didn't know about that.

The training involved a C-130 releasing drone targets, one by one, over time. Following the release of each drone, the lumbering C-130 — a cargo plane roughly 100 feet in length with a wingspan of more than 130 feet — turned 180 degrees and flew in the other direction. Meanwhile, fighter pilots would be on the prowl for the drone, lock on it, and wait to fire until they had approval from the safety officer.

What Heatley remembered most from that day was that one F-14 pilot had locked onto the wrong target. "I noticed on my radar that the target was moving a lot slower than it should have," he said, and that it wasn't in the proper range. He told the fighter pilot to hold fire and radioed the slower moving aircraft. It was the C-130, whose pilot told him that instead of pulling the 180, this time he thought he'd watch the drone explode. "I told him, it's yourself you're going to see explode!"

He wrote up both pilots, the C-130 pilot for disobeying a clear command, and the other for failing to recognize the differing ranges and speeds. "Oh, they were definitely debriefed," recalled Heatley.

But the filming had gone fine. Heatley thinks at least seven missiles were fired that day, and he got footage of them from varying angles. He said editors rejected what he thought were the best shots because the aircraft had different tail designs or insignias didn't match, which could be picked up on by moviegoers.

Shutting down principal photography

Wrap is the line where photography ends and post-production officially begins, but it's also the process, and a period of time, when a production is shut down. Everything leased or purchased over the previous months has to be returned, sold or otherwise accounted for. That process was under way in terms of shutting down the sound stages at the hangar at Burbank Airport, even as the skeleton crew went out on the USS Carl Vinson.

Because of the distinct phases of photography on *Top Gun*, the production office had already overseen a mini wrap process, meaning they were shutting things down all along, like the space at the Travelodge, even as they opened up elsewhere. Along the way they reconciled accounts, even though the numbers weren't final.[354]

Now all departments were permanently shutting down, returning camera, grip and lighting equipment, costumes and props, and whatever else, and providing documentation to the production department. There were hundreds of additional things to process, including damage reports. In shooting the insert that represented Goose's death, a second unit had cracked the canopy. The Navy needed compensation for that, and a lot of other things.

The accounting department had to reconcile all of it, an elaborate process that was just starting.

Chapter 11 - Endnotes

[345] Production Reports, September – October 1985. TGC.

[346] Schmidt, May 13, 2020 and September 4, 2021

[347] William (Bill) Coss, second assistant camera for *Top Gun*. Interview with the author.

[348] Badalato, January 26, 2020.

[349] U.S. Navy Communications Office, "Paramount Pictures Filming of 'Top Gun' USS Carl Vinson," memo and welcome packet, October 9-10, 1985.

[350] Schmidt, May 13, 2020 and September 4, 2021.

[351] Coss, September 21, 2021.

[352] Badalato, January 26, 2020.

[353] Heatley, December 1, 2020.

[354] Badalato, January 26, 2020.

CHAPTER 12
POST-PRODUCTION
OCT. 3, 1985 — MAY, 1986

If you diagrammed a pyramid to represent what people know about big movies, the pyramidion would be the actors. The next level would be the other people above the line, the director, the writers and the producers. The next would consist of the scores of people who work during principal photography, from accountants to assistant directors, camera operators to costumers, P.A.s to prop makers, and so on. At the base would be post-production, but its relative invisibility is no measure of its importance; post-production is where any movie truly comes together. With *Top Gun* significant changes were ahead.

While Weber and Lebenzon pieced together an assemblage of the movie, sound and visual effects were just ramping up. The sound department grew exponentially in post-production as sound effects were added followed by music, a layered and laborious process. Visual effects were different from special effects, which were done during photography. Visual effects — in this case planes exploding — were managed by Gary Gutierrez and his company, USVX, and eventually a crew of between 40 and 50 people.[355]

The effort over Labor Day weekend to organize the aerial footage had involved marking clips in the raw material for use in specific scenes. Those were handed over to Claudia Finkle, an assistant editor who oversaw three technicians. That team organized the marked sections onto separate reels so Weber and Lebenzon could work on individual sequences. They also catalogued shots, put "trims" away, and managed the overall organization of the footage. Working in film was labor intensive. "They were the ones that literally boxed up the film," said Weber.

Part of the process, enabled by the KEM editing machine, was a temporary soundtrack. They used "Born in the USA," Bruce Springsteen's chart-topping anthem, as the theme song while they cut the scenes. It would be replaced later when the original music was completed, but temp tracks made it easier to pace the scenes.[356]

Sound takes depth

The sound department working on set consisted of just three people, led by sound mixer Bill Kaplan. Their primary responsibility had been to capture dialogue. Now it was up to Cecelia "CeCe" Hall and George Watters II, the supervising sound editors, to create a layered, cohesive soundtrack. Music had its own team at work, and Hall and Watters focused on sound effects.[357]

Hall had worked on creating sound for two longer trailers about *Top Gun* that were to be used in-house. They ran seven or eight minutes and were designed to let people throughout the company know what the movie would look like. A large group of Paramount employees traveled to 5555 Melrose Ave. to see the trailers, the first real look at the movie by anyone not directly involved. They liked it, and Weber was asked to make 200 copies for wider distribution to employees of Paramount, which had offices all around the country at that time.[358]

The sound department also had challenges with the aerial scenes. To capture the sound of F-14s, other planes, and related ambient noise, they gathered up equipment and headed to Miramar for four days, followed by a trip to Nellis Air Force Base in Nevada.

The results weren't what they needed. "The jets were a problem in terms of getting them to sound dynamic," said Hall. "It sounds like distorted air. The engines of an F-14 have a much higher pitch, but that doesn't give you that definition and movement." To come up with "the drama of the actual sound effects" would mean inventing and manipulating sound.

Hall began building a library of "great animal sounds" that were more dynamic. She focused on animal roars, specifically lions and tigers, and mixed in monkey screeches and parts of an elephant trumpet to get a slight scream. "So if you see a jet flying across the screen it might be a mix of 15 or 16 monkeys and elephants," she recalled. "It was a lot of fun."[359]

That part of the process — replacing sound captured during filming with outside sound — is known as Foley. Sounds like jets landing on the aircraft carrier, the hook grabbing the cable, the roar of the jets when they surge forward "was all done on the foley stage," said Hall, the first woman to be hired in the sound-editing department at Paramount.[360] In 1987, Hall garnered an Oscar nomination for her sound effects editing in *Top Gun*, the first woman to be nominated in the category. She went on to become a senior vice president of post-production sound at Paramount.[361]

Sculpting visual effects

The visual effects team had started prepping months earlier. In the spring, Gary Gutierrez had flown from his home base in the Bay Area for the interview in the DeMille Building. Scott and the producers had already liked him for the job. He had done the visual effects for *The Right Stuff*, which featured scenes similar to the ones they needed. *Top Gun* only needed about 50 shots compared to that movie's roughly 400.

At their meeting at Paramount, Scott had shown him storyboards of jets plummeting to earth. "He told me, 'I don't know how much cooperation I'm going to get from the Navy, and what kind of things they're going to allow during air-to-air photography,'" recalled Gutierrez. Scott was pushing for as much as he could get on the Navy side, but he understood blowing up planes was not going to be in the mix.

That's where USFX would come in. Scott told Gutierrez he was hired and to come up with a shot list based on the script.[362]

He hired David Sosalla, a sculptor and model builder, to make the replicas of the F-14s and the MiGs they would blow up in the air. Sosalla had done effects, props and miniatures for *Star Trek: The Motion Picture* (1979). He had also been creature supervisor on *Star Trek III: The Search for Spock* (1984), and had worked as the stop motion technician on *Cocoon* (1985), a process that involves shooting a single image, then moving the subject and shooting it again and repeating the process until, frame by frame, the illusion of motion is created. All of his work involved bringing life to inanimate sculptures.

Sosalla's first job was securing the work that had already been done by another Los Angeles-based contractor and incorporating it into his plans. Armed with scale drawings of a real F-14 and more photographs than anyone dared to count, he began designing the replicas. The goal was to make the aircraft as close to the original as they could at a scale of 1:6, meaning one-sixth the length of the original jet. The first version, which Sosalla termed "carving a buck," was made of wood and wood fill.[363] From that they created molds to cast the fiberglass airplanes they would use in the scenes. These were lightweight enough to hang from thin wire, but looked convincingly solid. Some were made with perforations so that specific sections would break off, say, at the wing.

Over the months, the collection of jets grew. One model was nine feet long, while the others measured six feet. They were painted to match the shots of specific aircraft. For the flat-spin scenes they put together 18-inch models, which included remarkably detailed painting, right down to the helmets of the pilots inside.

The end of principal photography had answered the question about exactly what they needed to capture. Gutierrez was in contact with Weber and Lebenzon, who made sure he knew the specifics, based on footage. In the meantime, Gutierrez was steadily building his dozens of crew.

The main requirement for their location was a 360-degree sky view on a site without much brush. He found the perfect place on a hilltop in Oakland. "It was a housing project where the houses weren't in yet; graveled lots, paved roads. We didn't want to start a fire." It was also a "bowl of sky," he continued, "so we could have the sun where we needed it to be."

For the camera crew he sought out people who had backgrounds in documentaries. "I wanted guys who could grab a real event," which required a specific skill set. "They needed to be able to follow a fast move, find focus, deal with unexpected events and trajectories and still get a good shot."

Fall was approaching, and there was some concern about weather, but they pressed on. In early November they had two trailers in place. These were less like recreational vehicles than small buildings, like those used for portable classrooms. They set one up as a meeting and projection room, and the other as a workshop. While the models were fabricated elsewhere, they needed refinements and repairs, particularly once the crew started blowing them to pieces.

The week before they started filming was all testing. Some of it was tweaking lighting and backdrops, but most of it involved pyrotechnics. They tried different chemical mixes to determine which explosions they would create to get the effect they were after.

USVX operated independently but about a week in, Scott flew up. "Tony came up to the hilltop for one day, to see the dailies, give us his take on things, give us his blessing. It was just a nice, fun day," Gutierrez recalled, but there was one big takeaway. "He said how much he liked backlighting, where the sun is just out of frame, but in the direction in which we're shooting." Gutierrez liked it for another reason, too. Backlighting helps to hide wire. One by one they fashioned the clips of jets in flames that synced up to the story.

Large music team

Bob Badami was hired as music editor at the start of post-production. "It was pretty much at the end of shooting, when the first cut was being generated," he said. His job was to work with composer Harold Faltermeyer on the score and help tie in other musical elements. "You start experimenting, what style of music works, and bridge it with the work from the composer as it comes in," Badami said.[364]

Faltermeyer had been at work on the music since being hired by Simpson and Bruckheimer that spring. With the approval of the demo of "Top Gun Anthem" he had a solid tune and melodies to build on. He'd put together a full track and a longer instrumental version. "It was a big challenge to do a score like that, and we worked really, really hard," recalled Faltermeyer. "There's no padding underneath, instead it's percussive elements to bypass sound effects and dialogue." That involved trying a lot of different things. "Some of the talent we recruited on the fly; if we needed another percussionist, we'd get a session musician to do that."[365]

They worked out of Oasis Studios, owned by Giorgio Moroder. Faltermeyer's first "big break," had been working in Munich with Moroder, who produced Donna Summer and is credited with being a primary power behind disco. That experience led to Faltermeyer writing and co-writing songs for Summer, including "Hot Stuff," which anchored the *Bad Girls* album in 1979. He and Moroder then worked on *American Gigolo* (1980), another hugely popular soundtrack. That's where Faltermeyer had first met Simpson and Bruckheimer.

Marketable soundtracks were enormously popular in that era, and one had always been planned for *Top Gun*. The producers knew how important the music had been to the success of both *Flashdance* and *Beverly Hills Cop*. Scott, almost from the start, had told people about the driving music that would accompany the film.

Pulling 12 songs together was another thing, Badami said. By then they were watching a cut of the movie paced with the Bruce Springsteen track. Badami wouldn't confirm what it was because people tend to make too much of temp tracks. It's filler and in place for a short time — perhaps a couple of months in this case — while they sorted out what would replace it.

To get original music they invited a large group of musicians and songwriters to watch various scenes and submit songs. Kenny Loggins was one of a group of perhaps 100 artists. He thought they'd all be writing for the theme song, and a better strategy on his part would be to write for one of the less flashy scenes. He zeroed in on the volleyball scene.[366]

Badami remembers sitting around the studio with the group, including Simpson and Bruckheimer, with the task of going through the mountain of cassettes and listening to submissions. They would give each one at least five seconds. Anyone could stop it at that point, but if someone else said for it to continue, they played it longer. By the end, nothing had really spoken to them.

Moroder was nearby and he had some ideas. He might have turned to any number of people to work with, but a conversation with his mechanic had piqued his interest. The mechanic, Tom Whitlock, said he was also a lyricist. They teamed up to write "Danger Zone." For a time, it looked like the band Toto, which was very popular at the time, would perform it.

At around the same time, Moroder, a highly regarded producer who worked with several popular bands, was in the recording studio with the band Berlin. He had already written "Take My Breath Away," with Whitlock again writing the lyrics, and the producers liked the song, but not the rendition he played for them. During one of the sessions with Berlin, he asked if they would be interested in doing the song. Despite the reticence of some members of the band, which had only done original tunes to that point, they ultimately agreed.[367]

Kenny Loggins' submission, "Playing With the Boys," matched up well with the volleyball scene, and won favor with Simpson and Bruckheimer. Moroder was in the studio with Loggins producing that song when he learned that Toto had backed out of doing "Danger Zone." He asked Loggins if he was interested. "It was incredibly lucky for me," Loggins told an interviewer in 2004. "It helped my career when disco was taking over, and it was hard for established acts to stay alive." With the perspective of passing decades, "help" may be too tame a verb. "At the time [1985], it seemed like a pretty simple piece of rock and roll," the singer recalled in a 2020 interview. "It turned into one of the biggest songs of my career."[368]

Even with those songs in place and all the work done on the score to that point, they still needed perhaps five songs. That's when they found "Heaven in Your Eyes," by Loverboy, Badami said. They used just 12 seconds of it for the scene where Carole, Goose's wife, shows up, enough for it to be on the soundtrack. "That was a number two song," on the charts, he added.

There were some stressful moments, but they found ways to make it fun. At some point a golf ball driving game was erected. It had a net on one end, and an optical device that could clock ball speed to establish how far the ball would have gone. "It was Harold who started it, and they would just drive golf balls into the net," recalled Badami. "Don and Tony were competitive people, both of them, in a good sort of way. So they had a driving contest." He wasn't sure who won but he remembered a highlight. "Tony wore cowboy boots and he hit it so hard he slipped and fell on his ass."[369]

Somewhere in there, the studio put the pedal down. They needed to get the music done and were given a finite period to do it.

"Back then they didn't invest much in sound and mixing," Badami said. "We were breaking new barriers in terms of complexity of sound and mixing music. Then the studio said, 'you have to finish this, and you have a day and a half to do the last battle.'" They weren't done yet, and the choice was between walking away and working for free.

"Tony gave us what we needed to do our job," said Badami. "He paid for the time out of his own pocket."

Adding up the numbers

In the background the production accountant and Badalato had arrived at final accounting figures. The process had been a back and forth between the production and the studio as decisions were made on how to account for unusual circumstances. There wasn't a framework for doing business with the Navy.

To organize irregular elements of the production, Juli Arenson, production accountant, devised a system of five Special Units, distinct from the phases of photography.[370]

The largest of the special categories, Unit 1, comprised all air-to-air components in Fallon, along with the USS Carl Vinson, referred to as "the second carrier," which involved reshoots of jets. The total cost of the unit was $1.56 million. The flying was the biggest chunk of it. Badalato had budgeted $900,000 for that line item. The final cost of flying the jets in Fallon — the F-14s, F-5s and A4s — were under budget at $845,923. While in Fallon he oversaw daily cost reports, which deducted each day's total expense from the larger budget. That figure was checked with Navy representatives at the same time, so everyone was on the same page.[371]

But that didn't include the cost of operating in Nevada, where crew and maintenance and hotel, along with transportation and per diem, totaled $303,119. Unit 1 also comprised the Grumman package, which ran $129,375. Helicopters – both to ferry the crew, and use of the Navy's Sea Ranger – came to $75,877. The cost of Clay Lacy's Learjet landed at $43,000. Art Scholl Aviation was paid $9,878.

Unit 2 was the carrier at sea. One memo references an unexpected $126,264 bill, notated as "Navy costs for the carrier and planes used on carrier that monies were not originally allocated for per original Navy estimate."

Unit 3 was termed "Gimbel Sequence/ Burbank Hangar, $616,708.

Unit 4 covered aerial coordinators Dick Stevens and Tom Harmon, and related costs, weighing in at $89,130.

Unit 5 was the second San Diego trip — the added days at the end to get additional shots at Charlie's house, as well as those on base, came to $372,766.

The special units as a group were significantly over budget. An Oct. 2, 1985 cost report showed the special units were budgeted at $1,744,807, while the later report ballooned to $2,728,646, an increase of just under $1 million.

The precise amount paid to the Navy, while hard to nail down because of the way they accounted for it, is safely in the ballpark of $1.5 million. One of the wrap memos asked Simpson and Bruckheimer how they wanted to account for the additional $500,000 sent to the Navy.[372] That would have been on top of a reported $1 million deposit from Paramount. The memos, which included the accountants at Paramount, sorted through all of it.

One series of wrap accounting memos addressed approved and unapproved overages, determining whether the studio – Maguire – had agreed in advance. The reshoots in San Diego were a good example. They knew the shooting company would be going back, and had a good idea what it would cost. Maguire chose to approve just $150,000. The actual cost, which surprised no one, was $372,766. It still went down as an overage of $222,766.[373]

Then there was the special effects unit, which went completely beyond estimates. At $442,031, it was the largest single overage, next to the Navy. Studio post-production costs required an additional $294,797. This was convincingly explained in a memo from Paul Haggar, the legendary head of the department at Paramount for 50-plus years at the time of his passing. The sum pushed the amount allotted to post-production for *Top Gun* from $1.5 million to a little more than $1.8 million.[374]

The final cost of making *Top Gun* was $15,276,091, which was over budget by $1.4 million, according to the cost report. The budget was $13.8 million, which dated back to Maguire's edict during prep that the picture be held to $13 million, not the $15 million ballpark filmmakers understood. Badalato, who had promptly papered it to Simpson and Bruckheimer, noted they would be "lucky" to get out of it for less than $15.5 million.[375]

None of the overages in the final accounting were alarming to higher ups at the studio, who by now thought they had a hit on their hands. It was just a process of working it out on paper.

"Back then they would pressure you on every cost, and then, in post, when they thought they had a good picture, they'd throw money at it," said Badalato. "It used to drive us crazy."[376]

Meanwhile, the Navy did its own accounting. Willard confirmed that the figures he had overseen were later audited, making the time invested in carefully managing them at the time they were shooting worthwhile. The lessons learned from *The Final Countdown*, at all levels, had paid off.

Final numbers

Of the $15.3 million cost of making *Top Gun*, about $4.6 million stayed above the line, meaning with the writers, actors, producers and director. Some $1.85 million went to "principal players," while day players were in for $33,574, and "stuntmen," $7,477. Allowances comprised the rest.[377]

Background actors, still called "extras" in those days, earned $58,296. It's hard to guess what it would have been if the production had been required to pay Navy personnel, who made up the bulk of the background actors. Skaaren fared better than imagined in his original contract, which had been detailed in an April 26 Paramount deal memo. That provided him a $150,000 salary with bonuses, based on how he was credited. The tier structure diminished based on how much the credit was shared. At the low end was a $50,000 bonus if he ended up with no credit, plus 1 point of net profit.

While he lost the arbitration for a screenwriter credit with the WGA, he was given an associate producer credit. The studio noted in paperwork it filed that he had done four sets of revisions and a final shooting script. Paramount sent him a letter that further outlined what he had done for the movie that was outside the scope of a scriptwriter's job and into producer territory. That included watching dailies and weighing in on technical details from screen tests to lighting, as well as participating in things that came up in post-production.

The studio revisited his deal package. His total pay in 1985, which reflected salary, fringes, travel and living, was $356,950, according to a Sept. 6, 1986 memo that broke down approved overages.[378] (He was always considered an overage because he was hired outside the budget.)

But there was more. As they updated his deal, he kept the original 1 point of net profit. That 1 percent of NP from *Top Gun* translated to $330,000 between 1987 and 1990, when Skaaren died of bone cancer.[379] Skaaren's biographer, Alison Macor, serves on The Warren Skaaren Charitable Trust, which has been in operation since 1992. She calculated that one percentage point of the film's net profits translated to about $5,000 for every $1 million gross earned by the film.[380] Using that same calculation against the $357 million gross of *Top Gun* to date, Skaaren's one NP would factor out to a total of $1.8 million to date.

The trust gave out $106,000 in grants and scholarships in 2019, according to the trust's Form 990, the most recent available. Among other things, Skaaren's trust funds the Warren Skaaren Scholarship at Rochester Community and Technical College in Minnesota, where he studied for two years.

The 2019 filing for the trust also reflects royalty income of $16,010, although it isn't broken down. Skaaren wrote the screenplays for *Beverly Hills Cop II*, *Batman* (1988), *Beetlejuice* (1988), among others. He also had a stake in the *The Texas Chain Saw Massacre* (1974). The most likely scenario is that the royalties reflected in the 2019 filing stem from *Top Gun* and the *TexasChain Saw* franchise. Moreover, it's likely the new 990s will show an even bigger increase in royalties, given the boost in interest in *Top Gun*, with its 35th anniversary and sequel, and the latest installment of the horror movie, to be released in 2022.

The accounting cost report shows that producers as a group were paid $601,000. Simpson and Bruckheimer split $500,000, while Badalato was paid $77,000, or about $202,000 today with inflation. Simpson and Bruckheimer's profit sharing agreement appears in paperwork "per their Overall Deal," but likely between 10 and 20 percent NP. Badalato confirmed that as executive producer, he was not included in profit sharing on *Top Gun*.

Scott was paid the $400,000 salary reflected in his deal memo, which also showed he was in for 7.5 points NP. Using the Skaaren payment estimate of one NP being about $5,000 for every $1 million earned, and the present-day estimate of a $357 million take for *Top Gun*, Scott's portion would translate to about $13.4 million over the years.

Cash and Epps were in for 5 points NP, since they didn't have to share the credit with Skaaren. Cash and Epps portion, using the same measure, would be a total of some $8.9 million to date.

NP was eventually determined to be a little too flexible and fell from favor. A lot of above-the-line talent felt it was too easy to manipulate the numbers to show a movie didn't make a profit, and that they didn't get treated fairly. It worked out well with movies that made a lot of money, like *Top Gun*.

Paula Wagner was ahead of the curve on seeing the limitations of NP. She negotiating gross points into Cruise's deal for *Top Gun*. The final contract, the document with the $1 million salary that the then 22-year-old actor had pored over in his hotel room days before shooting began, included

5 gross points. A straight five percent of the reported $357 million gross to date of *Top Gun* would be $17.85 million.

Early audience, red flag

By April, Scott had approved a first cut of the movie for a test audience. It's a standard practice of high-level filmmaking to gauge audience reaction fairly early in the process. Anything can change at that point. The music wouldn't have been final at that point, and the audience would have been told as much. Weber said this was a private viewing, rather than a full screening, but it was still a pivotal review.

The audience, which had been pulled in informally, didn't get it. There wasn't any disagreement that the showing had bombed. Simpson called Scott's agent and told him he was thinking about firing the director, Bruckheimer told an interviewer some years later. Even Scott was worried.

Bruckheimer, easily the calmest of the three of them, had everyone step back. They went back to the editing room and "looked at every frame."

Scott believed the images were strong enough to tell the story, and that the driving music would carry it through, but it was too strong on music. The story happening in the sky wasn't clear. "The first time we played that movie, it was a complete disaster," said Badami. "Harold [Faltermeyer] wanted to quit and sneak away."[381]

Top Gun was a different kind of movie to get through post because it merged action and romance. It was intentionally loud. That early version was heavy with singing, so the lyrics of the music could be heard in the front of the mix. "There's only so much room on the soundtrack, and with all the music and sound effects, it was a train wreck."[382] The good news was that seeing it up on the screen brought clarity. They pulled back on some sections where there was singing, and worked to rebalance it, increasing sound effects or otherwise shifting things around.

The informal screenings enabled them to make adjustments before it went out on two official screenings. The first was in Los Angeles, and it went well. The second was scheduled for Dallas, but just before the screening the Space Shuttle Challenger exploded. There was concern that the audience might be overwhelmed by the tragedy and unreceptive to the movie. But it hadn't mattered. The audience loved it.

Editors began cutting a negative, which is the last step in finalizing the movie. It means precisely matching the picture negative to the film editor's final cut to create the high quality film print needed to produce the release copy. But there would be one more twist.

Top Gun was sent out to exhibitors in Los Angeles, New York, and Chicago. The purpose was to show theater owners and managers the movie so they would commit to screening it. Changes rarely happen at that stage. It went well in Los Angeles and New York, but in Chicago, there was a big hiccup.

Exhibitors thought the relationship with Maverick and Charlie was too light. "We felt we needed that sexual thing, for Maverick to bonk Kelly," Scott said in an interview years later, although by all accounts the director was not part of the "we" when it happened.

"Nobody thought it needed that," said Weber. "'We' were done."[383]

There had been some issue about whether they could even do reshoots at that point, given the incredibly short notice, but the actors found a way to make it happen — fast. Cruise was working on *The Color of Money* (1986) and McGillis on *Made in Heaven* (1987) at the time. They shot the two new scenes within a week of the exhibitor showing, Weber said. Cruise's now longer hair was obscured by slicking it back. McGillis wore a hat for the elevator scene, because her hair was longer and colored dark brown for the new role, one of the most often-told behind-the-scenes stories of the movie.

They backlit the love scene and the music editor turned up the lyrics of "Take My Breath Away" for the final version.

Then they cut the negative.

Badami said *Top Gun* took more work in the editing room than perhaps any other movie he had worked on in decades, and as a music editor he had a good vantage point on the editing process. The void in the aerial material, which had to be laced throughout the story, was incredibly problematic. "Tony, Billy and Chris really created that part of the story. There was no movie without that."

Chapter 12 - Endnotes

[355] Gary Gutierrez, supervisor of special photographic effects for *Top Gun*. Interview with the author June 27, 2021.

[356] Weber, April 10, 2020.

[357] Cecelia Hall, supervising sound editor for *Top Gun*. Interview with the author, August 22, 2021.

[358] Weber, April 10, 2020.

[359] *Danger Zone: The Making of Top Gun*.

[360] Carolyn Giardina, "Pioneering sound editor Cece Hall is set to be honored at the MPSE," Hollywood Reporter, September 18, 2019.
https://www.hollywoodreporter.com/movies/movie-news/pioneering-sound-editor-cece-hall-be-honored-by-mpse-1237786/

[361] Cecelia Hall faculty bio, UCLA School of Theater, Film & Television.
https://www.tft.ucla.edu/blog/2011/09/08/faculty-cecelia-hall/

[362] Gutierrez, June 27, 2021.

[363] David Sosalla, model department supervisor, USFX for *Top Gun*. Interview with the author June 28, 2021.

[364] Badami, August 27, 2021.

[365] Faltermeyer, July 3, 2021.

[366] Danger Zone: The Making of Top Gun.

[367] Cameron Adams, "80s electropop band Berlin admit the success of Take My Breath Away hastened their demise." News Corp Australia Network.
https://www.news.com.au/entertainment/music/80s-electropop-band-berlin-admit-the-success-of-take-my-breath-away-hastened-their-demise/news-story/51c88650c3be64d5237bbeabc085283e.

[368] Corey Irwin, "How Kenny Loggins Ended Up Recording 'Danger Zone' For 'Top Gun,'" Ultimate Classic Rock, February 9, 2020.
https://ultimateclassicrock.com/kenny-loggins-danger-zone-top-gun/

[369] Badami, August 27, 2021.

[370] This reporting is based on a nine-page cost report dated Jan. 21, 1986, crosschecked to other documents that identified line items, and many of the aforementioned memos.

[371] Julianna Arenson, "Analysis Report — Overall," undated, ca 1985. TGC.

[372] Julianna Arenson to Bill Badalato, "Top Gun Approved Overages," Sept. 5, 1985. TGC.

[373] Julianna Arenson to Frank Bodo, "Top Gun Overages," Inter-Communication, January 14, 1986. TGC.

[374] Paul Haggar to Dawn Steel, "Reasons for Overages on Top Gun Post Production," December 20, 1985. TGC.

[375] Bill Badalato to Jerry Bruckheimer, Don Simpson, "Top Gun," March 20, 1985. TGC.

[376] Badalato, January 26, 2020.

[377] Paramount Consolidation Summary, "Above the Line," January 20, 1986. TGC.

[378] Arenson, "Top Gun Approved Overages," September 6, 1986. TGC.

[379] Kevin Phinney, "Death of a Screenwriter," *Premiere*, March 1991, 98–99.

[380] Macor, Rewrite Man, 108.

[381] Badami, August 27, 2021.

[382] Ibid.

[383] Weber, April 10, 2020.

CHAPTER 13
LAUNCH, LIFESPAN

I f you were alive and aware at the end of 1986 you didn't have to see *Top Gun* to feel its effects rippling through American culture. Bomber jackets, white T-shirts, and gold-colored, metal-frame aviator sunglasses surged in popularity. Commercials for all sorts of products used fighter jet imagery, either directly from the movie if they'd licensed it or imitating it if not. Music from the soundtrack was all over the airwaves.

It didn't start out that way. *Top Gun* was widely panned by critics, and underestimated by the studio.

The release date for *Top Gun* initially was set for May 23, but without public notice, Paramount pushed it ahead by a week. The press, noting the change, asked studio reps why, and got a pat answer: "Tests showed that it really works well with all four categories: young male; young female; adult male; adult female," Sid Ganis, president of worldwide marketing for the studio, told the Associated Press on May 15. "So we're going to get a nice week's jump on the market."[384]

Top Gun opened on just over 1,000 screens on May 16, a relatively small number given other contemporary releases.[385] It topped the field with $8.4 million at the box office. By Memorial Day weekend, box-office receipts — a weekly metric still widely used to indicate a movie's success — had Warner Bros.' *Cobra*, starring Sylvester Stallone, in first place with $15.6 million, followed by *Poltergeist II*'s $12.4 million.[386] *Top Gun* brought in $9.4 million. While the dollar figures were accurate, they were also misleading. When it came to proceeds per-theater *Top Gun* was the leader.

The critics didn't help. Roger Ebert gave *Top Gun* 2.5 stars. "Movies like *Top Gun* are hard to review because the good parts are so good and the bad parts are so relentless," wrote Ebert, who had a column that appeared in hundreds of papers, as well as a syndicated television show, "At the Movies." He marveled about the lack of chemistry between Cruise and McGillis, which he noted as being odd, given that the actress's physical presence in *Witness* was "palpable."[387]

Movie reviews by Ebert — easily the highest profile movie critic of the era — were also repackaged in summary form and reprinted separately. These were indispensable to frequent moviegoers who used them in deciding what to see. They would read: "The photography of aerial combat is brilliant, but the earthbound parts are deadly predictable."

Martin Kohn of the Detroit Free Press criticized the screenwriters and the plot for the same reason and more bluntly. "*Top Gun* is a second-rate military [genre] — sort of 'triteness in uniform.'"[388]

"An empty-headed technological marvel," wrote Michael Wilmington in the Los Angeles Times. The overall impression left by the movie was that of a "Disco War," he continued. "Like disco, it evaporates from your mind minutes after you leave. Even though it's an irresponsible movie (but one that has hit written all over it), it's hard to get offended. The deepest impulses behind *Top Gun* are not political but sexual. You can tell by the number of scenes set in the shower."[389]

Bill Cosford, movie critic at The Miami Herald, considered the plot a redo of *An Officer and a Gentleman* but said the flight scenes made up for it, amounting to the "payoff" the earlier movie lacked. He singled out Meg Ryan for special praise, as did several other reviewers, but noted the script given to the actors, in general, was "used junk."[390]

Cosford's review also addressed an issue that had broad resonance: the glorious depiction of the U.S. military. "The film is the glossiest recruiting tool the Navy has enjoyed since John Wayne was a fighting Seabee, and vivid proof, if any more were needed, of how our heroes and times have changed: *Top Gun* could not have been made just 10 years ago, let alone made for the 'youth audience.'"

Viva voce, marketing, and repeat visits

Moviegoers were checking it out for themselves. In week two, going head-to-head, *Top Gun* leapt over *Poltergeist* to take second place, while the ultra-violent *Cobra* stayed on top.[391]

Top Gun had padded its lead on a per-theater basis, but few consumers who looked at the widely circulated weekly list knew box office numbers weren't apples to apples.[392] *Cobra* was showing on more than twice as many screens as *Top Gun*.

You can be sure the higher-ups at Paramount knew, and they worked to expand distribution. *Top Gun* was added to 474 more theaters by the end of the month. Now on some 1,500 screens, it handily topped the Stallone-written feature, which fell to third place. "*Top Gun* shoots down *Cobra* at box office," read one June 11 headline.[393]

Paramount reps were wise in negotiating the expansion with exhibitors. To get the picture, theater owners had to agree to show *Top Gun* for at least 12 weeks.[394] There were inherent risks to that kind of obligation, but theater owners knew by now it was performing well.

In July, Ganis repeated his earlier comment about the movie's popularity among various elements of the moviegoing population. This time he added that they had moved it up from Memorial Day weekend, the traditional kickoff date for a big release, because of its "playability."[395]

International

Simpson and Bruckheimer went to Europe in July to market the film. Marilyn Beck, the syndicated columnist who had already written about the movie, wrote that the producers had just returned from a "promotion trip abroad that has them convinced the film will be as big — or bigger — a hit overseas as it is domestically."[396]

Tapping international markets as a business strategy was still in its infancy. Simpson and Bruckheimer knew firsthand it was effective, given that *Flashdance* had done three times as much business abroad as it had stateside, Beck wrote. Others remained skeptical, even as they said they thought *Top Gun* could match what it had done domestically, which at that point was about $75 million. In August, once the rollout of the movie was finished on the continent, they took the effort to Japan and Australia.

Reviews abroad echoed a similar theme to the early reviews stateside, but with some cheeky British perspective. "For a classic American hero, you couldn't find anyone better than fighter pilot Pete 'Maverick' Mitchell," columnist Pauline McCleod wrote when the movie was released in Great Britain on Oct. 3, 1986. "He's about as manufactured as American processed cheese and his fellow countrymen just LOVE him!" Cruise had played the role "with great skill," she wrote, noting it was the No. 1 film in the U.S.[397]

The writer at the Sandwell Evening Mail, a paper in the West Midlands in central England, also noted record crowds but had "doubts" the movie would fare as well abroad.[398] They were wrong about that. The movie would take in about $13.6 million in the U.K. and have similarly robust numbers in other key foreign markets.[399]

During a 2014 appearance on "Jimmy Kimmel Live!," Kimmel asked Cruise about the first time he had traveled the world to promote a movie. The actor said that it was during the foreign press junket tour for *Top Gun,* which he said took four months. They'd spend weeks in every city they visited in Italy, France, and Japan. Cruise told Kimmel he was the one who came up with the idea of premiering films in other countries, though he said, "It took me a few years to get it going." Kimmel quipped, "So all these other actors must want to kill you."[400]

Tom Cruise answers questions about the movie on June 26, 1986, during an interview in his hotel suite in London.

Peter Stone/Mirrorpix/Newscom via ZUMA Press

Soundtrack soars

By mid-August, *Top Gun* was the top grossing film of the year, and its popularity was driven by more than word of mouth. A phenomenon had emerged that hadn't been seen before, certainly in numbers like this, and that was people returning to see it a second — and sometimes third — time. "*Top Gun* is getting tremendous repeat business," Ganis said. "Girls like it for Tom Cruise; boys like it for the action *and* Tom Cruise; kids are bringing their parents to see it!"[401]

He might have mentioned the music as well. The soundtrack had contributed mightily to the success of the movie. Radio was pervasive and influential in those days, before cable and the internet came to dominate the media, and "Danger Zone," crooned by Kenny Loggins, and "Take

My Breath Away" by Berlin, were in regular rotation. The soundtrack topped the charts that summer, staying in the lead position for five weeks.[402]

Between May 23 and Sept. 1, *Top Gun* booked $119 million, followed by *The Karate Kid, Part II* ($99 million), *Back to School* ($80 million), *Aliens* ($66 million), and *Ferris Bueller's Day Off* ($60.7 million.) *Cobra* was nowhere to be seen. The same story about box office numbers at the end of the summer reported that *Top Gun* had lost the top spot that week, bumped a notch by newcomer, *Stand By Me*.

While soundtracks were often popular with music buyers, there were no guarantees, David T. Friendly wrote that fall in the Los Angeles Times. Plenty of movie music collections quietly disappeared. Despite "lesser known artists," *Top Gun's* soundtrack album had soared. David Geffen, the head of the record label that bore his name, was interviewed in the piece.

"One of the reasons *Top Gun* has hung in there so long is because the music was so effective," Geffen told Friendly. "And it doesn't hurt to have a radio station saying 'Top Gun' eight times a day."[403] The soundtrack had sold nearly 3 million copies by October. Ultimately it became the best-selling soundtrack of 1986.

Across the industry, the box office had seen a slump in 1985, something blamed on the home video market, and at that time it looked like it might rally in 1986. That didn't turn out to be the case — revenue was down another 1 percent — but *Top Gun* had contributed more than its share to the totals.

"*Top Gun* came in first ... because of repeat business," wrote the Associated Press, in its end of summer summary. It was known that soundtracks could help boost sales of movies, but people returning to see them in such numbers was unusual.

In addition to having that year's top selling soundtrack *Top Gun* had also won the box office for 1986. Harder to document was the sale of bomber jackets, white T-shirts, Ray-Bans, and other gear that had been featured in the movie.

Costume designer Jimmy Tyson said that before the movie, bomber jackets were plentiful; after the movie, you could hardly find one anywhere, certainly not for a reasonable price.[404]

Sunglass maker Ray-Ban was only one of several companies to ink deals with Paramount. Another was The Shirt Shed, then a division of Nexus Industries, which licensed the rights to make *Top Gun*-branded T-shirts. They had been in bankruptcy protection in 1985, so it was a bold gamble, but one that paid off. The company reported a 33 percent increase in sales after the movie came out, jumping from $28.6 million in 1985 to $37.6 million in 1986. A company called Joy Insignia received the licenses for arm patches.

Those items have since become a cottage industry for a great many small businesses, most of which don't have licenses with Paramount, making the true economic impact of the film difficult to measure.

As for Simpson's and Bruckheimer's boast that they could beat the domestic haul for *Top Gun* in international markets, they came close. *Top Gun* has taken in an estimated $180 million in the U.S. and another $177 million abroad.[405]

Becoming Iconic

How is it that a 35-year-old (plus) movie, roundly rejected by critics, ends up so widely recognized that it remains a thriving brand of its own decades later? Locations from *Top Gun* around San Diego remain tourist destinations to this day. The movie has several thriving social media fan groups, just one of which has more than 10,000 followers. Retail items associated with the movie — not all of them sanctioned by the studio behind it — still sell in impressive numbers.

It's a rare feat that any single movie ends up with legions of followers decades later, and that was true before the long-awaited sequel, *Top Gun: Maverick*, advanced. For critics at the time, and to film scholars since, given the silence, *Top Gun* hasn't stood out as one of the important or critically notable films released in 1986.

That year's most highly praised movies included *A Room With a View*, *Children of a Lesser God* and *Platoon*, a gritty look at the life of American soldiers during Vietnam. *Platoon* dominated the top categories at the 59th Annual Academy Awards in 1987, earning four Oscars.

Top Gun had received four nominations: Billy Weber and Chris Lebenzon for film editing, Cecilia Hall and George Watters II for sound and for sound effects editing. It won for original song, for "Take My Breath Away," by Giorgio Moroder with lyrics by Tom Whitlock.

The clear winner at the box office that year, however, was *Top Gun*. It took in nearly $180 million, compared to *Platoon*'s $138.5 million, the only critically acclaimed movie to be on the list of top ten moneymakers. The fan favorite list included plenty of still-recognizable films or franchises: *Crocodile Dundee*, *Aliens*, *Ferris Bueller's Day Off*, and sequels *The Karate Kid Part II* and *Star Trek IV: The Voyage Home*. Films that got little attention from critics or crowds in 1986 but have stood up well include *Kiss of the Spiderwoman*, *Out of Africa*, and *Stand By Me*.

But whatever can be said of the other top movies of 1986, you won't find imagery from them on top-selling movie T-shirts in 2021.

Then and now

"It was a definite popcorn movie, but it was the rock and roll stars of the sky," is how Scott summed up the movie in an on-camera interview for a reissue of the movie. "It was great-looking guys, blue skies with silver jets and rock and roll music."[406] He made that comment, or some variation of it, over many years.

The quality of Scott's visual imagery, groundbreaking for its time, along with a best-selling soundtrack, were key to the film's success in 1986. The cooperation of the military, specifically the Navy, which supplied sets like the USS

Ranger, the USS Enterprise and the USS Carl Vinson, its own mega-star, the F-14 fighter jet — accompanied by great strides in aerial cinematography — meant truly fresh content. This was the MTV generation, and *Top Gun* saturated every sector of the cultural airwaves. The soundtrack remains on the top ten list of units sold to this day.

The reasons it was popular in the 1980s don't necessarily explain its longevity. The mega-stardom of Tom Cruise certainly plays a huge role, but so does the sheer luck of timing, both culturally and technologically. The marketing efforts of Paramount — which has strategically allocated money over the decades to promote it, upgrade it, and re-release it — have also been effective.

Vietnam

The Vietnam War had ended 11 years before *Top Gun* came out, but it was still in the forefront of the minds of Americans, particularly young people. Stories of the futility and immorality of the conflict were the rule, and it remained incredibly unpopular, even a source of national shame. That sentiment was reflected in the success of *Platoon*, which told a story without a shred of silver lining.

People were ready to feel better about the country, and *Top Gun* provided a vehicle for that. Its positive depiction of the military and its appeal as a vehicle for recruitment were dominant themes in early reviews.

"*Top Gun* is as well engineered as a beautiful machine, putting thrilling aerial sequences against the drama on the ground with stopwatch precision," wrote Malcolm L. Johnston, film critic at The Hartford Courant. "It's manipulative, but it sure works."[407]

Johnston took special note of the film's access to military hardware. "From the moment it begins aboard an aircraft carrier in the dawn's early light, one big question arises: Why hasn't anyone ever made a film about Navy fighter pilots before?" Catching planes in flight went back to *Wings*, the silent-era classic, he wrote. "Add in the almost supernatural presence of the leviathan carriers at sea and you have the makings of an exciting experience in big screen cinema."

But far more took issue with it being what they saw as an advertisement for the military. The Philadelphia Inquirer called *Top Gun* "…a thrilling new Navy recruitment film… guaranteed to make diehard conscientious objectors into raving warmongers."[408]

The headline on the review in the Boston Globe published that May read "Boy Meets Plane," while its jump headline read "'Top Gun' idolizes military hardware."

"The planes assume mystical, god-like qualities as their speed and power roar through the theaters," wrote Michael Blowen, who also might have been the first to state the movie's potential as an actual recruitment vehicle. He noted there was a "Pavlovian" response to hardware on the display at the theater where it was screened, although he didn't state exactly what he meant. "The Navy might have signed up dozens of gung-ho pilot trainees if they'd only had the sense to set up a table in the lobby."[409]

The military figured it out in no time. By early July the recruitment boon was meaningful enough to catch the attention of an Associated Press writer along with others.[410] It's easy to find references online to significant percentage increases in recruiting, some as high as 500 percent, but there is a lack of data to support specific claims. Certainly the Navy was cagey about it at the time. Stairs, involved with the movie on the Navy's behalf during production, used cautious language in an interview with the Los Angeles Times. Navy regulations prohibited even the appearance of it endorsing a commercial product, she told the reporter. The piece noted the striking uptick, as the movie continued to draw throughout the summer, often with military recruiters set up in front of theaters.[411]

Some recruits complained that the movie had given them a false idea of what they'd be doing in the Navy. The Miami Herald, which did a piece about the Aviation Officer Candidate School in Pensacola, helped set the record straight.

The Navy had granted nearly full access to Herald reporter Mary Voboril. Her piece explained the sheer difficulty of even becoming a pilot, much less the Topgun program. Her article pointed out that most people in the Navy never even touched an F-14. Incidentally, that piece also had recruitment officials admitting the "major impact," of *Top Gun* even if the (unnamed) chief of naval information in Washington, D.C., would supply no corroborating data.[412]

Crew who had worked on the movie, most of them surprised by its success, were aware of this effect. "Everybody was so depressed about the war," recalled gaffer Russell, who would go on to be director of photography for *Days of Thunder*, the next project on the horizon for Scott, Simpson and Bruckheimer. "Soldiers took such a hit when they came back, people telling them, 'Shame on you.' This was the first project that actually gave life and brought back pride to the military."[413]

Others were less comfortable with the pro-military motif. "We talked a lot about it," said music editor Badami. "It was along the lines of, 'what have we done.'"[414]

Actor Tim Robbins said in an interview in 1994 that he wasn't in a position to turn down roles at that point, but that he'd been unaware it would be such a recruitment film.[415]

Cruise was asked about whether it was pro-war repeatedly in interviews to promote the movie and made it a point to downplay any jingoism. "I think there are a lot of people who will project that in the piece, because of the political environment we are living in. We never were interested in making a war movie. The movie was about love of country, flight, and competition," he said.[416]

Timing technology in 1987

A little bit of the history of home viewing, beginning with the entry of a Japanese company called JVC, helps set the stage for what happened next.

The short version is that JVC introduced the VHS videocassette in the United States in 1977, and quickly licensed the format to companies making videocassette machines. In fairly rapid order it overtook the Sony Betamax format, and by the time of *Top Gun*, VHS could claim 90 percent of the home video market.

Videocassette machines, or VCRs, were commonplace in homes by then. The VHS rental market, aided by retailers like Blockbuster, was thriving, but the sale of individual copies of movies was something new. To own a personal copy of a movie at that point was expensive, typically in the range of $80 for a recent release. But pricing was under pressure, with Disney discounting the costs of its existing library on VHS as part of a year-end sales blitz. Paramount followed. Its next step was to dramatically lower the price for both *Beverly Hills Cop* and *Indiana Jones and the Temple of Doom* to $29.95.

"Almost alone in the industry, Paramount has tried to create a sell-through market for new movies," the New York Times reported.[417]

Paramount announced in January 1987 that when the VHS of *Top Gun* went on sale that March it would cost $26.95, the lowest price of any newly released movie to date. There was another first: The cassette would start with a 60-second Pepsi commercial, and the spot would debut at the February Grammy Awards. The marketing campaign for the movie, estimated to cost $8 million, would be split between the soft drink maker and the studio.

"This is as much or more than is usually spent to send a new movie into theaters, and millions of dollars more than has ever been spent to advertise a new video cassette," the New York Times reported.[418]

That March the numbers came out. Initial orders for *Top Gun* on VHS, with the Pepsi commercial, were in excess of 1.9 million copies. It handily topped the sales of *Indiana Jones*, which previously held the record at 1.4 million copies.[419]

Chapter 13 - Endnotes

[384] Bob Thomas, "The Annual Summer Movie Binge" *Monitor* (McAllen, Texas), 2B. https://www.newspapers.com/image/322069179/

[385] Ibid.

[386] Vernon Scott, "Cobra' biggest draw for box-office bucks," United Press International, May 29, 1986. Retrieved from *Sun Sentinel* (Fort Lauderdale, FL), 6E. https://www.newspapers.com/image/236638168/

[387] Roger Ebert, "Reviews: Top Gun," News America Syndicate, May 16, 1986. Retrieved from *Capital Times* (Madison, WI). 40. https://www.newspapers.com/image/521445556/

[388] Martin Kohn, "Top Gun never gets off the ground," *Detroit Free Press*, May 16, 1986, 4C. Retrieved from https://www.newspapers.com/image/99355485/

[389] Michael Wilmington. "High Tech Flyboys in 'Top Gun.'" *Los Angeles Times*, May 16, 1986, VI-1 and VI-22. https://www.newspapers.com/image/401994425/

[390] Bill Cosford. "'Top Gun: A miss for Cruise, McGillis." *Miami Herald*, May 16, 1986, 6D. https://www.newspapers.com/image/631234086/

[391] "'Cobra' muscles way to box office lead again," Associated Press, June 5, 1986, Retrieved from *Cincinnati Enquirer*, C10. https://www.newspapers.com/image/101782043/

[392] Jack Mathews, "Box office top 10: Who's engrossed?" *Los Angeles Times*, June 13, 1986, VI-16. https://www.newspapers.com/image/402409279/

[393] Vernon Scott, "Top Gun shoots down Cobra at box office," United Press International, June 11, 1986. Retrieved from *Tampa Bay Times*, 5D. https://www.newspapers.com/image/321047566/

[394] Mike H. Price, "Howard's egg a lesson in marketing," *Fort Worth Star Telegram*, Sept. 28, 1988, 4D. https://www.newspapers.com/image/639390978/

[395] Bob Thomas, "Release of films is an art," Associated Press, retrieved from *Merced Sun-Star* (Merced, California), May 20, 1986, 15. https://www.newspapers.com/image/785401470/

[396] Marilyn Beck, "Top Gun Aims at Foreign Markets," *Pensacola News Journal,* July 6, 1986, 3E. https://www.newspapers.com/image/267050602

[397] Pauline McLeod, "Girl in Tom's Sights," *Daily Mirror*, Oct. 3, 1986. https://www.britishnewspaperarchive.co.uk/viewer/bl/0000560/19861003/126/0026

[398] Fred Norris, "A Flight of Daft Fancy," *Sandwell Evening Mail,* Midlands, U.K, Oct. 2, 1986. https://www.britishnewspaperarchive.co.uk/viewer/bl/0002487/19861002/109/0015

[399] Revenues from https://www.saltypopcorn.co.uk/movies/top_gun; conversion from £ to USD https://www.poundsterlinglive.com/bank-of-england-spot/historical-spot-exchange-rates/gbp/GBP-to-USD-1987

[400] *Jimmy Kimmel Live!* (June 3, 2014). Tom Cruise, interviewed by Jimmy Kimmel. https://archive.org/details/KGO_20140604_063500_Jimmy_Kimmel_Live

[401] George Williams, "The long cold summer," *Sacramento Bee* (Sacramento, CA), Aug 31, 1986, Encore 16. https://www.newspapers.com/image/623052850/

[402] Billboard 200, Top selling albums, August 1986. https://web.archive.org/web/20130623100921/http://www.billboard.com/charts/1986-08-02/billboard-200

[403] David T. Friendly, "Seeking the groove in movie soundtracks," *Los Angeles Times*, October 2, 1986. Vi-6. https://www.newspapers.com/image/402854157/ [404] Tyson, June 6, 2020.

[405] Box Office Mojo, "Top Gun (1986)." https://www.boxofficemojo.com/title/tt0092099/

[406] *Danger Zone: The Making of Top Gun.*

[407] Malcolm L. Johnson, "Top Gun Flies High on Land, in Air," *Hartford Courant*, May 16, 1986, B2. https://www.newspapers.com/image/371937673/

[408] Carrie Rickey, "Film: 'Top Gun' enlists Tom Cruise as Navy Fighter Pilot," *Philadelphia Inquirer*, May 16, 1986, 20. https://www.newspapers.com/image/169265909/

[409] Michael Blowen. "Boy meets plane," *Boston Globe*, May 16, 1986, 24-25. https://www.newspapers.com/image/438808456/

[410] Mark Evje, "'Top Gun' boosting service sign-ups," *Los Angeles Times*, July 5, 1986, IV-10. https://www.newspapers.com/image/402865163/

[411] Ibid.

[412] Mary Voboril, "On a Wing and a Dare: It's a long way from Pensacola to Top Gun," *Miami Herald*, August 17, 1986, 1G. https://www.newspapers.com/image/631231706

[413] Russell, September 27, 2020.

[414] Bob Badami. Music Editor for *Top Gun*, interview with the author, August 27, 2021.

[415] Hillel Italie, "Tim Robbins mixes art, politics," Associated Press, March 1, 1994. Retrieved from *New-Journal* (Mansfield, Ohio), 2-B. https://www.newspapers.com/image/296479118/

[416] Diane Haithman, "'Top Gun' star disarms with old-fashioned cheeky charm," *Detroit Free Press*, May 16, 1986, 1C. https://www.newspapers.com/image/99355464

[417] Aljean Harmetz, "Marketing 'Top Gun' Cassette," *New York Times*, January 15, 1987. C-17. https://www.nytimes.com/1987/01/15/arts/marketing-top-gun-cassette.html

[418] Ibid.

[419] Dennis Hunt, "'TOP GUN' CASSETTE BECOMES TOP SELLER." *Los Angeles Times*, January 16, 1987, C25. https://timesmachine.nytimes.com/timesmachine/1987/03/04/275987.html

PART IV
TONY SCOTT, LIFE AND LEGACY, FANDOM

PHOTO: Armando Gallo/ZUMA Studio.

Tony Scott
June 21, 1944 – Aug. 19, 2012

CHAPTER 14
WHAT HAPPENED TO TONY SCOTT

Shortly after noon on Sunday, Aug. 19, 2012, Tony Scott brought his black Toyota Prius to a stop at the crest of the Vincent Thomas Bridge in the Port of Los Angeles. He got out, strode purposefully to the eight-foot-high fence atop a guardrail on the south side of the bridge, scaled it, and jumped off, plummeting nearly 200 feet to his death.[420]

It happened just that quickly, according to an observer whose first thought was that it was someone into extreme sports. Scott, wearing his trademark red shorts and a blue-gray shirt, had looked nervous, but aside from a quick look around, a passerby said he hadn't hesitated.

It was a shocking end to a brilliant, creative life, devastating to his family and close friends and legions of fans, as well as to hundreds of people who worked with him on his movies and commercials over decades. They were from all ends of the moviemaking spectrum, former production assistants, cameramen and other crew, as well as Tom Cruise, Jerry Bruckheimer, and producer David Ellison, who were beginning work on *Top Gun: Maverick*. Tony Scott was working with them on the sequel when he died.

Bruckheimer was asked about Scott's death at the School of Film and Television at Loyola Marymount University in 2015. He called it "a real shock… We were talking about doing another *Top Gun*, down in Fallon, Nev., meeting with Top Gun pilots." The interviewer, a journalist, asked if Scott had seemed alright. "He seemed okay, he seemed fine," Bruckheimer replied. "I got a call Sunday night he'd passed away."[421]

Scott's last days

That Friday, Scott, Cruise, and Bruckheimer had flown by private jet to the naval air station to meet with Navy brass.[422] *Top Gun* made stars of both Scott and Cruise, and they had done one more movie together, *Days of Thunder* (1985). Scott made six movies with Bruckheimer. Had Scott lived to direct *Top Gun: Maverick,* it would have been the first time Scott, Cruise and Bruckheimer had reunited on a project since *Days of Thunder.*

Scott referred to such trips as "reccys," the term used in the U.K. for scouting or reviewing locations, but its larger mission was to schmooze. As with the first *Top Gun*, the sequel had been cleared by the Pentagon, while its success would rest on support down the chain of command. To the filmmakers, it was familiar terrain, as most of the air-to-air scenes had been shot in Fallon in August 1985.

The training facility for the Navy's top pilots, the creative nexus of the story, had relocated from San Diego to Fallon in 1996. Meanwhile, operations at the base had grown dramatically. In 1985, it had a workforce of 1,345, with 780 military personnel; now there were closer to 3,000, with nearly 1,100 of them military. Almost everything was different.[423]

When the *Top Gun* movie production shot aerial scenes over two weeks in 1985, they didn't need the actors. The pilots, including Abel, took the actors up in F-14s in hopes of getting them on camera, but lacking training or acclimation to G-forces, they had predictably lost their stomachs. Instead, the actors were filmed in an F-14 mockup on soundstages.

For years fans had called for a sequel, and occasionally there were promising rumors, but it didn't start to come together until early 2012. Adam Goodman, president of Paramount Motion Pictures Group, told reporters in late April that a *Top Gun* sequel was on. "Jerry Bruckheimer would produce, with Tony Scott returning to direct. All parties are moving ahead," he said.[424]

The visiting group toured the base's aircraft, runways and hangars for the sequel. RADM Mark Vance, then commander of the Navy Strike and Air Warfare Center, hosted a lunch meeting, said Zip Upham, spokesman for Naval Air Station Fallon. Upham was taking a group of Cub Scouts and their parents on a tour when they saw Cruise outside the lunch hall. The actor had stepped outside to make a call. "The Cub Scouts didn't know who he was, but their dads did," said Upham. "It was a fun moment." [425]

The news of Scott's death less than 48 hours later left everyone at Fallon dumbfounded, but it left the film world stunned. Friends, colleagues and fans paid tribute to Tony Scott on social media. Actors who worked with him topped the list, many noting his contributions to film. Cruise issued a statement: "Tony was my dear friend and I will really miss him. He was a creative visionary whose mark on film is immeasurable. My deepest sorrow and thoughts are with his family at this time."[426]

Denzel Washington, who worked with the director more than any other actor, said it was "unfathomable to think that he is now gone." He called Scott "a great director, a genuine friend" and noted his "tremendous passion for life and for the art of film-making and was able to share this passion with all of us through his cinematic brilliance."

Unstoppable star Rosario Dawson addressed Scott personally in her post: "What a lovely, kind human being you were. I will love and miss you much."

Keira Knightley, who played the lead in *Domino*, described him as "one of the world's true originals." Tony Scott was "one of the most extraordinary, imaginative men I ever worked with," she said.

Said Gene Hackman, who starred in *Crimson Tide* and *Enemy of the State*: "We've lost a wonderful, creative talent."

Wrote Val Kilmer: "RIP Tony. You were the kindest film director I ever worked for. You will be missed."

Even critic Roger Ebert, who years earlier had taken a stick to some of Scott's work, called him "an inspired craftsman."

Tony Scott was buried in a large ceremony at Hollywood Forever on Aug. 24. There had been discussion about keeping it small, family only, but Donna felt it should be the opposite. She planned it, and the guest list, about 300 people. "My husband made so many people who they are, he really did," she said. "So many people loved him," she said.[427]

Ridley Scott, who had flown to the U.S. after it happened, organized a celebration of life the following February. It was at the Samuel Goldwyn Theater at the Academy of Motion Picture Arts and Sciences. Bruckheimer started the event off by welcoming attendees, while Denzel Washington, who had starred in more of Scott's films than any other actor, gave the introduction.

Then came special guest speakers from throughout Scott's professional life: Gary Oldman, *True Romance*, 1993; John Travolta, *The Taking of Pelham 123* (2009); Hans Zimmer, composer, *Top Gun* and three other films; Harry Gregson Williams, composer for Scott's last eight movies, starting with *Enemy of the State*; Skip Chaisson, producer on *Unstoppable* and other projects; Bob Gazzale, president and CEO of AFI; Tom Cruise; Tom Hardy, actor and family friend; and Dakota Fanning, *Man on Fire* (2004). Donna Scott spoke ahead of the reel of Scott's work, edited by Chaisson. Ridley Scott spoke last, encouraging everyone to stay for the reception that followed.[428]

News coverage

Scott's suicide was international news, given his prominence and the suddenness of his passing. The initial stories tried to piece together what happened, while next-day stories dug in for more. Several pieces noted how many projects Scott had on his desk. Two of the movies were about drug smuggling, "Narco Sub" and "Lucky Strike." Another was a remake of *The Wild Bunch* (1969),[429] the Sam Peckinpah classic. He was also considering "Potsdamer Platz," which had been pitched by producer and longtime associate Catalaine Knell.[430]

"Narco Sub" was with 20th Century Fox. "We had a meeting just two weeks ago and he was burning with the excitement of creating stuff," Tom Rothman, then chairman of 20th Century Fox, told the Los Angeles Times.[431]

The reports, while accurate, missed the degree to which the Maverick sequel had come online. "*Top Gun* became the priority, because they were getting the green light on that ahead of everything else," explained David Nowell.[432]

Nowell talked to Scott the Wednesday before his death about the aerial photography for *Top Gun: Maverick*. "He said, 'Whatever you want to do, mate,' and that he'd know more after he met with Jerry and Tom on Friday."

A few months earlier, cameraman Nowell had been working on *Oblivion* (2013) in Baton Rouge, La. "Tom [Cruise] was waiting for a shot and I reintroduced myself, said we'd met when we were doing Mission Impossible 3. The conversation turned to the potential sequel for *Top Gun*. "I told Tom I had just talked to Tony about it, and he said, 'Tony is going to crush it!'"

One news story had the effect of changing the long-term narrative around Scott's death among fans and even people who knew him. It was published by the online team at ABC News: "'Top Gun' Director Tony Scott Had Inoperable Brain Cancer."[433] The story, branded with the "Good Morning America" logo, used an unnamed source identified as "someone close to Tony Scott."

ABC News is one of the oldest broadcast news organizations in the world, with a strong team of journalists, one that other news and entertainment media follow. Numerous organizations picked up the story, including People, Vanity Fair, Huffington Post, Entertainment Weekly (EW) and TMZ. It surprised people who knew he'd had health issues but believed he had recovered.

Donna Scott, obviously in a state of shock and grief, challenged its accuracy, which was relayed to the press by state officials. "According to the family, to their knowledge, he did not have any issues with any cancers," Los Angeles Assistant Chief Coroner Ed Winter told reporters. "They don't know where that came from."[434]

ABC News ran another story at 5:40 p.m., this one without a byline: "Tony Scott Brain Cancer Report Appears in Doubt; Family knew of no cancer, coroner says." But while ABC News pulled the other story off the site, it didn't immediately retract it. That meant that other news organizations left it up, too. Some, like EW, reported that the story was in doubt, yet its headline still read: "Report: Tony Scott was suffering from brain cancer."[435]

Media watchdogs pounced on ABC News, with one critic noting several serious reporting errors in recent months. The use of a single, unnamed source for the brain cancer story while a named source — his wife — disavowed it, was problematic, and an ABC spokesperson said they were "investigating."

The Los Angeles County Department of the Coroner issued its final report on Oct. 11, 2012, which stated that the cause of death was multiple blunt-force injuries.[436] It detailed the physical damage to Scott's body from the fall, which had killed him instantly. It noted that therapeutic levels of Mirtazapine, an antidepressant, and Eszopiclone, used to treat insomnia, were in his system. The 24-page report was also important for what it didn't show, which was a diseased brain. In medical speak, Scott's brain wasn't herniated, and there were no signs of aneurysm. There was "no anatomic evidence of neoplasia (cancer) identified at autopsy," according to the coroner's office.

ABC News, which had stood by its story for nearly two months at that point, retracted it.[437] A retraction is different from a correction, which admits to a mistake contained in a story. A retraction is an admission that the point of the story was incorrect.

A spokesperson for ABC News, asked in October 2021 about the delay in issuing the retraction, noted that it followed the release of the coroner's report and that the network had apologized. They directed a journalist back to the network's statement in 2012.[438]

Retraction

Please Note: ABC News previously reported that director Tony Scott had inoperable brain cancer and cited it as a possible reason for his suicide. The Los Angeles County coroner's report on Mr. Scott's death listed no evidence of brain cancer. ABC News has retracted that Aug. 20 story and extends a formal apology to Mr. Scott's family and friends.[439]

Professional news organizations have strong policies about the use of unnamed sources. It is unlikely the network, particularly under pressure, would have stood by the report without strong reason to believe its source was unimpeachable. Higher-ups would have been aware of the source's identity because they, too, were standing by it. In other words, it is safe to take ABC at its published word, which was that the source was someone close to Tony Scott. "Close" suggests a member of his family, a publicist, or a personal assistant.

One thing for certain: ABC News isn't going to identify the source, because once a reputable news organization agrees to take information off-the-record, they can't in good faith back out, even if they were misled.

So who was the source, and does it matter a decade later? The answer is yes, for two reasons. The first is that the false story changed the public narrative of what happened, and the delay in correcting it contributes to the brain cancer story being widely believed today. People stopped asking the logical question about what happened in the days leading up to his death because it offered an explanation. Most weren't following along two months later to know the truth.

The second reason is more important, because the absence of correct information continues to fuel misinformation, in this case among people who were paying attention. One rumor has gained traction with a number of crew who worked with the director over the years: that Scott was told on the return trip from Fallon that he wouldn't be directing the sequel to *Top Gun*, which helped trigger his suicide two days later. Further, some believe Cruise or a supporter was behind the placement of the ABC News story, which served to deflect attention from the actor, who had been with Scott.[440] The basis for the rumor seems to be that one of the reporters behind the brain cancer story covered the actor and hence would have access to him.

Cruise, through counsel, stated unequivocally in November 2021 that Scott was on to direct *Top Gun: Maverick* at the time of his death, and referred a reporter to spokespeople for both Bruckheimer and Ellison, who confirmed the same thing. Cruise's counsel also provided a redacted email that stated Cruise and Bruckheimer would do the movie only if Scott directed. He vehemently denied any connection to the erroneous story put out by ABC News.

But it's also unlikely to have been Cruise for several other reasons. While Cruise and Scott were friends, they weren't "close" in the sense the actor knew Scott's medical issues. They were colleagues about to go into business together again. Donna Scott said in an interview in January 2022 that Tony Scott hadn't told *anyone* in the work sphere about his illness.

She declined to share her thoughts on who leaked the false story except to say she was "100 percent" sure it wasn't Cruise. "Tom Cruise had nothing to do with it," she said. "That much I can tell you."[441]

But there is a lot of misinformation out there about her husband's death. For one thing, Donna isn't convinced he meant to kill himself. There are several good reasons for that, even though he was suffering from depression and brain fog connected to prior cancer treatment, and even said he might jump.

Immediate family

Donna and Tony Scott were together for 24 years, the last 18 of those years married, and the last 12 raising twin sons, Max and Frank, who were born in 2000.

She and Scott met in 1989 when she landed an audition in Los Angeles for the role of Darlene, a "pit girl" in *Days of Thunder*, a story about the professional racing circuit.

Donna Wilson was 24, a smart North Carolina beauty queen with an impressive resume and one credit, a small role on *Vanishing America,* (1986) a comedy by Rich Hall.

She had begun competing in beauty contests in high school in Davidson, winning the title Miss North Mecklenburg, then Miss North Carolina National Teen-Ager in 1982. She was second runner-up in the national pageant that same year. As a student at the University of North Carolina in Greensboro, her studies included communication and dance, and she performed with a local dance troupe.

In 1983 she was declared Miss Mello Yello for the World 600, then in 1984, the N.C. Rhododendron Queen. As Top Gun was coming out on VHS in 1987, she was competing to become Miss North Carolina. She won the title, which made her the state's representative in the Miss USA pageant. That opened a lot of doors, and she went to New York, where she got plenty of work, primarily doing television commercials.

The audition in Los Angeles was a big break. "I read for Tony, and then he sent me down to read for Don [Simpson] and Jerry [Bruckheimer] together." She still recalls the producers' famous shared desk in the large office at the end of the hall.

Shortly thereafter Donna began dating Simpson. "I loved Don madly," Donna recalled, but that didn't mean she took him seriously.

Working on *Days of Thunder* was something different, and so was Tony Scott. "My big direction was 'Hey blonde, stick your tits out!' But it didn't make her mad. "He was so cheeky and charming. He could get away with it where someone else couldn't."

The movie production enjoys a storied status as one of the more wild off-screen adventures in filmmaking. "It was insane! It was Florida, and the whole vibe of the movie — everyone was having a good time," said Donna. Everyone except the leadership at Paramount, who was balking at cost overruns.[442]

One night during principal photography she was dancing with Jake Scott, son of Ridley Scott, at a nightclub taken over by the production. "Jake said [Tony] tapped him on the shoulder and said, 'This one is mine, get out.'" She didn't take Tony seriously at first.

"It was just fun for me, but that's where we started," Donna said. That was Easter weekend, 1990, but when the movie wrapped, they were still together. In 1992 they moved onto a Beverly Hills estate they called "Seabright," although it's better known to others as Bella Vista; it had been home to famed actor John Barrymore from 1927 until his death in 1942.

The movie business demands stamina, even of its laziest. Tony's level of energy was on the other end of that spectrum, rare among even the most committed of directors, according to numerous people who worked with him. Several people interviewed for the book commented that Tony worked harder than anyone, generally in regard to whether he was demanding.

In many ways he was fearless. He once made off with the wife of a bad-ass actor who might have hurt him if he'd found him in time. Bruckheimer described Scott, decades before he died, as someone who lived life to the fullest, a "real adventurer" who had wrecked four motorcycles. "In fact, he almost has a death wish, always pushing it right over the edge."[443]

People close to Tony knew that for many years he was prescribed and took Sustanon, a steroid used to treat testosterone deficiency, which obviously contributed to his high level of energy.[444] But he had always kept moving, and fast. That high energy characterized his youth and continued into his 30s when he was deep into a career making commercials. It was there in his early 40s when he was making *Top Gun*. It was evident in his 50s and 60s, both on set and off, in fast cars and on his Ducati, and also as a husband and father. And it was true on the last day of his life.

Donna recalled a story Tony told about getting pulled over in the U.K. while driving the Dino Ferrari he'd bought when he'd earned his first $1 million. He was a storyteller and so he painted the narrative with colorful details. He had been 28 at the time, and still living with roommates. They shared an apartment over an Indian restaurant that had a bathtub with a meter requiring coins for hot water. "He used to say they'd sweep the floors of the restaurant to get free food."

Tony had taken the new car for a drive and had just gone under a bridge when it was picked up on radar. "The police said they thought it was low-flying aircraft," Donna said. The fact that it had gone under a bridge made it clear the object was earthbound.

Donna could keep up with Tony in a way most people couldn't. That's what made their relationship work. She enjoyed the same kind of extreme outdoor adventure, albeit with less abandon. When they vacationed, it was to do things like rock climbing or SCUBA diving. "He was a badass," Donna said. "He really was."

One trip was to the Dolemites, where Tony had first learned to climb. The northern Italian Alps offer climbers various degrees of difficulty. The guide, whom Tony had known for years, came up with a plan for the family whereby they'd balance the challenging climbs he wanted to make with those more appropriate for the twins, who were eight. The group would split up, with Tony going on more extreme climbs that required tying in, while other guides would go with Donna, Max, Frank, and the babysitter who traveled with them, for rigorous but less-threatening climbs.[445] Everything was an adventure. Even the regular trip to brunch at their favorite Malibu restaurant involved riding bikes.

Most of all, Tony loved to shoot – commercials, but especially movies. "He was a workaholic," Donna said. "He would get depressed if he wasn't working."[446]

Donna had roles in a number of Scott's movies. She also acted in other movies, like *Get Shorty* (1995), *Austin Powers: International Man of Mystery* (1997), and *Water for Elephants* (2011), and has appeared in numerous television shows.

"We got married on *Crimson [Tide]*" she said, referring to the Denzel Washington thriller filmed in 1994. They'd been together for four years by then and she had adapted to his superstitious nature. He wanted chicken fajitas for dinner every night he was shooting. "I figured out on *Crimson* I could make the whole bunch on Monday night," and then they'd be ready for the rest of the week.

"He liked to follow the same patterns he had with earlier successful movies," she recalled. He ate half a tuna salad sandwich with jalapeno and Tabasco, washed down with a Coca-Cola. "He would have 10 versions of the same outfit, the same shooting vest." It helped minimize the time he had to think about anything other than the movie he was making.

They wanted to have kids, but there were health issues and it took some time. Max and Frank were born in 2000. By then they had turned the lavish Spanish colonial Seabright compound into their own. When the mural on the living room ceiling, – commissioned by Barrymore – needed to be touched up, they updated it with their own family and present-day greenery.[447] The Scott's annexed several neighboring properties over the years, a subterranean garage and land so no one could build adjacent to their home. Tony redesigned the two-story aviary built by Barrymore for live birds and animal trophies, converting it into bedrooms for the boys. "It was the last really nice thing he did," Donna said.

It was important to the couple that the boys have a traditional upbringing. The Scotts had staff to help with the estate but Donna regularly organized meals, either cooking herself or ordering from favorite restaurants. Once she called in the family dinner order to the Mr. Chow's in Beverly Hills from Buton, an island in Indonesia. She had reminded Tony in a phone call that she was on the other side of the world, but he wanted her to order the dinner anyway. The chain of fine-dining Chinese eateries was a favorite of the family. Ironically, the last time she spoke with Tony was when he asked if she would call in the family's regular order at the restaurant.[448]

They'd had a row on Thursday night; he'd got back late from the scout in Nevada on Friday. Saturday she had dinner out with friends, which is when she and Tony talked on the phone about the food order.

She played all of that out, every word, ad nauseam, the same as almost anyone who has a loved one who takes their own life.

August 19, 2012

That Sunday morning Donna was asleep at Seabright when Tony kissed her on the head. She stirred for a moment, and as soon as she woke up she went looking for him to tell him it was sweet and that she loved him. But when she went to his office at the bottom of the stairs to look for him, she found the door locked. Donna tried to call Tony on his cell and at the office at RSA Films, which was closed for the weekend.

She checked his buckslip schedule book, which showed he planned to take the boys and some of their friends on a reccy for a Pepsi commercial featuring the band One Direction. But he'd left without them, telling the nanny he'd be back by noon.

Noon was still well more than an hour away, and for a moment she felt relief, but it didn't last long. She resumed calling Tony, now "psycho dialing." She called both his assistants, before getting one who offered to go look for Tony. He lived closer to the bridge, which connects San Pedro to Terminal Island, than she did. Donna told him to hold off while she turned her efforts to tracking Tony's car and phone, which came up empty. She called him back and said, yes, please go look for Tony.

Eventually Tom Moran, Tony's primary assistant, arrived at Seabright. Donna waited for him before unlocking the office, and they went in together. They found a note to Donna and the boys. It was hand written, personal, and alarming by its presence but it could also be read as just a loving note to his family.

After a while the other assistant rang in. He told Donna the authorities wanted to speak to her, and gave her a number. She called only to be put on hold and transferred three times, her stomach sinking lower each time. Finally, someone came on to say they'd have to call back. The next call was from investigator Kristy McCracken, who told her what happened. It was 5:50 p.m., according to the report.

Donna's memory is a bit blurry. She remembers breaking down, but regaining her composure to continue the call. The boys, then 12, were nearby, well aware by then that their dad was missing. One of them asked her not to tell him what happened.

Donna asked if she needed to identify the body, and as told it wouldn't be necessary if she could confirm a tattoo. McCracken described a tattoo on his right buttock, one Donna has as well. They got the matching tattoos in Santa Barbara in 1992 when Tony was shooting *True Romance*. The characters at the center of the Quentin Tarantino script had matching body art to proclaim their love for each other. It featured a cherub holding a heart with a banner in it. Tony and Donna dropped the cherub in their design. Theirs was of two hearts with a banner featuring two names underneath, illegible from the passage of time, of the kids they still wanted to have at that point.[449]

The information was all McCracken needed, given other evidence, including Scott's Prius, which had a short, facts-only note with Donna's name and numbers for the home and her cell, along with the cell number of one of his assistants. The official report quoted the short note but blocked out, or redacted, the words.[450]

The report stated that co-workers at his company came to the bridge and talked to investigators. They'd taken a cell photo of a note he'd left at the office, and said there had been another one showing he was going to the bridge. Investigators noted that the 33 miles would have taken 42 minutes to drive.

But Donna doesn't think it is that clear-cut. Neither of the notes expressly stated he planned suicide. The one in the car — which he had left running — said, "If anything happens," and listed her name and both the home and cell numbers, as well as Moran's number.

Donna's heart checked when she saw the note in his office that day before she received official word. "When I saw that, not good. Did I see that as a suicide note? Considering that he had threatened to jump on two other occasions, yes. And, no." He could be quite dramatic, she explained, even "sensationalist." They were serious climbers — the whole family — and there were many times Tony would, on the spur-of-the-moment, climb a wall or the face of a rock or even a billboard. Donna believes he might have climbed the bridge not thinking he would actually jump, and perhaps passed out.

Which leads to another part of the story that few know, and even those close enough who can guess have done so with little accuracy. Tony hadn't been well. No, he didn't have brain cancer, and it's irritating to Donna that so much of the world thinks that so many years later.

But he was suffering from prolonged side effects of cancer treatment. Tony had cancer twice in his life, once as a young man, and more recently, a rare form that took root in his hip. He'd been in remission for 18 months, which is why the coroner's report showed him to be free of cancer.

The effects of the treatment —— a "cocktail" of pharmaceuticals including chemo and various other drugs —— had taken a serious toll. The couple had been forewarned about one drug in particular, Donna recalled. Adding it to the mix could help with his recovery, the doctor told them, but its side effects included persistent brain fog that could last as long as two years. "Tony wanted to get better, so he said okay."

They thought about the doctor's warning as symptoms persisted. "His brain wasn't healed from the drugs," Donna explained. "When someone is mad about their lives, they take it out on the people closest to them." Pressure for the Scotts was heightened because of the decision to keep quiet about his illness. Tony had to maintain with everyone else so there were few places to vent.

Twice when Tony was frustrated he said he might jump off the bridge, so Donna called the doctor. There was still hope for it to get better, given the 24-month time frame.

"We were fighting a lot – it was hard," she recalled in the January 2022 interview. "He could be so hard on me, and I can take a lot." She would escape to the guest cottage on Seabright and he would eventually find her. "He would see me so devastated, and be so sweet. He had a really good heart, and tears would roll down. He had awareness, but he couldn't stop himself." It happened numerous times, to the point the kids asked them not to fight in front of their friends. "He had no ability not to do it or even regulate. It was like the Tasmanian devil."

Donna replayed what happened for years in her mind. Her priority, and what has helped her the most, has been the boys. The family moved out of Seabright to Encintas after Tony died. She sold the Bella Vista estate in 2021, although she keeps some property in the area, in case the boys ever want to live there again.

Donna still occasionally acts and produces select projects while working on personal real estate projects. She splits time between the West Coast and two places on the East Coast: North Carolina, where her family still lives, and New York, where the twins attend film school. A lot of her closest friends stem from the time Tony was shooting *Days of Thunder*. She's cordial with several people connected to *Top Gun* and other movies Tony made.

Frank and Max are now young men in college. They struggled with what happened in a way that's easily imaginable to anyone, even if hard to fathom. Donna acknowledged there is one thing they've had to deal with that is unique, which is the degree to which people talk of their father in familiar tones. Tony Scott's personality was such that many people considered him a friend, and even a close friend. But no one was closer to him than his family, and it can be hard to take.

The Bruckheimers, Jerry and wife Linda, have been very kind to them, Donna said. Max and Frank went to work in post-production on *Top Gun: Maverick* for a few days. When they arrived, they were shown to a couch outside Bruckheimer's office to await PA instructions. They were soon engrossed in their phones, when a recognizable voice roused them. It was Tom Cruise.

"He told them, 'I loved your dad so much!'"[451]

It meant the world to them, and to Donna. She hopes to honor Tony with a star on Hollywood Boulevard. She's designed his headstone, which stands as a memorial to him at Forever Hollywood. On one side of it is a list of all of his films, and on the other, a mountain climber using lines to ascend it.

The inscription reads: "A loving husband and father."

Chapter 14 - Endnotes

[420] Andrew Blankstein and John Horn, "Director jumps to his death," *Los Angeles Times*, Aug. 20, 2012, AA1. https://www.newspapers.com/image/203884787/

[421] "The Hollywood Masters: Jerry Bruckheimer," Q&A at LMU School of Film and Television in Los Angeles, hosted by Stephen Galloway of *The Hollywood Reporter*, November 2, 2015.

[422] Pamela McClintock, "Tony Scott Spent Final Days Working With Tom Cruise on 'Top Gun 2," *Hollywood Reporter*, August 20, 2012.

[423] Zip Upham, Fallon Naval Air Station Fallon. Interview with the author, April 30, 2021.

[424] Pamela McClintock, "Tony Scott Spent Final Days Working With Tom Cruise on 'Top Gun 2."

[425] Upham, April 30, 2021

[426] "Tom Cruise leads tributes to director Tony Scott," BBC News, August 21, 2012. https://www.bbc.com/news/world-us-canada-19322540

[427] Donna Scott, interview with the author, March 13, 2022

[428] Program, Tony Scott, Celebration of Life, undated.

[429] Ben Fritz and Steven Zeitchik, "Movies that were left behind," *Los Angeles Times*, August 21, 2012, D1. https://www.newspapers.com/image/203875636/

[430] Knell, April 18, 2020

[431] Blankstein and Horn, "Director jumps to his death."

[432] Nowell, May 12, 2021.

[433] ABC News, "'Top Gun' Director Tony Scott Had Inoperable Brain Cancer," *Good Morning America*, August 19, 2012, courtesy of WaybackMachine.

[434] ABC News, "Tony Scott Brain Cancer Report Appears in Doubt," August 21, 2012. https://abcnews.go.com/Entertainment/tony-scott-brain-cancer-report-appears-doubt/story?id=17045816.

[435] Hillary Busis, "Report: Tony Scott was suffering from brain cancer," *Entertainment Weekly*, August 20, 2012. https://ew.com/article/2012/08/20/tony-scott-brain-cancer/

[436] "Autopsy Report. Scott, Anthony, 2012-05503," Office of the Coroner, County of Los Angeles, August 20, 2012.

[437] Julie Moos, "Two months after Tony Scott's suicide, ABC News retracts story claiming he had brain cancer," Poynter Institute, October 24, 2012. https://www.poynter.org/reporting-editing/2012/two-months-after-tony-scotts-suicide-abc-news-retracts-story-claiming-he-had-brain-cancer/

[438] ABC spokesperson requested anonymity.

[439] Unbylined story and retraction, "Tony Scott Died From Blunt Force Injuries, Report Finds," ABC News, October 23, 2012. https://abcnews.go.com/Health/tony-scott-died-blunt-force-injuries-report-finds/story?id=17544365

[440] This story was repeated several times to the author over the course of reporting, including by people who believed it enough to be on the record.

[441] Donna Scott, interview with the author, December 5, 2021.

[442] "2 of Paramount's Costliest Top Guns Lose Their Jobs," Alan Citron and Nina J. Easton, Los Angeles Times, November 16, 1990.

[443] Bruckheimer, AFI's Harold Lloyd Master Seminar, ©1988, used courtesy of American Film Institute.

[444] Off the record, March 1, 2020; additional confirmations.

[445] An Adventure with Tony Scott," Enrico Maioni, Guidedolomiti.com, retrieved March 1, 2022. https://www.guidedolomiti.com/en/true-stories/tony-scott-climbing/

[446] Donna Scott, January 5, 2022

447 "Historic Bella Vista Property," Open House TV, YouTube, retrieved March 1, 2022.
https://www.youtube.com/watch?v=BeYKqVD8IFo
448 Donna Scott, March 13, 2022
449 Ibid.
450 The LAPD took more than five months to deny an open records request for a copy of the police report, checking a box on a form letter that said only the investigating detective division can release reports of victims of crimes other than traffic reports. "Relatives of deceased victims must provide legal documentation as proof of relationship through Power of Attorney."
451 Ibid.

CHAPTER 15
TONY SCOTT'S LEGACY

I f *Top Gun* were a crime scene, Tom Cruise would appear on the security cameras while almost all of the DNA investigators found would link to Tony Scott. Fans, partly because of the cultural focus on celebrity and partly because of Scott's untimely death, often overlook the depth of his artistic ownership of the movie. When a prominent creative commits suicide it ends up in the lead paragraph of every story that follows, even overshadowing their work. Scott's work is due another look.

Scott learned to manage the abundance of critics at the outset of his career in features. "I stopped looking at reviews after my first movie, *The Hunger*, because I got slagged off so badly," he told the BBC a few years before his death. "With my movies I reach for difference and I reach for change and I think — especially the American press — they're not up for change. They're too comfortable with what they know."[452]

Much of the derision over time stemmed from the view the action genre movies were empty-headed entertainment. Scott preferred the term "popcorn" movies, happy to own that particular criticism. In the wake of *Top Gun*'s success, he told interviewers he knew it wasn't a "deep-thinking" film. "I don't want to go off and make *War and Peace*. I like making a hard core audio visual experience."[453] Few could have predicted in the 1990s that by the 2020s' action would take over the landscape, populating the hills with franchise McMansions.

There were endless comparisons to his brother, Ridley Scott. The logical parallels were numerous, starting with going to the same schools, and springing from the world of commercials, and being business partners. Both were termed "visualists," meaning they placed more importance on the shot than the story, a comment that wasn't generally made with love. At the same time, the comparisons belied vastly different choices in projects, and styles, both on screen and on set.

Films Directed by Tony Scott

Unstoppable (2010)
The Taking of Pelham 123 (2009)
Deja Vu (2006) Domino (2005) Man on Fire (2004)
Spy Game (2001)
Enemy of the State (1998)
The Fan (1996)

Crimson Tide (1995)
True Romance (1993)
The Last Boy Scout (1991)
Days of Thunder (1990)
Revenge (1990)
Beverly Hills Cop II (1987)
Top Gun (1986)

Top Gun is the very rare movie that retains relevance 35-plus years after release, and it is just part of what Tony Scott contributed to cinema.

Ridley and Tony

Tony Scott was six years younger, so he naturally followed his older brother. Both graduated from the Royal College of Art in London, although it took Tony two tries to be admitted. "It's been a brother-mentor relationship," Scott said shortly before his death. "But Rid and I are as tight as it can get."[454]

Ridley Scott started his commercial production company in 1965, and "five years later I made my brother join me," he told an interviewer with the British Academy of Film and Television Arts in 2019. Ridley Scott Associates (known as

RSA Films) was successful from the start. But the plan from the outset had been to make a feature, it just took much longer than he ever thought it would. "I kept getting turned down," he said. "At that moment the feature world could not connect with a director who had only done 30, 60 seconds."[455] Nearly 13 years passed before Ridley Scott made his first picture, *The Duellists* (1977), but he was off from there, making *Alien* (1979), and *Blade Runner* (1982), a pace he has kept up since.

The Scott brothers were part of an influx of British directors who came to Hollywood in the early 1980s, and they shook things up. It was Ridley Scott, Alan Parker, who directed *Midnight Express* (1978), *Fame* (1980), and *Evita* (1996), and Adrian Lyne, who directed *Flashdance* (1983) and *Fatal Attraction* (1987).

"The American movie had gotten so traditional, wide shot, medium, close-up, do this and be done," said Ward Russell, who was gaffer on *Top Gun* and cinematographer on *Days of Thunder* (1990) and *Last Boy Scout* (1991). "They were more interested in the impression they left rather than character development."[456]

He described it as "a whole new attitude that changed the style of filmmaking in the United States."

The ideas brought forth with the influx of talent from across the Atlantic Ocean gradually became the new normal. "They brought an English style of moviemaking, different visuals, stylish looks and fast-moving action, and fast-action editing."

Schmidt, a cameraman who worked with cinematographer Russell and Scott, also described it as a change to the status quo. "Before, it was old school, how you'd always done it. Whereas a regular director would say, "This is what I want to see," and the DP would get a 35 [millimeter lens], Tony would tell them to get an 85 [millimeter lens.]" To explain it he used the example of a camera aimed at a car with people in it. The focus of the lens would be on the people in the car, while things outside of it were distinctly out of focus. "Tony didn't want everything to be in focus," and that was different.[457]

"The thing with Tony and somewhat with Ridley, too, was that they liked long lenses," Schmidt continued. Changing the depth of field was a very different look. "Most directors would start with 18 or 20 lenses. Tony would start with 50."[458] That was a big difference in the '80s.

A lot of veteran movie crew ended up working with both Scott brothers over the course of their careers, and several noted a difference in command styles. "Both are great, and they're totally different," said sound editor Badami. "Ridley is like the general who stands on the hill and overlooks the battlefield. Tony is the colonel at the lead of the troops charging, and the bullets are whizzing over his head, and people are dying all around him, and you follow him."[459]

Ridley Scott, who didn't respond to a request for comment, might challenge that. He told the BAFTA interviewer he'd been the operator on virtually all of the roughly 2,000 commercials he had made in his life. "I was told this is not the way we do it, directors stand back and say "action, darlings," and shit like that," he told the interviewer in 2019. "I don't do that. I actually back off and say hey, come here, and will walk and talk to them."[460] The director's relationship with the camera operator is imperative, he said, because of their intimacy with the person in front of the lens.

The competition between the brothers was legendary. Two cameramen who regularly worked for Tony Scott recalled being hired to work on a commercial by Ridley Scott. They joked that Ridley hired them to learn how Tony got certain shots, because Tony certainly wasn't going to tell him.

When a BBC interviewer asked Tony what other director he'd most like to see work, he answered it was Ridley. "I've never seen him at work because we might kill each other on the same set. He and I are so very close in terms of family and business so we couldn't be on the same set."[461]

Early career

Scott used to joke that after *The Hunger* flopped he "couldn't get arrested."[462] He spent the next two years making commercials at RSA. After *Top Gun*, when he was the talk of the town, the joke shifted. Scott started telling people he was busy not returning the calls of people who hadn't returned his calls during those feature-lean years. Next up was *Beverly Hills Cop II* (1987) followed by *Revenge* and *Days of Thunder* (both 1990). Scott was to make six movies with Bruckheimer.

Scott's vision was such that he had to do it his way. Russell recalled he and Scott being called into a meeting in the producer's office about spending on *Last Boy Scout*. "[Joel Silver] was going over the budget, saying "too many days," and Tony sat there and listened to the whole thing," he recalled. Finally the producer asked Scott how he was going to get it under control. "Well, we gotta do it right," the director replied. "What else do you want me to do?"[463]

Russell said Silver shook his head, and that he and Scott went back to work. They didn't change a thing. "Tony was a perfectionist, and it was going to take as long as it was going to take to do it," said Russell. He acknowledged there were department heads that grew weary of Scott's tendency to micromanage. "There wasn't any other way for Tony to do the job. He was that dedicated."

The first time Quentin Tarantino stepped onto a Hollywood movie set it was *Last Boy Scout*. It was a spring day in 1991 and the production company was setting up a scene in a Los Angeles alley. In the scene, the Bruce Willis character uses humor to disarm the thug who is there to kill him, whereupon he kills the thug.

Only the actors weren't out yet. "They were taking forever to shoot it because Tony was setting up six cameras," said Tarantino, then 28. He had marveled at the six monitors, and the fact they were getting six pieces of coverage right away. "I was, 'Holy Shit, this is how they do it?'"

The visit to the set was arranged by Knell. After working as Scott's assistant on several films she was doing development work for CinTel Films, which had optioned one of Tarantino's screenplays. He was like thousands of other young people trying to break into the movie business, she said. He worked at a video rental store, a good fit given his love of movies. "Quentin was very poverty-stricken," recalled Knell. "He went everywhere by city bus."[464]

But his talent was unmistakable. "You know by page five if someone is a writer. And he was a writer," she said. CinTel hired Tarantino as a script doctor on another screenplay. Meanwhile, Knell took her praise for the young writer to Scott. The director met him during his visit to *Last Boy Scout*, although he didn't have time to talk.

The next thing Tarantino knows, he's invited to a birthday party for Scott. "I'm spinning. Now I'm invited to his birthday party, and it's this little, intimate thing," the two-time Academy Award winning writer-director recalled.[465] He wanted to bring a gift and found a bus-stop size poster of *Revenge*, one of his favorite Scott movies. Before he left the party, Scott told him he wanted to read his work.

"I've met a lot of people I thought were cool, and heard they were writers, and I've never said, 'Let me read your work,'" said Tarantino. "In fact, I can't even imagine me saying that." It was a big milestone for him. "It's such a huge thing to get your shit read. It's the hurdle. All the other hurdles seem little after that."[466]

Once *Last Boy Scout* wrapped, Scott got on a plane for Italy with two of Tarantino's screenplays. He read both "Reservoir Dogs" and "True Romance" by the time he landed. When he called Knell, he told her he wanted to do "Reservoir Dogs," which Tarantino had figured out how to do on his own. "He said, okay, let's do "True Romance." That's kind of how it started," recalled Tarantino.[467]

They shot *True Romance*, a violent, character-driven getaway drama, during the last three months of 1992. The $13 million budget wasn't that much less than *Top Gun*'s, but a lot less than other films Scott had shot since it wrapped. By way of comparison, *Beverly Hills Cop II* had been made for $28 million, *Revenge* for $22 million and *Days of Thunder* for $60 million. It had taken a different investor's belief in the script for *True Romance* to make it happen.

Visualist

Tarantino made his comments at a talk at The Los Angeles Film School a week after Scott's death. The tribute, called "Writing for Tony Scott," featured him and Richard Kelly, who wrote the screenplay of *Domino* (2005), along with screenings of both movies. The event was helmed by Jeff Goldsmith of The Q&A podcast and Backstory digital magazine, and was one of the most substantive of a thousand tributes to the director that week.

The most common accolade paid to Tony Scott was that he was a visualist, while people overlooked that he was a good director of actors, Tarantino told the audience, citing Scott's pairing with Denzel Washington. A lot of times it wasn't positive. "I was always criticized for being so visual, until I realized actually it's an advantage, because we're dealing with pictures," said Ridley Scott. "Hang on, it's not a radio play, we're actually dealing with pictures, so if the pictures are narrative, that's good. Some of the greatest films tend to be more visual, than wordy."[468]

Tarantino gave several examples of how Scott made *True Romance* visually stimulating, not all of which Tarantino said he liked at the time. At first the younger director hadn't understood why he was using a giant billboard as a set. The scene, right after the young lovers spend their first night together, has Alabama duck out the window of the apartment behind the billboard, followed by Clarence. Tarantino had the conversation happening on a couch. He realized later that there were two other scenes in which the conversation takes place on the couch, and the billboard made the scene visually interesting.[469]

Another example was the use and location of a swinging lamp for a scene where the pimp is killed. There were floor to ceiling fish tanks in the set, which didn't get blown up. Another blood scene featured white feathers. "That's cinema, and when it works, it works and you don't have to fucking explain anything."[470]

A question about whether Tarantino's script for *True Romance* had been reworked was illuminating in terms of who Scott was as a director. Tarantino's version of the script wasn't on a linear time frame. It moved around somewhat like *Pulp Fiction* would a few years later.

Scott put the narrative in chronological order but didn't rewrite it, leaving the characters, dialogue, and story intact. There was one significant change, however, and that was to the ending. Scott refused to kill off the young couple in the end. Tarantino wasn't happy when he found out and confronted him, saying, "I put the script in your hands, and you're wimping out for commercial bullshit, man!" Scott said he couldn't kill them. "Quentin, I'm not doing it to be a commercial fuck. I'm doing it because I love these fucking kids." Scott paraphrased words Tarantino had written in the script, they deserved to get away with it.

Reservoir Dogs (1992), released before *True Romance* (1993), put Tarantino on the map, which had most reviewers focusing on Tarantino rather than Scott, who had directed it. "Even when it got good reviews, they wouldn't give Tony the credit for it," recalled Tarantino.[471]

But Scott was called upon to defend the violence in his movie. "Violence should not be glorified. It certainly isn't here," he said at the Westwood Hotel during the *True Romance* press junket. "There's much more a sense of desperate people living on the edge, right between living and dying."[472] It wasn't known at the time that the movie would have been more violent, had Scott not changed the ending.

Mid-career

In the mid-'90s critics didn't get Scott as well as studios did, but they were coming around. His next movies, which all cast Black Americans in leading roles, came with big budgets. *Crimson Tide* (1995), his first teaming with Denzel Washington, cost about $53 million and brought in $157 million. *The Fan* (1996), starring Robert De Niro and Wesley Snipes, cost $55 million to make but performed poorly at the box office. *Enemy of the State*, starring Will Smith and Gene Hackman, had a budget of about $90 million and returned $251 million.

Next up was *Spy Game* (2001), which put Robert Redford and Brad Pitt together on the big screen at a cost of about $115 million, and returned about $143 million. "Unlike his older brother, Ridley, Tony Scott mostly shoots swift, snazzy thrillers without much substance, but here he's at his best," wrote Michael Wilmington at the Chicago Tribune. "The younger Scott knows how to make a movie move and he has a sharp eye for framing and actors." *Spy Game* was "never boring and rarely predictable," Wilmington concluded.[473]

Between features Scott made commercials and shorts. He used them as a laboratory where he experimented with techniques he might incorporate into his movies, said cameraman David Nowell. "He experimented with techniques he wanted to try. If it worked, he would incorporate it into his movies."[474] He did that regularly with his commercials. A prime example was Scott's 2002 short, *Beat the Devil*, which was commissioned by BMW to promote its cars.

That 10-minute story directed by Scott and based on a concept by David Fincher and Fallon Worldwide, starred James Brown, Clive Owens, Danny Trejo, and Gary Oldman. Scott cranked things at different speeds to create subtle variations in the spot, which created a unique feel. "Those techniques ended up being something he used in *Man on Fire*."[475]

That 2004 movie was a project Scott had in the works for decades. The action thriller, about a retired CIA agent freelancing in Mexico, had been on his desk since 1980. Jamie Portman of CanWest News Service wrote that the movie belonged in a "special category" because of its combination of talent.[476] The $70 million *Man on Fire* was directed "by the visually flamboyant Tony Scott, one of the most bankable directors in the business," wrote Portman, and starred Washington. It brought in about $131 million.

Passion projects

Richard Kelly was struck by how collaborative Scott was on *Domino*, a semi-true account of a woman who came from high society and rejected it to be a bounty hunter. Scott initially hired the scriptwriter to pick up a start to the story. It had no third act when Kelly first read it, and his ideas on how to fix it landed him the job.

Scott gave him a lot of material he had collected to use in the process. "He was an aggressive, aggressive researcher, in a wonderful, inspiring way," recalled Kelly. "He was all about making the experience as accurate as possible."[477] As part of his research in writing the script, Kelly did a four-hour interview with Domino to better understand why she would abandon a life of privilege to pursue the meaning of life in the underbelly of LA.

Second AD Sharon Mann also noted Scott's pursuit of authenticity. She recalled being on a location scout in one of the Miramar hangars during prep where Scott saw mechanics at work. "They were greasy and sweaty, wearing well-aged uniforms, and Tony said, "I want to work with these guys! Can we have them?" Mann said they were soon signed up to work as background. "They show up in clean uniforms, anxious to look their best for camera. We had them go change."[478] Even as some areas of *Top Gun* were contrived, he tried hard to capture the pilots at their core.

Sound editor Cecelia Hall, who along with George Watters II was nominated for an Oscar for their work on *Top*

Gun, also noted Scott's interest in people and teamwork. "He wanted to know what your opinion was," she recalled. "Tony was an incredibly generous collaborator" with a willingness to "try anything."[479] In her case it was the sound reel that used a melding of wild animal sounds to bring life to the sounds of jets in flight.

For Kelly it translated to sitting in a director's chair next to Scott's while on the set. Scott had him rewrite scenes or polish the dialogue of characters played by Mickey Rourke and Tom Waits, and generally included him in the process. "Usually a screenwriter is not invited to set," explained Kelly, and certainly not for stretches of time.[480]

Scott's humanity was evident in his affinity for Domino, both the character, and the young woman it was based on. "I saw this bond between them," said Kelly. "He looked at her kind of like a daughter, very close with her, and supported her over the years." She was born in England, and she wasn't impressed when she arrived in Los Angeles, he said. Her attitude was, "who are all these phonies and assholes? She identified with the poor people, and minority culture," said Kelly. "[Scott] felt the same way in a lot of ways."[481]

Scott told a funny anecdote from shooting *Domino* that also speaks to collaboration. Scott said he was "winging it" in a scene where Choco, played by Edgar Ramirez, is in the launderette. "The scene where he strips down to his underwear wasn't in the script, but I thought it would be an interesting idea so I asked him to take his jeans off," recalled the director. "He was wearing this terrible, grubby pair of Y-fronts. So I gave him my Speedos." He told the story after being asked what was the stupidest question he had: It was "We gather Edgar is wearing your underwear?"[482]

Final three movies

As the popularity of the action thriller genre grew, informed criticism did, too. Some critics even understood the influence of Scott's distinctive style. *Deja Vu* (2006), which cost $75 million to make and returned $180 million, didn't feel like science fiction. Gary Thompson at the Philadelphia Daily News wrote that Scott's "wide-screen compositions, acrobatic camera moves and staccato editing have been established as bedrock elements of the modern Hollywood movie." *Deja Vu* was an ambitious mindbender that succeeded. "In key ways Scott is the ideal guy to make visual sense of the movie's complex story, which moves from past to present quickly, fluidly, and in a way a viewer intuitively understands."[483]

The Taking of Pelham 123 (2009), a $100 million remake that grossed about $150 million, also netted positive if mixed reviews. "Scott serves a lightning-fast thriller that feels completely plugged in to our modern anxieties about terrorism, political corruption and Wall Street money men run amok," wrote Christopher Kelly of McClatchy News Service. "Always a technophile, Scott films the gleaming transit control center that borders on the obsessive. The result is unexpectedly beautiful and frequently transfixing." Kelly concludes that the movie didn't reinvent the action thriller, but perhaps better, it "pays the genre its due."[484]

Nowell said Scott pursued cinematic innovation his entire working life. He worked with him on a spot for Dodge, which was done right before they began shooting *Unstoppable*. "He loved doing the commercials, and it was highly lucrative for the company. But it was a testing facility for him."[485]

That commercial was also a good example of the extent to which Scott collaborated, Nowell continued. "He told us what he wanted, then he said, "You guys get this, and you guys get that." Basically, everyone was in charge of their own little movie," he recalled. "Tony was testing the crew, letting us run and gun. Then he put it all together."[486]

Unstoppable brought praise from critics. Some noted the demands of the movie-going public had changed, and that computer-generated imagery was taking over. In hindsight, it might turn out that Scott was one of the last great directors to use real action.

"Scott makes no nonsense, breathless, muscular movies, and Unstoppable promises a runaway train picture and delivers," wrote Barbara Vancheri at the Pittsburgh Post-Gazette. "What moviegoers really want to see are crazy stunts, runaway trains, fiery explosions, near or actual collisions, and Mr. Scott delivers with real engines and cars, not computer-generated models that always have a whiff of artificiality."[487]

Washington starred in all three of those movies and by then obviously knew Scott well. The director's suicide had to have been particularly painful for him. Reshoots for *Unstoppable* were shot in a railroad yard underneath the Vincent Thomas Bridge. He called the director a "genuine friend" and said it was "unfathomable" to think he was gone. "He had a tremendous passion for life and for the art of filmmaking and was able to share this passion with all of us through his cinematic brilliance."[488]

The following year when Washington was promoting *The Flight* (2013), an interviewer asked what he missed about Scott. "His passion, his energy, his shorts — that pink hat." The actor received a note from Scott just three or four days before he died, about doing another film, his passion evident. "He would cry at emotional scenes," recalled Washington. "He was just a wonderful, wonderful man."[489]

Scott was a trained artist first, who told people that if he weren't a director he would be painting canvases. As it was, he did his own storyboards. On *Top Gun* he sketched every day with clarity that was easily understood by people working on the movie.

"[I]t would be difficult to deny the visual, aural, narrative, thematic, and energetic consistency of Scott's films, from his first effort ... all the way through to his last," wrote film scholar Michael Loren Siegel, in a chapter about post-cinema,[490] a term that loosely refers to cinema ceasing to be the dominant media after more than a century.

"As a person who watched him work — I don't know what comes across to other people — I see the painter in him, the artist," said Daniela Scaramuzza, Scott's personal photographer. "I think you can lower the volume on any of his movies and look at the image, and know the story. The images are just one painting after another," she said. "That is what makes the difference to me. He has an eye, the ability to translate a cinematographic image into an art piece."[491]

Pushing to be better

Badami, who was sound editor on *Top Gun* as well as *Crimson Tide* and *Taking of Pelham 123*, called the director "an inspirational person," and said it was fun to be around him. "Tony brought a kind of humor to all of his movies. There was that troublemaker; a wink and a nod."[492]

"Tony was part of the crew," said Jack Cooperman, another veteran cameraman who worked with Scott on commercials as well as movies. "You knew he was the director but you could talk to him." More than that, Cooperman said, he wanted you to talk to him.[493]

"He was always asking more than what you thought you could deliver, and you were always surprised when you actually could do it," said Knell. "He did it with an energy, stories and images, that was phenomenal at the time. You wanted to see the world as he saw it."[494]

"With Tony you never worked harder," said Schmidt. "But you never had more fun."[495]

Mann noted Scott's use of filters to "increase sky drama," as if it still amazed her. "Tony was a driven man, wild and passionate. He would go for the biggest and the best shot every time, the most dramatic, the best lighting, everything. And he got it."[496]

Scott was beloved by the people who worked with him, with relatively few outliers. That's noteworthy given the nature of directing. It requires managing a lot of intensely creative people amid the stress of time and fiscal constraints. It's probably not the norm that everyone who works on a movie leaves wrap with fondness for the director, particularly one that worked them to the end reel.

Budget limitations with *Top Gun* put Scott and the executive producer in opposite corners, Scott pushing to spend more, and spending more, and sometimes paying out of pocket. Even with the inherent conflict, "It was impossible not to like Tony," said Badalato.[497]

Chapter 15 - Endnotes

[452] Papamichael, "Getting Direct With Directors: No.33, Tony Scott."

[453] Jamie Portman, "British director proves mastery of US razzmatazz," Southam News Service, July 29, 1987, retrieved from *Star-Phoenix* (Saskatoon, Saskatchewan, Canada). D8. https://www.newspapers.com/image/511172591/

[454] Stephen Galloway, "Tony Scott's Unpublished Interview: 'My Family Is Everything to Me'," *Hollywood Reporter*, August 22, 2012. https://www.hollywoodreporter.com/news/general-news/tony-scott-death-ridley-scott-interview-364528/

[455] On Directing, "Ridley Scott on the Biggest Challenge of his Career," BAFTA, November 18, 2019. https://www.youtube.com/watch?v=Crc1mlZK-Ng

[456] Russell, September 27, 2020.

[457] Schmidt, September 4, 2021.

[458] Ibid.

[459] Badami, August 27, 2021.

[460] *"On Directing,"* Ridley Scott on the Biggest Challenge of his Career."

[461] Papamichael, "Getting Direct With Directors: No.33, Tony Scott."

[462] Portman, "British director proves mastery of US razzmatazz."

[463] Russell, September 27, 2020.

[464] Knell, April 18, 2020.

[465] Jeff Goldsmith, "Writing for Tony Scott: A Quentin Tarantino & Richard Kelly Q&A," Q&A with Jeff Goldsmith, August 29, 2012. http://www.theqandapodcast.com/2012/08/writing-for-tony-scott-quentin.html

[466] Ibid.

[467] Ibid.

[468] *"On Directing,* Ridley Scott on the Biggest Challenge of his Career."

[469] Goldsmith, "Writing for Tony Scott."

[470] Ibid.

[471] Ibid.

[472] Dan Bennett, "Quentin Tarantino does violence with a real flourish," *North County Times* (Oceanside, California), September 3, 1993, 4. https://www.newspapers.com/image/573090727/

[473] Michael Wilmington, "In flashy CIA thriller, Robert Redford has a role that spotlights quiet heroism," *Chicago Tribune*, November 21 2001. 5-1.

[474] Nowell, May 12, 2021.

[475] Ibid.

[476] Portman, "British director proves mastery of US razzmatazz."

[477] Goldsmith, "Writing for Tony Scott."

[478] Mann, April 29, 2020.

[479] Hall, August 22, 2021.

[480] Goldsmith, "Writing for Tony Scott."

[481] Ibid.

[482] Papamichael, "Getting Direct With Directors: No.33, Tony Scott."

[483] Gary Thompson, "Baffling 'Deja Vu' gets high-tech dazzle from director Tony Scott," *Philadelphia Daily News*, November 22, 2006, 30.

[484] Christopher Kelly, "'123' adds up," *Fort Worth Star-Telegram*, June 11, 2009, A23. https://www.newspapers.com/image/654870798/

[485] Nowell, May 12, 2021.

[486] Ibid.

[487] Barbara Vancheri, "'Unstoppable' rides on high-octane action and suspense," *Pittsburgh Post-Gazette*, November 12, 2010, E-1. https://www.newspapers.com/image/96479020/

[488] Natalie Finn, "Denzel Washington Remembers "Genuine Friend" Tony Scott," E News Online, August 20, 2012.https://www.eonline.com/news/339553/denzel-washington-remembers-genuine-friend-tony-scott

[489] TheCelebFactory, "Denzel Washington talks about Tony Scott," February 14, 2013. https://www.youtube.com/watch?v=anr6S2haKgc

[490] Michael Loren Siegel, "Ride into the Danger Zone: TOP GUN (1986) and the Emergence of the Post-Cinematic," in *Post-Cinema: Theorizing 21st-Century Film*, eds. Shane Denson & Julia Leyda (Falmer: REFRAME Books, 2016). 666.

[491] Scaramuzza, April 25, 2021.

[492] Badami, August 27, 2021.

[493] Cooperman, September 4, 2021.

[494] Knell, April 18, 2020.

[495] Schmidt, September 4, 2021.

[496] Mann, April 29, 2020.

[497] Badalato, June 13, 2020.

CHAPTER 16
FANDOM

Keeping the legacy of a movie alive takes legions of fans. *Top Gun* has far more than most, and they seem to fall into three categories.

The majority of people who like the movie, or even loved it when it came out, will watch it again if it shows up on a channel they stream. There's a sense of nostalgia, even with younger people who saw it for the first time in the late '90s as children at their uncle's house, but they aren't going to take a special trip to Oceanside to see the beautifully restored Top Gun House or travel to San Diego expressly to see various locations where the movie was shot or to have a meal at Kansas City Barbeque.

The next group are people who have seen the movie multiple times, either back in the day or over the longer stretch, and certainly at least once in the last decade. Pilots and military people fit into that category, as does anyone who loves aviation, for obvious reasons. They might have visited some place significant to the movie, especially if they happened to be somewhere nearby. They'll likely have some kind of merchandise associated with the movie, maybe a t-shirt or a personal copy of the movie, whether on Blu-Ray or in an online cue.

Then there are the uber-fans who watch *Top Gun* often. They might even have it cued up right now. They know the lines, the trivia, they might even debate whether the movie would have been just as great if Val Kilmer had played Maverick, instead of Tom Cruise, or failed completely.

All of that translates to dollars, from the sale of patches and bomber jackets, to destination travel that includes museums with a display about the movie or actual locations brought back to life, like the Top Gun House.

Here's a look at some of the fan leaders, locations, props and events that live on.

Top fans

Top Gun Day, the official day the movie was released, falls on May 16, and it does not go unnoticed, even in off years. True fans will even explain why that's the correct date — when it went into wide release — and not Memorial Day, as others claim.

In 2021, the 35th anniversary of the movie, there were numerous fan events. Paramount had *Top Gun* back in theaters, posting clips on Twitter and links so fans could find a nearby theater, while Tom Cruise tweeted something masterful that connected the event to the new movie.

Fans didn't need to leave their homes to celebrate. There was a livestream event that was a joint effort between Michael Sherriff, who created The Top Gun Movie Fans group on Facebook, and Michael "Taco" Bell, who has an aviation-history podcast. Some 1,200 people tuned in to what turned out to be five extended segments featuring pilots and people who worked on the movie.

Sherriff and Bell were on different continents when they saw *Top Gun* for the first time, but they had parallel experiences: They loved it and wanted to see it again. Both have remained fans ever since, part of a select group of super fans helping to keep the movie alive.

"There have been very few movies that I can say changed my life," said Mitchell "Taco" Bell, who works as an airline pilot and hosts a podcast on the side called "Tall Tales With Taco."[498] It primarily focuses on the military from World War II to the present. He's done several episodes linked to *Top Gun*, including one that featured Pete.

Bell described seeing the movie as an "epic, life-altering experience." He was already interested in F-14s, thanks to an uncle who had been a RIO, which had prompted him to pursue an "air contract" with the Marines. That meant they would put him through pilot training, if he graduated and passed certain tests, which he did. "My VHS tape of that movie was the sole motivator that would get me through the tough papers or studying for a test," he said. He watched it so many times, especially the dogfights, that the VHS wore out. He thought it was one of the best examples of flying at the time, which he says "still holds true today."

Sherriff was also taken by *Top Gun* as a young person. "There's something magical about the film," explained Sherriff, who was 13 and growing up in Leicester, England, when it came out in theaters.[499] He saw it for the first time on video a couple of years later, and he was hooked. His parents rented it for him so many times that they bought him his own copy when it went on sale. "That got wore out because I watched it over and over again. I memorized it word for word. I couldn't help but deliver the next line and it ruined it for anyone else."

"I thought I was on my own, but then I found there were other people…I couldn't believe there were other *Top Gun* nerds!" He founded his fan page in 2018 and discovered how many there were. By March 2022, the group had 43,400 members.

"It's not just another FB group. I am building a community of actual *Top Gun* fans, bringing in the people who can give the information no one else can." To join the group requires answering questions. One asks the name of the character who died in the movie. "A *Top Gun* fan would know about that. It's quite an easy question to answer, really," said Sherriff.

John Merritt, who operates Skid Voodoo's Hard Deck, an Instagram page with 7,300 followers in March 2022, beefed up his coverage. He saved up unique items for the anniversary, and went out to see the movie at a local fan event. He followed the movie when it came out. "I read about it in the Hollywood Reporter and Variety, and I knew of Tony Scott because my father was in advertising," and he knew who Simpson and Bruckheimer were. "I was a film student, I guess, and I had a sense about what these guys were doing, and it was in the town I lived in, and a topic that I liked."[500]

The Instagram fan page happened by accident. He had the page, but it was more of an art site, when he posted a picture of himself being interviewed on television. He had gone down to watch them shoot *Top Gun: Maverick* and was interviewed. He posted it on the page and within the week he had added hundreds of followers.

Tom Cruise on Top Gun Day

The star of the 1986 movie, and the sequel, weighed in on May 16, 2021 courtesy of Twitter.

"Top Gun Day is created by and dedicated to the fans. I can't wait for you guys to see *Top Gun: Maverick* later this year."[501] His tweet included a not-yet-released still from the new movie. Maverick, now pushing 60, stands in a hallway of photos to gaze at one of them. It's from a scene in the movie where he stands in front of the still photo of the original *Top Gun*. In it, Maverick and Iceman, played by Val Kilmer, grasp hands. The still is from a scene toward the end of the movie, when the two pilots have resolved their conflict and celebrate a successful flight.

Mark Zabielinsky, 29, thinks he first saw the movie as a toddler on the VCR at his grandparents house. "I was always intrigued by aviation," he said, and his whole family loved the movie. He runs the Instagram page top.gun.movie on the side. It had 23,400 followers. It started as a personal account in 2015. He set it aside for a time but has been running it steadily since 2017, and by March 2022 had more than 1,440 posts.

Zabielinsky, who works as a police officer in Florida, said it was a fun pastime. "It's making relationships with cast and crew, and hunting and finding behind the scenes photos, collecting tidbits of information."[502]

Paramount leads the social media pack with its official site for the new movie, @topgunmovie.com on Instagram. It had 109,000 followers with 36 posts at the same time.

Top Gun House
Oceanside

When principal photography on *Top Gun* kicked off on June 2nd from the beach in Oceanside, no one could have imagined that the house would end up a landmark. Or that it would have to be moved to best do that.

PHOTO: Citation Press

The Top Gun House was moved from its original location down the street to anchor a resort across from the Oceanside Pier.

Referred to as "Charlie's house" in production documents, the house at 102 N. Pacific St. needed significant upgrades to be used as a location for the scenes between Maverick and Charlie. "Top Gun House," as it is now called, is now the centerpiece of the brand new 384-room Oceanside Beach Resort across from the pier.

The house has drawn fans of the movie from all over the world, said Leslee Gaul, president and CEO of Visit Oceanside, the conference and visitors center for the city. It was enough of a beacon that nobody liked seeing it fall into disrepair as it did over the years. A coat of paint had noted a mention on the visitor center site in 2014. "We couldn't be more thrilled to have it restored and once again accessible to the public," said Gaul.[503]

S.D. Malkin Properties, which built the new resort property, spent $1 million to restore and physically relocate the Victorian house.[504] It involved substantial work, from structural improvements to cosmetic detailing. Significant thought was given to what paint color was to be used, thanks to a project preservation consultant. After scraping through the paint layers at key locations on the house "they were able to confirm that the '*Top Gun*' blue and white scheme was not the original color scheme, nor was it appropriate for a Victorian house."

That didn't stop them from painting the Top Gun House blue when the time came.

Maverick's jet

When the time came to take the F-14 offline in 2006, the Department of Defense didn't just retire it, they scrapped it. That meant they destroyed a lot of the aircraft. There was a reason for that, which was to make it harder for Iran — which continues to fly the aircraft — to find parts.

As a result, there are just over 100 of the original 712 airframes still in existence, according to Matt Lawlor, an aircraft historian and consummate fan of *Top Gun*. Some time in 2017 he began efforts to find planes featured in the movie that were still intact. He pored over a list of Bureau Numbers, or BuNos, which are serial numbers assigned to naval aircraft. By then, most of the planes had been destroyed. "Some were shredded back in the 1980s; a few had crashed, unfortunately."[505]

Then he got a major hit with BuNo 160694. It was one of 20 aircraft on display on the flight deck of the floating USS Lexington Museum in Corpus Christi, Texas. He excitedly reached out to the powers that be. "I said you have this plane, with both military and film history, film markings!" A nice response was forthcoming, but it felt to him a little like, "Thank you, but who the hell are you to tell us that?"

Lawlor, who has the Facebook page Top Gun Props and Costumes Forum, continued on the mission anyway. Over the next year or so he emailed people in the Navy for records and other aircraft historians. He viewed, and re-viewed, flight scenes in the movie, sometimes stopping frame by frame. He dug up stills from the movie as well as other deployments of F-14s. He hit the research jackpot when he interviewed F-14 pilot Bozo Abel, who still had his logbooks. Abel confirmed, among other things, that BuNo 160694 had been the plane he flew to buzz the tower in the famous scene.

"It was the most heavily used aircraft in the movie," used by multiple pilots, said a jubilant Lawlor.

Steve Banta, executive director of the USS Lexington Museum, explained its aircraft are in a scheduled rotation for refurbishment, and when it came time for BuNo 160694 they noted it to the public.[506] Lawlor reached out when he saw it, making the case they should restore it to its movie star look. He also offered his assistance in re-creating it, and offered up his, by then, detailed information. It was good material, Banta said, noting that the history of the plane was known because its service, including having flown in the movie, was detailed in the paperwork that accompanied it when it first came to the museum. It was the extent of the enthusiasm of fans that came as a surprise.

The plane. There were some in the camp that believed it should carry its original paint scheme. Some believed it should be restored to its VF-1 Showbird Design, which was more aviation history, less Hollywood. Others, particularly the marketing side, thought it would be a boon for the museum to have the original *Top Gun* plane. It was under review when Lawlor and others took to social media. They started a hashtag, #PaintMavsJet.

Then it took on a life of its own. More people joined in the effort. "They're super fans, really," said Banta. In April 2020 the museum conducted a poll, with Maverick winning by a mile.

PHOTO: Citation Press

This F-14, featured in Top Gun, draws interest from many visitors to the popular USS Lexington Museum in Corpus Christi, Texas.

Lawlor was a "great resource," said Banta, who flew helicopters in the Navy until he retired in 2018. "He sent us graphics that we blew up in our office to put on the plane. He had been doing the research for at least a year," and they spent time getting the paint just right. The museum has a full time staff that does refurbishment for its aircraft. Corpus Christi is on the Gulf of Mexico, and weather takes a toll. It takes months to "sand it down, remove the corrosion, prepare and then repaint an aircraft. Given the size of the F-14, and the detailed paint job required to match it to its role in the movie, it took time. "Really, it was a great labor of love," said Banta.

It's hard to quantify the added draw Mav's jet has brought to the museum, given there is a flat price to access it, but it is significant, Banta said. "That plane is a big deal for us, and the connection to the movie is great."

Friendship, community, party!

Lawlor and John Merritt have formed an ultra contemporary friendship: They're in touch constantly, either online or via text but as of September 2021 had never met in person or even spoken on the phone. Their shared passion and seriousness about *Top Gun* launched the relationship. They team up to share things on their respective online sites at the same time and communicate almost daily.

Merritt has a special love for San Diego, which celebrates its ties to the movie. The USS Midway Museum held its first Top Gun Night in 2009, which was the 40th anniversary of the Topgun school, said David Koontz, director of marketing. The hybrid museum-attraction is "the number one thing to do in San Diego, as per Trip Advisor," he said, with more than 1 million annual visitors. The October weekend where they screen the movie each night is its biggest draw.[507]

"Tom Cruise, as Maverick, was flying off of a San Diego based aircraft carrier," said Koontz. "We are the location for that."

The movie night(s) became an annual event in 2015. They show the movie on a giant inflatable screen and attendees are encouraged to dress up. The 2,000 tickets available for each night, which also features a DJ and dance floor, sold out within 45 minutes in 2019, Koontz said. "It's the most anticipated night of the year, that's for sure."

Last time Merritt dressed as Maverick, and this time he'll go as Jester. He has the appropriate helmet and flight suit for Jester. "It's a lot of fun," he said. "You're sitting on the deck with a bunch of people who love the movie, and everybody knows every line. It's a shared experience — the Comicon of *Top Gun.*"[508]

Kansas City Barbeque

It's possible Cindy and Martin Blair knew the staying power of *Top Gun* before anyone else. The owners of Kansas City Barbeque provided a key location for the movie, and they've made note of it ever since. The neighborhood has changed dramatically over the years, and the bar restaurant has been upgraded, but it still has the feel it had back in 1985, and fans appreciate it.

The bar was used for the double date with Maverick and Charlie, and Goose and Carole, a scene best known for the group singing "Great Balls of Fire." The Blairs enjoyed the day the movie shot there, and were delighted when Tony Scott wanted to return for the final scene, when Maverick is alone at the bar and Charlie arrives and plays "You've Lost That Lovin' Feelin'" on the jukebox.

They found it exciting and illuminating as to how Hollywood worked, but they also knew it was good for the restaurant. They had an event linked to the San Diego premier. "We had 30 people here." They had drinks and went to the movie at Horton Plaza not knowing what they'd find. "We didn't know if our scene was in the movie!" They cheered when it started.[509]

They have kept the restaurant marketing aligned with the movie ever since. "The first 10 years we had a lot of Navy pilots," said Martin Blair. "The Topgun school would come down and have offsite meetings here." That lasted until 1996 when the flight training school relocated from Miramar to Fallon. "It's been a big military bar because of where we are," he said, noting the impressive Navy hat collection. He's heard his share of grumblings from people who joined the Navy because of the movie who didn't end up flying.

The Blairs also have one of the best *Top Gun* memorabilia collections, starting with the upright piano, which was theirs to start, but there are many other keepsakes and mementos as well. Most of what's in the restaurant are copies of the originals, which they keep elsewhere. That proved to be a wise bit of planning when they had a fire in 2011. They lost a lot of stuff, but not the piano, thanks to it being in a separate section of the restaurant.

When the restaurant reopened, amid great fanfare, it re-committed to *Top Gun*. "We have tour groups come in all the time," he said in 2020. He said it's especially popular with the Japanese who visited regularly before the pandemic. "They just love *Top Gun*," he said, adding that he'd seen young girls crying as they looked at the pictures." T-shirt sales remain strong. "That we're still selling them says there's still a lot of interest."

The sequel has only helped. "It's exciting," he said.

"Anything that regenerates interest in the brand is good for us."

Chapter 16 - Endnotes

[498] Mitchell "Taco" Bell. Interview with the author, May 17, 2021

[499] Michael Sherriff. Interview with the author, April 24, 2021

[500] John Merritt, operator of Skid Voodoo's Hard Deck, an Instagram page. Interview with the author, September 14, 2021

[501] @TomCruise (Tom Cruise), *Twitter*, May 13, 2021, https://twitter.com/tomcruise/status/1392872330842542080

[502] Mark Zabielinsky, Interview with the author, May 20, 2002.

[503] Leslee Gaul, president and CEO of Visit Oceanside, Interview with the author, June 24, 2020

[504] Chris Jennewein, "Oceanside's 'Top Gun House' Moved to Permanent Home at New Resort," *Times of San Diego*, May 21, 2020. https://timesofsandiego.com/business/2020/05/21/oceansides-top-gun-house-moved-to-permanent-home-at-new-resort/

[505] Matt Lawlor, operator of Top Gun Props and Costumes Forum, aircraft historian, and artist. Interview with the author, August 11, 2021.

[506] Steve Banta, executive director, USS Lexington Museum in Corpus Christi, Texas. Interview with the author, August 11, 2021.

[507] David Koontz, director of marketing, USS Midway, San Diego, CA. Email and interview with author, September 16, 2021.

[508] Merritt, September 14, 2021

[509] Cindy and Martin Blair, proprietors of Kansas City Barbeque. Interview with Martin Blair, June 29, 2020

ACKNOWLEDGMENTS

I f you've worked with me, you've probably heard me say that movies are a collaborative art form. It seems obvious, yet we still know more about the visible one percent of people above the line than all the others, a group filled with stellar artists, artisans, managers and business people.

This book is about *all* the people who made *Top Gun* (1986), what it took, and how they did it, and it could not have been written without them. Thanks to every person who contributed. I'm an annoying reporter who calls back, so double and triple thanks to those who indulged second, or even third, interviews. Not that three was a cap on how many times I called some people back. I appreciate your patience.

There are challenges in writing about anything that happened decades ago, and movies are no exception. I had a distinct advantage from others who've done it because so many of the people who worked on *Top Gun* weren't in the industry. Sincerest thanks to the pilots and RIOs and others who helped me understand the Navy side of the equation and for their very different perspective. It's a remarkable group that includes Lloyd "Bozo" Abel, Dave "Bio" Baranek, C.J. "Heater" Heatley, John "Smegs" Semcken and Bob "Rat" Willard.

Donna Scott, wife of Tony Scott, wasn't around for the making of *Top Gun* — she met her husband during the making of *Days of Thunder* (1990) — but her contribution to this book is significant. She took time to fact check areas she knew about and patiently recalled many of the director's stories of making *Top Gun*. I can't thank her enough.

I was fortunate that so many people and organizations were willing to contribute or license images for use in this book, and for the help of Citation Press photo editor Chelsey Schaffeld. Shout out to Matt Lawlor, a researcher who also does amazing illustrations for use in his documentation. He did the artwork for patches used on flight suits, as well as the F-14 camerabird. He's part of a remarkable group of fans who love *Top Gun*. Collectively they provided a lot of fuel to keep me going.

When it comes to facts, there's nothing like old-fashioned documentation. Many people contributed to the boxes of material that sat on a six-foot folding banquet table in my office. I'm grateful so many wanted the real story of the movie to be told, and that some could contribute paperwork. Writing an independent biography of a contemporary film, with communication happening in so many different venues, seems like it would be much harder.

Numerous libraries, repositories and databases widened the picture for *Top Gun Memos*. An echoing thank you to Wayback Machine, which takes snapshots of websites that amount to screen grabs of history. It is an incredible resource that, among many other things, makes it easier to trace media missteps.

Early on, Leighton Bowers at Western Costume dug through company archives to unearth photos about Cruise's costume fittings, verifying costume work done there. Thanks to Carol Lloyd, director of Churchill County Library in Fallon, Nev., and the Churchill County Museum, and to both the USS Midway Museum in San Diego and the USS Lexington Museum in Corpus Christi, Texas. The Harry Ransom Center at the University of Texas at Austin, which holds the paperwork and recordings of screenwriter Warren Skaaren, was incredibly useful. Thanks to Alison Macor, author of *Rewrite Man, The Life and Times of Warren Skaaren*, who helped put that in context. Thanks also to the Margaret Herrick Library and its staff, who were working during the pandemic even as visitors were prohibited.

The American Film Institute (AFI) provided audio of a talk given by Simpson and Bruckheimer, which felt like being dropped into a 1988 time capsule. Another audio felt like being dropped in 2012 a week after the loss of Tony Scott, thanks to Jeff Goldsmith, of The Q&A podcast and Backstory digital magazine.

Much appreciation is also due the following folks: The Horton family for sharing *What a Life*, the family memoir written by John E. Horton, who helped *Top Gun* navigate Washington D.C.; Cindy and Martin Blair, owners of Kansas City Barbeque, for generously sharing their time, files and photos; and Leslee Gaul and the organization she heads, Visit Oceanside.

All of the research in the world doesn't matter without people. I'm beholden to editor Lynn Medford, a stellar journalist and editor. She was a steady hand on those occasions where I felt the tightrope swing. John Keeney jumped in with a stringent copy edit, proving that my friend from 8th grade English had been paying attention. Brandyn Briley contributed line and technical edits with flare and creativity. Jeremy Kinser, another highly skilled editor, read from there. Rasel Khondokar came in with formatting and design for the finish.

Lawyers are important, too. Thank you, Cynthia Counts, for your assistance with this book, and for your commitment to the First Amendment. Thanks also to Molly Murphy for her legal insights.

Thanks to various colleagues and friends, starting with everyone in The Creatives, a weekly zoom meeting during the pandemic, and including Michele Adair, Michael Crosby, Gary Romolo Fiorelli, Lisa Fitzpatrick, Kathy Gaschk, Rick Hubbard, Carolyn Johnston, Anna Kula, Mandy Main, Tom Minderhout, Martin Prew, Jennifer Smith, and most of all, Kay Zuna. You made a difference.

Family enables it all, from heaven-side parents, Robert Paul Jordan and Jane Taylor Jordan, to my earthbound siblings Rob Jordan and Julia Jordan, niece Grace Maniglia and nephews Jordan Maniglia and Max Maniglia, as well as the brilliantly creative Melanie and Oliver. A nod also to Gwen Cowden, Stephanie Oberhelman, Virginia Jordan Russo, Jack and Uschi Taylor, Dan Taylor, and the entire Taylor clan, including Grace Unruh. It is a foundation that continues to bring richness to my life.

Rolling!

PRIMARY SOURCES

ources for this book include original documents and primary materials held in both private collections and public archives, as noted below. Quotations, background material, and biographical information was obtained primarily through interviews with former executives, cast, crew, and military consultants who worked directly on the production of *Top Gun*. Supplementary information was sourced publicly from secondary materials such as newspapers, magazines, videos, books, and industry websites.

The following abbreviations appear throughout notes to distinguish the source of quotations and specific information.

TGC	The *Top Gun Collection* encompasses material loaned or given to the author for use in the book by several people with private collections of material stemming from the movie. Examples of that material include Paramount Pictures internal studio memos, production memos, and other related documents, most of which have not been widely circulated.
MSP	Margery Simkin Papers, Academy of Motion Picture Arts and Sciences, Margaret Herrick Library, Beverly Hills, CA.
WSP	The Warren Skaaren Papers, Harry Ransom Humanities Research Center, The University of Texas, Austin, TX.

PEOPLE/ROLES

Name	Description	Credit*
Abel, Lloyd	Additional Crew	F-14 aerial coordinator / aircrew (as LCDR Lloyd 'Bozo' Abel)
Alavardo, Nick	Camera and Electrical Department	Aerial camera operator
Altman, Scott D	Additional Crew	F-14 aircrew (as LT Scott 'D-Bear' Altman)
Arenson, Julianna	Additional Crew	Production auditor (as Juli Arenson)
Arquette, Rosanna	Actor considered or auditioned	
Badalato, Bill	Produced by	Executive producer
Badalato, Billy	Additional Crew	Assistant: Mr. Simpson
Badami, Bob	Music Department	Music editor
Baker, Wayne	Camera, underwater	
Baranek, Dave	Additional Crew	TOPGUN instructor and MiG pilot (as LT Dave 'Bio' Baranek)
Baron, Fred	Location coordinator	Uncredited
Bell, Mitchell "Taco"	Fan/Podcast "Tall Tales With Taco"	
Blair, Martin & Cindy	Owners / Operators	Kansas City Barbeque
Blanford, Larry	Camera and Electrical Department	Aerial camera operator
Blue, Michael	Additional Crew	TOPGUN instructor and MiG pilot (as LT Michael 'Vida' Blue)
Bruckheimer, Jerry	Produced by	Producer
Callan, Cecile	Actor considered or auditioned	
Carr, John	Vice chairman of Grumman	
Carr, Patti	Additional Crew	Assistant: Mr. Badalato
Cash, Jim	Scriptwriter	Written by

Name	Description	Credit*
Cassidy, T.J	Self (as Admiral T.J. Cassidy)	Cooperation and support (as RADM T.J. Cassidy)
Stewart, Catherine Mary	Actor considered or auditioned	
Gilyard, Clarence Jr	Actor/LTJG Marcus 'Sundown' Williams	Actor
Clark, Ron	Actor, Inquiry commander	Uncredited
Clarkson, Lisa	Casting Department	Casting associate
Connolly, Tom	Retired vice admiral of the Navy	
Connor, John J	Camera and Electrical Department	Camera operator (as John Connor)
Cooperman, Jack	Camera and Electrical Department	Aerial camera operator / underwater camera operator
Cosgrove, Patrick	Second Unit Director or Assistant Director	Second assistant director
Coss, William	Camera and Electrical Department	Second assistant camera (as William F. Coss)
Cruise, Tom	Actor/LT Pete 'Maverick' Mitchell	Actor
DeCuir, John Jr.	Production designer	Production Design by (as John F. DeCuir Jr.)
Duff, Patricia	Actor considered or auditioned	
Duggan, Jim	Camera and Electrical Department	Second company grip (as James Michael Duggan)
Edwards, Anthony	Actor/LTJG Nick 'Goose' Bradshaw	Actor
Faltermeyer, Harold	Composer	Music score by
Fiorentino, Linda	Actor considered or auditioned	
Foster, Jodie	Actor considered or auditioned	
Fox, Christine	Consulting Analyst on contract to Department of Defense.	
Furie, Dan	Paramount Attorney	
Garrow, J. A	Head of CHINFO	Cooperation and support officer: U.S. Navy (as RADM J.A. Garrow).
Gaul, Leslee	CEO of Visit Oceanside	
Gelfan, Greg	Paramount Business Affairs	

Name	Description	Credit*
Gilbert, John	Camera and Electrical Department	F-14 camera consultant
Goodman, Adam	President, Paramount Pictures Corp. in 2012	
Greenberg, Jeff	Casting Department	Casting assistant
Greist, Kim	Actor considered or auditioned	
Gutierrez, Gary	Special Effects by	Supervisor of special photographic effects
Hall, Cecelia	Sound Department	Supervising sound editor
Hall, Allen	Special Effects	Special effects coordinator
Hamilton, Linda	Actor considered or auditioned	
Haney, Connie	LCDR Connie Haney	Uncredited
Harmon, Thomas R	Additional Crew	Aerial consultant
Hays, Ron	Admiral Ron Hays, Vice CNO for Navy Air	Uncredited
Heatley, C.J	Camera and Electrical Department	Aerial camera operator (as LCDR C.J. 'Heater' Heatley)
Hess, Susan	Actor considered or auditioned	
Holloway, James L. III	Additional Crew	Cooperation and support officer: U.S. Navy (as ADM James L. Holloway III USN ret.)
Horton, John	Paramount's representative in Washington	Government relations
Hubley, Whip	Actor/LT Rick 'Hollywood' Neven	Actor
Hunt, Helen	Actor considered or auditioned	
Ironside, Michael	Actor/LCDR Rick 'Jester' Heatherly	Actor
Kaplan, William B	Sound Department	Sound mixer
Kauber, Jim	Navy rescue swimmers	Uncredited
Kauber, Mark	Navy rescue swimmers	Uncredited
Kelley, William E. Jr	Camera and Electrical Department	Aerial camera operator (as William Kelly)
Kelson, David	Sound department, cable operator	Utility sound

Name	Description	Credit*
Kilmer, Val	Actor/LT Tom 'Iceman' Kazansky	Actor
Kimball, Jeffrey L.	Cinematography by	Director of photography (as Jeffrey Kimball)
Kirkpatrick, David	Production executive, Paramount	
Knell, Catalaine	Additional Crew	Assistant: Mr. Scott
Kolsrud, Dan	Second Unit Director or Assistant Director	First assistant director (as Daniel P. Kolsrud)
Koontz, David	Director of marketing, *U.S.S Midway*, San Diego	
Lacy, Clay	Camera and Electrical Department	Air to air photography (as Clay Lacey)
Langland, Liane	Actor considered or auditioned	
Lawlor, Matt	Fan/Facebook page, "Top Gun Props and Costumes Forum;" Aircraft Historian	
Leahy, George P.	Camera and Electrical Department	F14 camera consultant (as George Leahy)
Lebenzon, Chris	Film Editing by	Film editing
Lehman, John F. Jr.	Thanks	Special thanks (as The Secretary of the Navy - The Honorable John F. Lehman Jr.)
Leigh, Jennifer Jason	Actor considered or auditioned	
Leo, Melissa	Actor considered or auditioned	
Lloyd, Carol	Director/ Churchill County Library in Fallon, Nev	
Loggins, Kenny	Vocals for "Danger Zone;" lyrics and music for "Playing with the Boys."	Soundtrack
Loughlin, Lori	Actor considered or auditioned	
Lynch, Pamela	Actor considered or auditioned	
MacDowall, Andie	Actor considered or auditioned	
Macor, Alison	Author of *Rewrite Man* biography of Warren Skaaren.	
Madsen, Virginia	Actor considered or auditioned	

Name	Description	Credit*
Maguire, Charlie	Studio executive, Paramount	
Mann, Sharon	Second Unit Director or Assistant Director	Second assistant director
McGillis, Kelly	Charlotte 'Charlie' Blackwood	Actor
McGovern, Elizabeth	Actor considered or auditioned	
Merritt, John	Fan/Instagram page, "Skid Voodoo's Hard Deck"	
Milligan, Richard "Dick"	Grumman Aerospace deputy director of public affairs, liaison to *Top Gun* production.	Uncredited
Moore, Demi	Actor considered or auditioned	
Moroder, Giorgio	Oasis Studios, owner and music producer for *Top Gun* soundtrack	
Morris, Haviland	Actor considered or auditioned	
Nelson, Ralph	Camera and Electrical Department	Still photographer (as Ralph Bahnsen Nelson) (the Cruise thumbs up photo)
Nishino, Ken	Camera and Electrical Department	First assistant camera (as Kenneth Nishino)
Nolan, Terry	Consultant (Volleyball)	Uncredited
Nowell, David B.	Camera and Electrical Department	Aerial camera /Astrovision® operator (as David Nowell)
Otterbein, Thomas	Capt. Thomas 'Otter' Otterbein, commander Miramar in 1985	Uncredited
Pasdar, Adrian	LT Charles 'Chipper' Piper	Actor
Penn, Sean	Actor considered or auditioned	
Peters, Randy	Transportation Department, Stunts	Transportation coordinator, Stunts
Pettigrew, Pete	Perry Siedenthal	Actor
Pettigrew, Pete	Additional Crew	Technical advisor (as Peter 'Viper' Pettigrew) RADM. Rear Admiral USNR (Ret.) Pete Pettigrew.

Name	Description	Credit*
Pfeiffer, Michelle	Actor considered or auditioned	
Phillips, Julianne	Actor considered or auditioned	
Pollan, Tracy	Actor considered or auditioned	
Prophet, Tom Jr.	Camera and Electrical Department	First company grip (as Thomas Prophet Jr.) [key grip]
Proser, Chip	Screenwriter	Uncredited
Read, Bobbie	Costume and Wardrobe Department	Costume supervisor: women
Robbins, Tim	Actor/LTJG Sam 'Merlin' Wells	Actor
Rondell, R.A.	Stunts	Stunt coordinator / stunts
Rossovich, Rick	Actor/LTJG Ron 'Slider' Kerner	Actor
Rourke, Mickey	Actor considered or auditioned	
Russell, Ward	Camera and Electrical Department	Chief lighting technician
Ryan, Meg	Actor/Carole Bradshaw	Actor
Samson, June	Script and Continuity Department	Script supervisor
Scaramuzza, Daniela	Photographer	
Schlichter, Mark "Slick"	RIO, flew with Lloyd "Bozo" Abel	Uncredited
Schmidt, Gregory J.	Camera and Electrical Department	First assistant camera (as Greg Schmidt). Several interviews
Schneider, Ben	Additional Crew	F14 aircrew (as LT Ben 'Rabbi' Schneider)
Scholl, Art	Thanks (stunt pilot)	Dedicatee
Scholl, Judy	Aviation partner, wife of Art Scholl	
Scott, Ridley	Director, brother of Tony Scott	
Scott, Tony	Director	Directed by
Semcken, John Henry	Additional Crew	Cooperation and support officer: U.S. Navy (as LT John Henry Semcken)
Sherriff, Michael	Fan/Facebook page, "Top Gun Movie Fans"	

Name	Description	Credit*
Sillas, Karen	Actor considered or auditioned	
Simkin, Margery	Casting By	Casting
Simpson, Don	Producer	Produced by
Skaaren, Warren	Produced by	Associate producer
Skerritt, Tom	Actor/CMDR Mike 'Viper' Metcalf	Actor
Sosalla, David	Visual Effects by	Model department supervisor: USFX
Stairs, Sandy	Additional Crew	Navy public affairs (as LT Sandy Stairs)
Steel, Amy	Actor considered or auditioned	
Stevens, Richard T.	Additional Crew	Aerial consultant (aka Dick Stevens)
Stockwell, John	Actor/LT Bill 'Cougar' Cortell	Actor
Stroud, Duke	Actor/Air Boss Johnson	Actor
Tilly, Meg	Actor considered or auditioned	
Tolbert, Gary	Camera and Electrical Department	Aerial camera operator
Tolkan, James	Actor/CMDR Tom 'Stinger' Jordan	Actor
Tubb, Barry	Actor/LTJG Leonard 'Wolfman' Wolfe	Actor
Tyson, James W.	Costume and Wardrobe Department	Costume supervisor: men
Upham, Zip	Spokesman for Naval Air Station Fallon, 2012	
Valentine, Joseph F.	Camera and Electrical Department	Steadicam operator (as Joe Valentine)
Vance, Mark	RADM and CDR of the Navy Strike and Air Warfare Center, 2012	
Wade, Mark	Art Department	Property master (as Mark Robert Wade)
Wagner, Paula	Agent/Tom Cruise	
Watters, George II	Sound Department	Supervising sound editor
Weber, Billy	Film Editing by	Film editing
Weis, Aaron and Adam	Actor, Bradley Bradshaw	Uncredited

Name	Description	Credit*
Weintraub, Barbara	Additional Crew	Assistant: Mr. Bruckheimer
Wheeler, D. Michael	Camera and Electrical Department	Second assistant camera
Wheeler-Nicholson, Dana	Actor considered or auditioned	
Whiteley, Frank	Bodyguard to Tom Cruise	Uncredited
Whitlock, Tom	Lyricist, "Take My Breath Away" [and "Danger Zone"]	Soundtrack
Willard, Robert	Additional Crew	Navy aerial coordinator / top gun instructor and MiG pilot (as LCDR Robert 'Rat' Willard)
Winningham, Mare	Actor considered or auditioned	
Yonay, Ehud	Author, "Top Guns," California magazine	
Young, Sean	Actor considered or auditioned	
Zabielinsky, Mark	Fan/Instagram page "top.gun.movie"	
Zuniga, Daphne	Actor considered or auditioned	

* If applicable.

ABOUT THE AUTHOR

Meredith Jordan is an award-winning journalist who has been writing about the art and artistry of behind the scenes movie and TV production crew since 2012. Her first book, *Below the Line: Anatomy of a Successful Movie* (2019) was published by Citation Press.

When each woman was finally covered, warm, and somewhat protected from the cold, Eric and Abe filled a backpack with supplies from the van: Water, canned goods, matches, and weapons.

"We need these supplies." Abe placed the backpack on the side of the highway next to the immobile figures but didn't release his grip.

"Don't even think it." Eric balled his fist.

Abe put his hands to the sky in mock surrender.

Eric squinted and tried to decide a safe place for the non-responsive women. With a shrug of his shoulders, he sat them on the side of the road.

"The water's here." He pointed to the large plastic containers taken from the back of the van.

"Here." He offered them some expired jerky. Both grabbed for the food and water but remained silent.

Eric directed his gaze toward Abe. "We can't leave them."

"Nothing else to do."

"Even with weapons, they're defenseless. They might not be able to find more food for themselves." Eric kicked at the gravel and lowered his voice. "They'll be dead in days."

Abe sauntered away. "We have to get going. The van has close to a full tank of gas and I have the keys so we're taking it for now."

Eric followed, hating himself for doing so. "You're really going to leave them here?"

"Yes."

"Alone on the side of the road?" He bit his bottom lip.

"We've been through this."

"What about food and shelter?"

"For us or them?" Abe retorted.

"Them."

"We go into a town and the Streakers will get them sooner and maybe us too. Out here is as good as anywhere. Realistically, what are their chances?"

"We could bring them with us."

"We discussed this. Get in the van or stay with them. Your choice."

Eric glanced over at the two women. He was unable to protect them, barely able to stay alive himself. Reluctantly, he headed towards the vehicle.

He stared out the front window as the van drove away, the smell of death still lingered on his skin and soul. The two women sat on the side of the road, uncaring, as if they had already departed this earth.

Eric focused on them until their figures were dots, and then they were gone.

"Think forward," Abe said.

"What?"

"Think about the future. The van brings us one step closer to finding your friends and family."

"We left them."

"We left them, but we also saved them."

"Abe, you don't make any sense."

"It will soon enough."

Eric shook his head. "I want it all to end. I hate the world, the killing, and what I'm forced to do. Leaving the women is dead wrong. I'm taking a nap. Wake me if you need me."

"I will. We might just make it somewhere important today."

9

CHALLENGE IN CHINCOTEAGUE

The sign read Chincoteague Inn. Once a stately manor house, the inn now lay in ruins. White exterior paint, now gray and peeling clung to weathered boards. Shingles and shutters had fallen loose but the tall, dead grass buried them from view. A rusted metal gate surrounded the property, but it was open and invited them closer.

"Why are we here?" Eric huffed angry words. He hadn't forgiven Abe for leaving the women. It had shaken his faith in the man, and all he wanted was to reach the High Point Inn.

"I need certain items before we reach your friends. I want to arrive prepared."

"Maybe it's about time to reconsider your plan."

"Trust me."

"Not sure I can anymore." The words started barely audible but grew louder. "I'll find my friends. I will not forget them, even if they didn't do the same. If this is more important, and you don't want to keep searching, I get it."

"I told you, I'd stay with you, but I wanted to make a stop here. We'll be at your Inn tomorrow. The next day at the latest."

"Fine."

"These old bones are getting mighty weary." Abe gave Eric a hard slap on the back. "I think your reunion is due for an early celebration. Let's see if we can scrounge up something special, maybe even something to take the rough edges off."

"Old bones my ass. You whip my butt in combat any day."

"Remember you said those words." Abe scrutinized the rambling porch. "Let's find out if anyone left us a present inside." He drew out his blade and jogged up the steps. The front door was ancient wood and stained glass. The large central pane had lost many of the colored pieces, but at one time must have been a picturesque, flowered design. The top of the door fell in rather than opened, as the wood disconnected from the hinge.

Abe entered and Eric followed.

The room, full of windows, shimmered with dust and cobwebs. The deep silence drew them deeper inside. Eric brushed away the webs that found his hair and eyes after clinging, undisturbed, to the corners of the doors and the rafters of the ceiling.

The grand wooden stairs in the center hall had caved in, forming a pile of rubbish.

"Appears deserted. No shoe prints. There's a lot of undisturbed dust on everything. Probably been picked over good one too many times to be worth returning, and yet here we are." Abe pointed. "We'll search this floor first and then move upstairs next. Maybe if the place is as quiet as it looks, we'll bunk here tonight."

"Whatever." Eric headed towards the first door.

The large, gourmet kitchen was a shell of its former glory. Stainless-steel appliances remained but had been toppled and damaged. The floor had been painted brown with blood and food.

The two searched but found the cupboards empty. The rooms on the first floor proved equally as barren. With the grand central staircase no longer functional, Eric led the way up the rickety, narrow back stairs.

A huge fireplace had once been the center-piece of the first bedroom they entered. Now pieces of a flat screen television and the stuffing of a queen size mattress, all but destroyed, littered the floor.

"What's in the fireplace?" Eric pointed at a white spear sitting amid the ashes.

"I don't know." Abe stepped on the mattress, sinking into the remains as he walked. "Let's take a look."

With the edge of his blade Abe rocked the white sphere and toppled it in.

"Don't." Eric guessed what it was.

Abe stabbed his knife into the hole at the bottom and pulled it closed. Abe blew on the ashes and the flakes flew into the air.

Abe twisted the object, revealing a human skull.

"I can't take this. We leave women at the side of the road. Find human skulls in the fireplace. If you want to search, great. I'm done. I want a place to rest for a while." Eric wanted nothing more than to get away.

"Let's head back downstairs and get out of this hotel. I doubt there is anything worth searching for in the rooms. I'll explore the town after we decide where to stay."

Eric retreated down the back staircase with Abe behind him. He stood for a second in what had once been a large meeting room, contemplating where he should go next.

The sound of wood cracking and glass shattering startled Eric.

"We have a friend," Abe pointed to the collapsed front door.

The bloated corpse toddled like an obese baby. Outstretched hands grabbed at whatever object invaded occupied space in front of it.

The creature, after staggered into what had once been the reception area, stopped. It faced Eric and Abe and, if possible, grinned at its next meal.

"Our new friend has a friend." Abe pointed at the scarecrow undead with straw hair, remnants of a flannel shirt, and twigs embedded in its dry, wrinkled flesh that entered the room.

"Can my day get any better?"

The smell of rancid meat followed the corpses.

Eric stood behind Abe, crowbar in hand. He whacked it against his palm in preparation. Sensing movement, undead eyes were upon him. Part of the scarecrow's skull had been ripped away, exposing the rot underneath. Even without a working brain, it lumbered forward and stumbled over the other creature in its path.

The first Streaker outpaced the scarecrow, targeting Abe.

It reached for him and Abe's blade hacked into its arm. The limb dangled uselessly and at a 90 degree angle. With another slice, Abe dissected it from the undead's body.

It plopped on the tile and twitched. The creature shambled closer. Abe guided the creature away and Eric readied himself to face the scarecrow, crowbar clasped in his sweaty palms.

Eric stepped away from Abe and the scarecrow followed like a puppy chasing a chew toy. Ooze dripped from its nostrils and eyes.

Hoisting the crowbar, Eric swung and was rewarded with the sharp crack of metal against bone.

The creature's head split, but not at all phased by the blow, it inched forward. Eric pounded the zombie's face with his steady swing.

"Back. Get back." Eric yelled the words even with the understanding the words would not be comprehended. When the crowbar rammed through skin and muscle, and shattered the bone housing the undead's brain, it stuck there momentarily. The scarecrow shook it's head, wrenching the weapon from Eric's grasp.

Deformed fingers gripped Eric's jacket and wrenched him close.

The smell of sewage leaking from the undead's mouth made Eric gag. The close proximity of the scarecrow's black lips and rotted teeth filled him with terror

Nearby, the older man ducked as the Streaker reached out with its pustule covered hand, swiping over his head. Abe swung the sword low and hard. The weapon sliced deep into the creature's midsection, releasing leaking guts and an intolerable smell, but did little to stop its slow steps closer.

Unable to aim, Eric smashed into the zombie's chest, fingers sinking deep into rotting skin, but the undead was stronger. Eric's saw his death upon him as he was propelled forward. He continued to wrestle with the scarecrow.

I can have survived everything to die like this.

Something moved behind him.

Had Abe disposed of the other Streaker? Was Abe winning, or was the second zombie now ready to attack from behind?

Eric spun the scarecrow around. In the turning, he and the undead became a tangled mess and landed in a heap on the floor. The Streaker's rotten breath was in his ear. Teeth gnashed near his eyebrow. Eric kicked out and pushed the undead back.

He rolled away and crouched, ready to spring up. The Streaker's face, eaten away by slow decay and mold was layered with crevices, pockmarks, blemishes and dark spots.

Scarecrow's hand, Eric noticed when it grabbed his pant leg and dragged him across the floor, was the same.

Eric faced death.

10

REUNITED

Outside, Eric and Abe diverted from the main street.

"We need to find a quieter place. I don't know how many undead inhabit the area and I don't want to find out."

"Okay." Eric wheezed in a breath. He stood for a moment, trying to overcome the dizziness that hit him.

"Relax. Breathe deep. You did good. I wasn't sure if I'd need to step in and take care of the ugly son of a bitch, but you came back strong once I gave you the crowbar."

"It's all a blur."

"That last swing to the head when it's eye popped out showed how strong you've gotten."

"Great." Eric eyed his bloody hands and the disgusting crowbar he carried. He wished he could drop the weapon on the ground, but any weapon was hard to come by.

"Let's find a home away from the center of town. This place is busy, but not in a good way. It'll be easier for me to find what I need with you safe, tucked in bed somewhere." Abe detoured off the main street.

He read the street signs as they passed. "Bunting Road. Next, we have Flower Lane, and here we have Greenway Drive. Why can't they just do first, second, and third street."

Abe stopped at an old, ramshackle colonial. A large six-foot wooden fence surrounded much of the land and a screened in porch provided some protection. Even better, boards crossed all the doors and windows.

"This looks good," Abe said.

"Whatever. As long as I don't have to kill anything to take a nap or get a meal." He hoisted the crowbar not sure he could take on any other adversaries right now. Eric wouldn't tell Abe, but the women in the van left him questioning a lot more than the lack of sense in the world. He felt downright existential.

Abe led the way through the yard. The front door was boarded up. They crunched through the overgrown grass as they made their way toward the back

The crowbar became Eric's crutch as he followed.

The back door was boarded and locked, bolted from the inside.

"We could pry off the boards and break a window," Eric raised the crowbar halfheartedly.

"Let's look for a hatch first." Abe pointed Eric in the direction of the ground-level doors.

The heavy doors weren't bolted shut from the inside and lifted. Abe switched on his flashlight and peered down the stairs into the damp, dark cellar that smelled of rotted apples and rain.

"As good as it gets. There might be Streakers inside, but I can take care of them. Let's go." A narrow set of stairs led into the basement. Eric climbed an additional set of steps to the main floor of the house.

They explored the house and settled in without the need to fight Streakers and ate a meal that lifted Eric's spirits enough so that when Abe went out to find for what he needed, something he refused to reveal, Eric retrieved *Lord of the Flies* from his backpack.

He righted the couch and repositioned the cushions, surprised that most looked in descent condition. The old house had kept out the rain and while the mice had invaded and possibly an owl, the interior was in decent shape. Someone had managed to survive here for a while.

He relaxed and reread the dogeared pages.

Abe returned a couple hours later.

"Success?" Eric asked.

"Maybe." Abe grunted as he sat on the couch. "Let's spend the first night together in the living room. A bed sounds tempting, but they'll be there tomorrow. There could be a lot of nocturnal Streaker activity. I want to be able to communicate quick if zombies decide to pay us a nighttime visit."

"I guess that means you get the couch, being older and all."

Abe stood. "You take it tonight. You earned it."

Eric thought it would be hard to sleep. Images of the women had plagued him, yet darkness took him quickly. He was disoriented when he woke, but then the noise. Something creaked in the basement.

Footsteps or worse? A dog bark? Can't be.

He woke Abe and the two stood the kitchen door, weapons posed, waiting to fight evil if it found its way upstairs.

The door inched open.

A dark head peered into the kitchen.

"It can't be." Eric dropped the machete. It clanged on the wood floor.

Caleb rushed from behind Jenna.

"Stop!" The words rang through the room. Jenna pushed by Caleb and threw herself against Eric.

"You're alive." Jenna crushed him in a hug. "Is it really you?" Her laughter mixed with tears.

He melted against her.

"How is this possible?" Caleb asked. "I was at the movie theater. I saw the Streakers swarm you. How are you alive?

SNEAK PEEK OF BOOK 2

Dying is anything but rosy.

I wake with Caleb at my side. Having someone next to you during the zombie apocalypse is always a comfort. That is until he explains a mysterious illness almost finished the job of the undead and ended my life.

It can always be worse, and it is.

. . .

Outside the fortified High Point Inn, the zombies keep coming. There's turmoil within the ranks, and my best friend, Lilly, has been kidnapped.

I slept through it all. Sure, I was suffering from an unknown malady, but that's no excuse.

Unable and unwilling to sit in bed, I develop a rescue plan. As soon as I'm recuperated, Caleb and I are off into the wilderness to find Lilly.

Zombies, I expect.

The other surprises nearly send me to the grave again. Some days, it's hard to face the ugly truth, but I realize that not every monster is evil and not every human has a soul.

Hordes of zombies, mysterious illnesses, and the death of friends. Now there's a kidnapping. How much can one person take?

1

WAKING THE LIVING

Dying is anything but rosy.

Jenna sat in bed and gulped air. The dream receded unwillingly, scratching and clawing in its attempt to remain present. The effort of sitting caused the room to spiral. Black invaded the edges of her vision.

She fell back against the sheets and stared at the dull-streaked ceiling. Rubbing the sleep in her green eyes, Jenna hoped to clear her vision, but instead, the motion only brought pain. She whimpered, closed her eyes, and rolled into a fetal position.

A squeak had her peering through slitted lids. She watched a blurry figure rise from the chair, pad close, and then sit on the bed corner. Black hair escaped the edges of a hoodie.

"Caleb?" Jenna croaked. "Are the horses safe?"

Her last memories were of leaving the High Point Inn and traipsing through the field to go check on the Clydesdales.

"Another nightmare? You've been having a lot of them." He brushed damp bangs off her forehead. "The horses are fine. Of course, that would be your first concern."

"Where am I?" She pulled herself up to her elbows, then a bout of nausea erupted. Sinking back down, she twisted and dry-heaved over the bedside.

She recognized the rug and peering up, took in her room at the inn.

Caleb caressed her back. "You scared me and everyone else. We were all worried about you. How do you feel?"

This feels anything but all right. Why don't I remember what happened?

Her rumpled t-shirt was soaked with sweat. "Peachy. Ready for a marathon." Her stomach rebelled at her words. When it stopped, she sputtered, "What h-happened?"

"Don't you remember?"

"Not everything." The memories were slow to emerge. "I couldn't sleep and went to visit the horses in the barn."

Caleb wore his favorite hoodie and snug jeans. Although the hoodie was large, it didn't hide the muscles underneath. "You should have come to me." He handed over a glass of water.

"They're the best medicine most days." She grasped it, and her hand shook. The tepid liquid tasted like heaven.

"You were alone out there. Anything could have happened."

"What's going on?" An uneasy sensation washed over her. "What don't I remember?" Jenna bit her lower lip and waited. "You're making me more nauseous than I already am."

"Funny." His eyes held no mirth. "Not funny."

"Tell me what happened. All I remember is that I was queasy and sleepless. I went to the barn to get some fresh air and check the horses. What else is there?"

"Billy found you in the morning, unresponsive. We can't figure out why, but you've been comatose for three days."

"Three days?" His words shocked her. "At least I got some much-needed beauty sleep. Wanted to look good for you when I woke up." She sent him a small smile.

"Trying to be funny? You must be better."

"You love my sunny disposition and wit."

"Can't live without it."

Jenna grabbed his hand and held on tight. "I

remember the dream if nothing else."

"Tell me." His eyes radiated red, a trademark of the New Race. At this moment, those beautiful eyes regarded her with love and concern.

"Eric's alive and calling for help."

"We've been over this. You can't feel guilty about his death. He chose to fight."

"He was only a child."

"Childhood is a thing of the past. He was strong and able and willing to fight the Streakers." Caleb brought a cold cloth from the nightstand to her forehead.

"What happened to the optimistic person I remember?"

"You scared him away when you were fighting for your life. This is what remains." He fussed with the cloth.

"I'll take what I can get from you." Jenna grabbed his hand to still its restless momentum. She enjoyed the feel of their interlaced fingers.

Caleb shifted sweaty hair off her cheek with his other hand.

"Enough coddling me." She attempted to sit again. "I'm fine. Fit as a fiddle." She waved a hand in front of him. "Hand me a weapon and watch the damage I'll do."

"Only to yourself. You have to take this illness,

whatever it is, seriously."

"Fine. In all seriousness, you're lucky I'm too weak to laugh at you perched like a mother bird protecting her young. Who knew you were such a nurturer?"

He slumped in his chair. "You're evil when sick." He rubbed his brow and pushed his hair, straight and shoulder length, back. Worry still shined evident in his eyes.

"Hey, don't say such blasphemy. Streakers are vile. And some New Racers fit the bill. Me, I'm more of the cute and cuddly type."

Caleb snorted. "Cuddly, not so much. I'd say you take cute to a whole new level. Maybe not today after three days in bed being sick, but normally cute is not the word I'd use to describe you. Cute is a kitty. You're a tigress."

"Tell me more." Jenna thought the same of Caleb, unable to get enough of what she considered an art masterpiece.

Disheveled midnight black hair framed a straight nose and his angular cheeks. By the looks of his hair, he needed a shower as much as she did. That did little to distract from Caleb's lips, which were set in a straight line at the present. It didn't matter. They demanded kissing. Unfortunately, her rollicking stomach said otherwise.

"I'm really back from the dead?" She studied his face. "That's good news. So, why aren't you smiling?" A pause of silence fell between them. "What haven't you told me?"

"Tell me you're better." He refused to meet her eyes.

Jenna touched his cheek with a finger, nudging his gaze to her. "You're stalling. There's bad news, and you're trying to delay."

"How about you go first. Tell me more about the dreams. Was it only the one about Eric or were there more?" His hand grazed the overzealous stubble on his chin. "You've been having them often, sometimes crying out. Most nights calling out for Eric, but you called for Lilly too, which was odd."

God, he was stubborn, a trait Jenna normally loved. Today, she wanted to find out what was going on at the inn. She'd give him the momentary win, for now, but then, soon enough, she'd find out what Caleb refused to divulge.

"If you must know, and it seems you must, the dreams are realistic. They're terrifying but when I wake, sometimes they fade away too quickly to remember. Eric keeps calling out for me to save him. That, I can't forget."

"Do you remember the details from the last one?"

"I saw Eric in the dream. He seemed like his old self, but different too. In the dream, he'd grown stronger and taller. Things surrounded him when I tried getting close—not Streakers, but equally as scary."

Jenna tilted her head. It began to throb.

"Some new evil, these shadow creatures. They circled and engulfed him. He called out for my help. I yell, *I'm coming for you. I haven't forgotten. I didn't leave you!*"

"What do you do in the dream?"

"Nothing. I kept screaming at him, telling him not to move, but when I finally manage to get closer, he's dead. His eyes terrify me. They hold a world full of evil."

"It's only a dream."

"It's not. I just can't figure out what it all means. There's a crow or a raven too." Her fingers twined together in a restless motion. "The dream means something. Maybe Eric's alive."

"Don't go there." Caleb pulled Jenna in for a hug. His solid frame should have radiated heat, but it was cool. "You need to drink, eat, and rest. That's priority number one. Even a few days in bed, and you've dropped too much weight. You feel skeletal."

"Way to cheer up a girl."

"I want to run and find you food right this

moment. I'd cook you a gourmet meal if you'd let me." His eyes spiraled into crimson.

As one of the New Race, Caleb survived the pandemic that decimated the world. It hadn't killed him or turned him, but it had not left him unscathed.

"Are you hungry?" He stood.

"Not hungry."

"Have you been hunting?"

Most of the poor souls killed by the virus returned as zombies, which the group like to call Streakers. A few humans had been changed in other ways. They weren't human but tended not to gut and disembowel people. They survived off blood, whether by hunting animals or from humans. In that way, they were similar to Streakers. However, they did not kill humans for their blood.

"We're talking about you right now. I'm the healthy one."

"More water." Her voice squeaked. "Too much speaking."

All this talking and thinking was exhausting. I must really be sick.

He handed her the glass of water, she gulped, and hacked.

"You have to get better." Caleb took a long, slow breath. "I'd bear the sun for you. I can't live in this world without you."

"Those words scare me more than anything." Jenna said when she caught her breath.

Who could have guessed Caleb would turn into such a softie?

"Believe them." Stronger and faster, the New Race healed quicker, but there were many challenges for them.

For one, they were unable to venture out into the sun, skin blistering so bad, it might lead to their deaths if out in the bright light long enough.

"I'm fine," Jenna said. "Or I'll get there in a few days. You don't need to worry about me or baby me."

"There's something else I need to tell you. Something important. I'm not sure you're ready for it, but I don't want anyone else spilling the news."

Here is comes

"Tell me what?" A shiver ran through her.

His hand threaded through her tangles. "You shouldn't have to find out this way. Lilly's gone. So is Gunnar."

"What do you mean, gone?"

"The same day we found you with the horses, they disappeared." He rushed through the end of the story. "Gunnar must have kidnapped Lilly because there's no other logical reason for Lilly to leave."

"Lilly's gone?" Jenna echoed the haunting words. "I'm going to stake that bastard if it kills me."

2

CAN'T EVER GO HOME

A breeze stroked her face and sent brown leaves scurrying along the ground. The sun had left behind a full moon to bask the meadow in. Wrapped in a blanket and perched in a deckchair at the edge of the field, Jenna enjoyed her time outside.

So happy to be out of bed even for a few moments.

Jenna closed her eyes, and a distant whinny of the horses greeted her. She rested, ignoring the annoyingly cute but hovering Caleb.

Love him but wish he'd go inside and give me a few minutes of peace. There's only so much caretaking a person can take.

In the distance, a gunshot punched through the air. Shouts followed in the wind.

"Streaker," someone yelled from the woods. "Heading to the inn."

She sat straight in her chair. Her gaze focused on the direction of the voices.

"Stay here. I'll keep you safe." Caleb disappeared from her side.

A few quiet beats passed before she heard the faint, inhuman moan. Still too far away, the Streaker hid in the shadows.

Door slamming shut, Caleb returned holding a scythe, his weapon of choice. He plopped a gun in her lap and handed her bullets. "You remember how to load it?"

"I was sick, not suffering from dementia."

A Streaker shuffled from behind a line of conifers. Another zombie stumbled out of the woods behind it. Behind them, two men from the inn battled a few additional undead.

"Can you see it in the dark?" Caleb asked.

"When did the apocalypse become clothing optional?" Jenna asked, staring at the naked form lumbering her way.

Standing, her legs wobbled.

The Streaker's pock-marked breasts lurched in step with the creature. If that wasn't bad enough, the other skeletal monster had decomposed to where bones poked from putrefied skin.

A stench of rotten-fish-in-a-dumpster filled her nose.

"Oh, man, that's just . . ."

She put an arm to her face in hopes of muffling the smell, but nothing could stop the overpowering stink.

Caleb ran through the night, and the fight between him and the undead blurred.

Loading the gun, she took glances here and there, watching him wrestle with the zombie. The scythe slit through the skin and muscle of its arm, but the monster continued to attack. A second Streaker stumbled past Caleb, nearing the porch.

Hands shaking, Jenna held the loaded gun at shoulder's length, took aim, and pulled the trigger. The first bullet missed.

The undead lumbered closer.

Caleb hacked the undead's kneecaps, then turned, leaving the animated corpse struggling to stand. He launched himself at the bag of bones nearing the porch.

The two crumbled to the ground in a heap.

The Streaker rolled and stood over Caleb. Close by, another undead crawled and reached out for Caleb. Its decayed hand grasped his foot. Those same undead fingers slipped away. Decaying flesh streaked his black boots.

"Watch yourself." Jenna's words drew the

standing zombie's attention. It turned its emaciated head in her direction and gnashed its teeth.

Hate that sound.

The monster released a spitting hiss and took a step, but Caleb grabbed at its back leg. The skin peeled away, and the Streaker hobbled closer with a snarl that displayed a mouthful of decayed teeth, yellowed and full of pulpy bits of bloody flesh.

With a single mindedness, one focused on the terrible hunger driving it, the rattling bones reached the bottom of the porch steps.

Jenna steadied herself and took aim. The shot shattered the bones in its leg, dropping it to the ground. She sank back into the chair, depleted—her chest heaving.

The other Streaker managed to stand.

Caleb circled the gray-skinned, sagging bit of anatomy. Machete high, he sliced through the air. The weapon stuck in the creature's neck.

The skeletal smile never left the zombie's lips. Its head lobbed forward, still attached by a thread of bone and muscle.

He snarled, swung again, then slammed into the undead's neck one more. The swing of the weapon sliced separating head from body. The bottom half of the corpse crashed to the ground. The head lolled next to it.

With fluid movements, he turned to the undead at the bottom of the steps struggling to crawl and beheaded it as well.

Jenna sat tall. "Any more of them?"

"Don't think so, but let's get you back inside."

"Thank God. That's enough excitement for the night. This recovering patient isn't as well as she thought she was. What the hell is wrong with me?"

Caleb opened his mouth to answer.

Jenna put up a warning hand. "Stop. Don't even start."

3

DETONATION

The dream detonated in her mind like a bomb.

Heat. Pressure. The burning.

A small room full of night closed in on her. In front of her, a big window exposed the moon. The shadows enveloped her, and Jenna was both repulsed and seduced by them. Part of her wanted to let go and stay shrouded in the black oil, hidden from the light, but she also wanted to fight the darkness.

Don't want to go.

Gunshots exploded in the distance. Something moved outside the window in her dreamscape. Startled, she jumped. Tripping, one foot entangling the other, she staggered, but then soon regained her balance.

A shadow—the decrepit silhouette of a creature

—etched itself across the floor like the strokes of a paintbrush.

Heartbeat loud in her ears, Jena stared as the shadow grew to a mammoth proportion: fuzzy, distorted, and utterly terrifying. She shifted her eyes away hoping to find courage and let her gaze return to the window.

A large black crow perched on the sill, high-lighted by the moon.

No monster, just a bird.

Yet, it stared at her with wicked intent, cackling, like how the three witches had eyed Macbeth on their first encounter.

Crows don't speak. But she was sure this one said, "Eric."

Upon hearing the name, she jumped. The crow, indifferent and unflustered, took off into the night.

Voices erupted around her. Jenna recognized one. Eric wailed in pain.

"Eric," she screamed, racing, searching for him in the oily fog.

She fought the mammoth wings of the crows that swooped from the shadows.

Eric turned to face her, empty sockets where eyes should sit now dripped maggots.

"*Don't you remember me?*" he asked. "*Why did you*

leave me? I haven't forgotten you. I've come to be with you, always."

Events from the past shuffled themselves in front of her. Jenna found Caleb, Eric, his brother, and a group of survivors, the movie theater where they'd been swarmed by Streaker's, and Eric being swarmed by the undead.

There's no way he survived. Unless?

Stomach churning like she was on a carnival ride, the scene in her dream changed. Eric and Billy, his twin brother, squabbled loudly on a roof, exuding youth and innocence. The twins had been some of the youngest members at fifteen.

Fair-haired and optimistic, she'd formed a special bond with them, happy to take on the role of big sister.

Sadness hit her. The boys ought to be anywhere but in the middle of the apocalypse.

The landscape changed again. An old-fashioned silent movie played in her fevered brain. Scenes rapidly changed. The twin's heads bouncing in unison, Eric throwing pebbles from the roof, the boys trying to outdo each other at target practice, both getting into trouble. Billy telling stupid knock-knock jokes. Eric playing cards with Jenna and making her laugh even though she had been mourning all she had lost in her previous life.

All of the vivid movie scenes blurred, and several images, turning chaotic and violent, erupted like a volcano. Eric in dirty overalls fighting the undead, trying to rescue Victor in a dilapidated movie theater, Streakers ambushing him, and finally, Caleb telling her the undead were feasting on his flesh.

Eric screamed and his body surged out of a mass of Streakers. He wasn't dead, and he reached out an arm for her.

Someone else grabbed it.

"Stop making so much noise," Lilly demanded. *"There's something here trying to get us. We need a way out of here. We need you, Jenna."*

Lilly reached out her hand, but Jenna moved away.

The woman's skin decayed in front of Jenna, flaking off Lilly's arm in moldy patches. A wide-open mouth revealed mossy, snapping yellow teeth. An infected, open wound on Lilly's check revealed the red crust of a scab and muscle underneath. Lilly's face was pale, drawn, and splattered with blood.

Jenna couldn't ignore her even like this. She had tried so hard to remain distant, but the twins, Caleb, and Lilly had wormed their way into her heart even when the thought of getting close to anyone again had been foreign.

Everyone had already settled at the High Point

Inn when Lilly had arrived with a group of strangers. Of all the new additions, Lilly, who was close in age to Jenna, had become a friend.

Now, in the dream, Lilly beckoned for her to follow. Slivers of skin from Lilly's arm fell to the ground. From where the skin stuffed off, the arm oozed black blood and bone protruded.

Lilly smiled. Her lips cracked and blood ran down her chin. *"You have to find me and Eric, or this is what we become."*

"Can you show me the way?" Jenna wandered, searching through the haze. *"It's hard to follow."*

The fog deepened and she momentarily lost sight of the other woman.

Jenna ran through the beating wings and the endless darkness. She saw a figure ahead and reached out, grabbing at the hand.

Lilly's skin slithered against her fingers like snakes.

ABOUT THE AUTHOR

Lisa Acerbo is a short-story writer, novelist, and former journalist. Her work has been showcased in numerous anthologies such as Asylum, Carnival of Strange Things, and Scary Snippets. Her science fiction stories and story podcasts have appeared in Ripples in Space magazine. Her novels include Twelve Months of Awkward Moments, Wear White to Your Funeral, and Remote. She writes romance under her pen name Dakota Star.

Lisa enjoys teaching high school and is an adjunct at Norwalk Community College and Post University in Connecticut. She is a graduate of the University of Connecticut where she earned a BA in English Education before going on to earn her EdD from the University of Phoenix. When not reading, writing, hiking, drinking coffee or wine (depends on the hour), she spends her time with her husband and two rescue dogs.